The European Union's policy towards Mercosur

Manchester University Press

European Policy Research Unit Series

Series Editors: *Simon Bulmer, Peter Humphreys, Andrew Geddes* and *Dimitris Papadimitriou*

The European Policy Research Unit Series aims to provide advanced textbooks and thematic studies of key public policy issues in Europe. They concentrate, in particular, on comparing patterns of national policy content, but pay due attention to the European Union dimension. The thematic studies are guided by the character of the policy issue under examination.

The European Policy Research Unit (EPRU) was set up in 1989 within the University of Manchester's Department of Government to promote research on European politics and public policy. The series is part of EPRU's effort to facilitate intellectual exchange and substantive debate on the key policy issues confronting the European states and the European Union.

Titles in the series also include:

Globalisation and policy-making in the European Union   Ian Bartle

The Europeanisation of Whitehall   Simon Bulmer and Martin Burch

The agency phenomenon in the European Union: Emergence, institutionalisation and everyday decision-making   Madalina Busuioc, Martijn Groenleer and Jarle Trondal (eds)

EU enlargement, the clash of capitalisms and the European social dimension   Paul Copeland

The power of the centre: Central governments and the macro-implementation of EU public policy   Dionyssis G. Dimitrakopoulos

Creating a transatlantic marketplace   Michelle P. Egan (ed.)

Immigration and European integration (2nd edn)   Andrew Geddes

The European Union and the regulation of media markets   Alison Harcourt

Children's rights, Eastern enlargement and the EU human rights regime   Ingi Iusmen

Managing Europe from home: The changing face of European policy-making under Blair and Ahern   Scott James

The politics of fisheries in the European Union   Christian Lequesne

The European Union and culture: Between economic regulation and European cultural policy   Annabelle Littoz-Monnet

The Eurogroup   Uwe Puetter

EU pharmaceutical regulation   Govin Permanand

Regulatory quality in Europe: Concepts, measures and policy processes   Claudio M. Radaelli and Fabrizio de Francesco

The European debt crisis: The Greek case   Costas Simitis

Unpacking international organisations: The dynamics of compound bureaucracies   Jarle Trondal, Martin Marcussen, Torbjörn Larsson and Frode Veggeland

The European Union's policy towards Mercosur

Responsive not strategic

Arantza Gomez Arana

Manchester University Press

Published by Manchester University Press
Altrincham Street, Manchester M1 7JA
www.manchesteruniversitypress.co.uk

British Library Cataloguing-in-Publication Data
A catalogue record for this book is available from the British Library

Library of Congress Cataloging-in-Publication Data applied for

ISBN 9 78 0 7190 9694 5 hardback

First published 2017

Typeset
by Toppan Best-set Premedia Limited
Printed in Great Britain
by CPI Group (UK) Ltd, Croydon, CR0 4YY

To my parents, Marisol and Torcuato.

Contents

Boxes, figures and tables

Tables

Acknowledgements

I would like to thank everyone who has helped me to develop this monograph. The comments, attention to detail and help provided at different stages of the process by Professor Alasdair Young has been vital and I am extremely grateful to him. The comments of other academics, including Professor Maurizio Carbone and Dr Chad Damro and several anonymous external reviewers have also helped to shape this book during its final stages. I would like to thank also the participants of the panel on this topic at the Society of Latin American Studies Conference in 2010 for their helpful and kind comments.

I would like to send a special thank you to all my interviewees for being so generous with their time; I cannot mention you by name for obvious reasons but I am in debt to all of you. The fieldwork conducted on both sides of the Atlantic has been partially supported by UACES and the University of Glasgow, and I would like to thank those institutions. I would also like to thank the staff members of the European Library (Brussels), Mercosur's Library (Montevideo) and in particular to Silvana Asteggiante from ALADI's library for her incredible generosity during my time in Montevideo.

I would like to thank all the proofreaders and my editor Anthony Mason and his team at Manchester University Press for their help and patience. Finally, I would like to thank everyone who has supported me and/or commented on my work in one way or another through this long project, including Dr Stephen D. Ashe. Unless otherwise stated, all translations of quotations from non-English-language works are my own. Obviously I am the only one responsible for any mistakes that this monograph might contain.

Abbreviations

ACP	African, Caribbean and Pacific Group of States
ASEAN	Association of South East Asian Nations
CACM	Central American Common Market
CAP	Common Agricultural Policy
CCP	Common Commercial Policy
CCT	Common Customs Tariff
COPA	Committee of European Agricultural Organization
COREPER	Committee of Permanent Representatives
EDF	European Development Fund
EIB	European Investment Bank
EMIFCA	Europe–Mercosur Inter-regional Framework for Cooperation Agreement
EP	European Parliament
FDI	foreign direct investment
FTA	free trade agreement
FTAA	Free Trade Area of the Americas
GATT	General Agreement on Tariffs and Trade
GSP	Generalized System of Preferences
IRELA	Institute of European-Latin American Relations
MEBF	Mercosur-EU Business Forum
Mercosur	Common Market of the South
NAFTA	North America Free Trade Agreement
OPP	Ouro Preto Protocol
QMV	qualified majority vote
UN	United Nations
WTO	World Trade Organization

1

Introduction: the study of European Union relations with Mercosur

Introduction

This monograph seeks to examine the motivations that determine the European Union's (EU) policy towards the Common Market of the South (Mercosur), which is the most important relationship that the EU has with another regional economic integration organization. In order to investigate these motivations (or lack thereof), this volume will examine the contribution of the main policy- and decision-makers, the European Commission and the Council of Ministers, as well as the different contributions of the two institutions. This will make it possible to show the degree of 'involvement'/'engagement' reflected in the EU's policy towards Mercosur, which is the dependent variable in this study. The analysis offered here examines the development of EU policy towards Mercosur in relation to three key stages: non-institutionalized relations (1986–1990), official relations (1991–1995), and the negotiations for an association agreement (1996–2004 and 2010–present). The degree of engagement will be measured as low, medium or high. The outcome of the measure is created by analysing two factors: the level of 'ambition' and the level of 'commitment'.

'Ambition' reflects how far the EU is trying to shift from the status quo. In order to assess the level of ambition at the different stages, it is necessary to contrast:

- EU policy pronouncements
- negotiating mandates
- plans for the future of the relationship
- promises to Mercosur

with the status quo. Once the 'ambition' has been measured, it will be possible to analyse 'commitment'.

'Commitment' reflects how hard the EU is willing to try in order to realize its objectives, and how much it is willing to pay in order to achieve these objectives. In order to assess the level of commitment it is necessary to pay attention to different indicators:

- the frequency of meetings and the importance of those meetings held by the EU: official level, ministerial level, heads of state level,
- the amount of aid or funding provided by the EU towards the different aspects that compound the relationship is worthy of consideration,
- the willingness to compromise during the negotiations.

To complement this analysis, this book compares the different arguments in the existing literature on EU policy towards Mercosur in relation to the three key stages, in order to examine their explanatory capacity over time.

The importance of this analysis is based on the fact that EU–Mercosur relations are the first of the new phenomenon of inter-regionalism. Moreover, they included the first negotiations for a free trade agreement (FTA) between two regions. As such, the EU–Mercosur relationship has a prominent place in the literature on the EU as a global actor.

This monograph argues that the dominant explanations for this relationship in the literature – counterbalancing the US, global aspirations, being an external federator, long-standing economic and cultural ties, economic interdependence and the Europeanization of Spanish and Portuguese national foreign policies – all fail to explain the trajectory of EU policy adequately. In particular, these accounts tend to infer the EU's motives from its activity. Drawing extensively on primary documents, this book argues that the major developments in EU–Mercosur relations – the 1992 Inter-institutional Agreement and the 1995 Europe–Mercosur Inter-regional Framework for Cooperation Agreement (EMIFCA) – were initiated by Mercosur. Moreover, an FTA was included in the latter agreement whereby negotiations finally started in 1999 at the insistence of Mercosur. This suggests that rather than the EU pursuing a cohesive strategy, as implied by most of the existing literature, the EU was largely responsive. This analysis echoes the work of Jorg Monar (1997) which suggests that third parties were the ones demanding upgrading and policy developments from the EU.

How the EU responded to Mercosur's overtures, however, has been influenced by some of the factors highlighted in the literature, most notably the Europeanization of Portuguese and, particularly, Spanish foreign policies. This corresponds with the general debate on EU external relations, based on the special links upheld by EU members with their former colonies, as is the case of Iberian and Latin American members (for example, on this debate see Ravenhill 2002 and Marsh and Mackenstein 2005). Furthermore, the Commission's role as external federator has also influenced EU policy towards Mercosur, although to a lesser extent. Overall, however, these supposedly causal factors have provided only a very weak impetus for EU policy, which in large part explains why the relationship is much less developed than the EU's relations with other parts of the world.

As mentioned above, according to the literature, the Europeanization of Spanish and Portuguese policy, and the role of the Commission as external federator are not the only possible influences on the EU's actions towards Mercosur. There are four other main possible drivers put forward. First, the EU's actions could be seen as strategic behaviour to oppose or counterbalance the US in Latin America. A second influence is the development of a global agenda by the EU, with Mercosur being part of that global strategy. A third is the increase in socio-cultural values shared by the EU and Mercosur after the democratization process in South America. And finally, the growing economic interdependence of a globalized world which would lay the basis for an increase in trade between the EU and Mercosur could be a motive for the EU's policy towards Mercosur. In this study, each of these factors are considered at each of the three stages of EU policy development in order to understand to what extent they could offer a satisfactory explanation for the development of EU–Mercosur policy.

Beyond providing a distinctive and empirically rich account of the EU's relationship with Mercosur, this monograph contributes to the literature on the EU as a global player, particularly the extent to which it is a strategic actor, and to the literature on the Europeanization of national foreign policies of member states from a bottom-up perspective, particularly in reference to the case of Spain and Portugal. The significance of this work is enhanced because it speaks to this wider literature by offering a reinterpretation of the EU's relations with Mercosur, the central point of this volume.

In order to better understand the Europeanization process, it is necessary to explain a concept that is clearly linked to it – path dependence. It starts with an historical event that creates a 'before' and an 'after'. The historical event creates a path that will be followed and this creates a dependency on the path because there is not a second 'lane' to follow or a Plan B. Pierson (2000: 2) explains that 'path dependence refers to the causal relevance of preceding stages in a temporal sequence'. Pierson also draws on Sewell's definition of path dependence which suggests that path dependence means 'that what happened at an earlier point in time will affect the possible outcomes of a sequence of events occurring at a later point in time' (Sewell 1996: 262–263).

In the case of Europeanization, this is certainly not a new concept; it has been used in many studies. However, very few scholars have tried to provide an exact definition of Europeanization (Featherstone and Radaelli 2003). Wong (2008) argues that the notion of there being a Europeanization of foreign policy was initiated by Ben Tonra (2001). Therefore, the definition of Europeanization will echo the definition used in the area of foreign policy. Tonra's defines Europeanization as 'A transformation in the way in

which national foreign policies are constructed, in the ways in which professional roles are defined and pursued and in the consequent internationalisation of norms and expectations arising from a complex system of collective
European policy making' (Tonra 2001: 229; cited in Wong 2008: 323.

A key question in the study of European foreign policy relates to the
concept of 'movement'. The concept of Europeanization itself is about
movement, particularly when speaking of 'transformation'. When examining the issue of 'transformation', it is important to ask what is actually
being transformed. In other words, 'what is changing and what are the
mechanisms and direction of change (top-down from the EU to the member
states, bottom-up, or socialization?)' (Wong 2008: 323). As regards 'what
is changing', the discussion is about the changing of either procedures or
the substance of the foreign policies of individual member states (Wong
2008). In line with the discussion above, this relates to the idea of a member
state trying to influence EU foreign policy in a particular area and, as a
result, the EU uploads the policy.

The rest of this book is divided as follows. The next chapter provides
the analytical framework. It presents an extensive review of the existing
literature on EU policy towards Mercosur. Also, it examines the links
between that literature and the arguments related to the EU as a global
actor. Furthermore, this chapter will also outline the methodological
approach for this monograph. The discussion in Chapter 3 will focus on
outlining the EU's policy towards Mercosur by examining how the EU
internal mechanisms operate in this area. In doing so, the legal basis for
EU–Mercosur agreements and the consequent policy and decision-making
rules will be outlined. Chapters 4 to 7 correspond with each of the three
key stages in the development of EU policy towards Mercosur: the non-
institutionalized relations (1986–1990) will be discussed in Chapter 4, the
official relations (1991–1995) will be analysed in Chapter 5, and finally,
the negotiations of the association agreement (1996–2004) will be examined
in Chapters 6 and 7 (2010–present). Chapter 8 will sum up the conclusions
of this work.

The remainder of this chapter is divided into sections which aim to
contextualize broadly the different aspects of this study and to have a clear
overview of it. In the next section the discussion focuses on the concept of
the EU as a global actor. This will enable us to assess whether or not the
EU behaves as a global actor towards Mercosur. The importance of understanding this concept for the monograph is vital since this volume assesses
not only whether the EU has a strategy towards Mercosur but also how
behaving strategically relates to whether the EU is a global actor or not.
This will contribute to the discussion in and around one of the most keenly
contested topics in EU foreign policy – EU global 'actorness'. After analysing this issue, the discussion will turn to focus on the development of the
criteria which help us to identify what it means to be a strategic actor. This

will provide the necessary framework to enable us to determine whether or not the EU can be referred to as a strategic actor. In the conclusion, these discussions will be revised and linked to the findings of the book. After that a section is dedicated to the historical background; a short historical overview of regional politics in Latin America and the links to Spain, Portugal and the US until the mid-1980s is provided. Finally, an overview of Mercosur countries and Mercosur institutions is provided.

What is understood by EU global 'actorness'?

This section will focus on the discussion of global 'actorness'. Many consider the EU to be a global actor, and its relations with Mercosur are central to this argument. This position assumes a sort of EU activism and strategic behaviour. This monograph questions the strategic behaviour of the EU towards Mercosur and therefore will make a contribution to the general debate about the EU as a global actor. In order to understand the central point of the discussion of EU global 'actorness' and its assumed strategic behaviour, this section is divided into two. The first part will focus on the concept of EU global 'actorness' through the work of Bretherton and Vogler (2006), whereas the discussion in the second part will concentrate on the issue of the EU as a strategic actor.

The EU as a global actor

The discussion of the EU as a global actor emerged over a decade ago with the work of Bretherton and Vogler (1999 and 2006). Bretherton and Vogler (2006: 17) drew upon the work of Gunnar Sjöstedt (1977), citing Sjöstedt's work in relation to the concept of 'actor capability', which he defined as the 'capacity to behave actively and deliberately in relation to other actors in the international system' (Sjöstedt 1977: 16). According to Bretherton and Vogler (1999 and 2006), the EU's presence is almost everywhere, to different degrees. Other scholars who focus on the presence of the EU are Hill and Smith (2005) and Soderbaum and Van Langenhove (2005). Soderbaum et al. (2005) contend that there are many questions on the nature and impact of the EU as a global actor. One of those questions is whether the EU is part of the international sphere. At the very least, the EU is considered 'a force' in the international arena: 'The EU has become a force in international affairs, especially in trade, development cooperation, the promotion of regional integration, democracy and good governance, human rights and, to an increasing extent, also in security policies' (Soderbaum and Van Langenhove 2005: 250). Although it is accepted that the EU is involved in all of these areas, this does not imply 'actorness' or 'presence'. According to Bretherton and Vogler (2006: 27), there are three characteristics of EU's 'actorness': opportunity, presence and capability.

Opportunity

> [Opportunity] refers to the external context of ideas and events that enable
> or constrain EU action. Our concern, from the outset, has been with the very
> considerable changes to the external environment since the early 1980s. In
> the early years two major sources of international stability – Cold War
> bipolarity and the monetary stability provided by the US-dominated Bretton
> Woods system – combined to ensure that opportunities for and expectations
> of EU external action were relatively limited. (Bretherton and Vogler
> 2006: 24)

Linked to this characteristic is the discussion of globalization and interdependence which gained traction in the early 1990s. Mercosur was initiated at the beginning of the end of the Cold War in the mid-1980s and
took off in 1991. Therefore, the opportunity for the EU to benefit from the
increase in complex interdependence became more promising. At the same
time, by 1991 all Mercosur states were democratic and pursuing, from an
economic point of view, open regionalism – in contrast to their past of
import-substituting industrialization.

Presence

> [Presence] conceptualises the ability of the EU, by virtue of its existence, to
> exert influence beyond its borders. An indication of structural power, presence
> combines understandings about the fundamental nature, or identity, of the
> EU and the (often unintended) consequences of the Union's internal priorities
> and policies. Thus presence does not denote purposive external action, rather
> it is the ability to shape the perceptions, expectations and behaviour of others.
> (Bretherton and Vogler 2006: 27)

In that sense, the size and degree of influence of the EU is attractive as well
as projecting an image of security and efficiency. It will be interesting to see
to what extent the EU's presence has had an impact on Mercosur's prioritization of its relations with Europe, and, moreover, to what extent Mercosur
sees the EU as a structural power capable of counterbalancing the US
structural power in the whole American continent.

Capability

> [Capability] refers to the internal context of EU external action (or inaction)
> – those aspects of the EU policy processes that constrain or enable action and
> hence govern the Union's ability to capitalise on presence or respond to
> opportunity. Our framework has included ... the ability to formulate priorities
> and develop policies and the availability of and capacity to utilise policy
> instruments. (Bretherton and Vogler 2006: 29)

The capability issue has been discussed elsewhere as part of the capability–
expectations gap discussed by Hill (1993). It seems that in general there

is a problem in the EU in terms of using all its potential in the area of external relations. The expectations in relation to the capacity of a group of countries that involves such a large group with economic and political power are large; however, this capacity is not used in the area of EU external relations. This argument will be analysed in more detail in the proceeding chapters.

The EU as a strategic actor

It has been shown above what it means to be a global actor and the various ways that the EU is expected to behave if it is to aspire to being a global actor. This discussion has been developed further in the general literature, using the concept of the EU as a strategic actor. In other words, the literature studies to what extent the EU is not only an actor that develops external relations, but also an actor that plans, organizes and develops a strategy for a specific objective. As early as 1993, Hill claimed that the main problem of EU external policy was that 'There is now a large gap between what is expected and what can be achieved' (1993: 326). Hill suggested two changes that were designed to cope with this situation. First, the EU needs to be more realistic about what it can and cannot do, which involves not trying to replace the US in certain crises. Second, the EU needs to accept the 'complex interdependence' that affects foreign policy, therefore the EU will have to cooperate with other states. Could Hill have been calling for multilateralism?

In 2003, the EU launched the European Security Strategy. Much of the discussion in the literature about the concept of the EU as a strategic actor has been developed in relation to this policy. For example, Quille (2004) takes from the European Security Strategy the main goals of the EU as being: to tackle perceived external threats, to extend the zone of security around Europe and to strengthen the international order. However, he argues that the EU is failing as a strategic actor because it does not yet have the necessary 'strategic culture'. It could perhaps be argued that the problem now is not necessarily a lack of capabilities but a lack of will. In fact, in the European Security Strategy, the EU very much accepts that 'it should be more capable and responsible' (Aggestam 2008: 1).

Howorth (2010) offers one of the most detailed accounts in relation to the concept of the EU as a strategic actor, explaining how the EU has not acted in the strategic way that it could have done. Comparing the EU to major players, Howorth argues that:

> The big players may make strategic mistakes – even tragic ones – but at least they are lucid about their aims and objectives. They are, in short, playing chess. The EU, to date, has essentially been playing ping-pong. This is all the more regrettable in that the sort of chess game now being engaged in by the other players is *not* of the traditional Westphalian type, dominated by military

power and territorial acquisition. It is a game which involves the deployment of a vast range of instruments in new and unprecedented ways – a game in short for which the EU is comparatively well equipped. (Howorth 2010: 464–465)

According to Howorth, the EU has shown a distinct lack of will in terms of developing a strategy. This monograph will show how Mercosur is another example where the EU does not demonstrate the will to become a strategic actor.

This study will contribute to this debate by offering an analysis of the EU's behaviour towards Mercosur. In order to do so, it is necessary to conceptualize the EU as a strategic actor in the area of EU external policies. Borrowing extensively from Michael Smith and Huaixian Xie (2010: 5), this book will argue that if the EU is to be referred to as a strategic actor, it must comply with the following criteria: 'It must demonstrate the capacity to extract and mobilise resources from its Member States and other relevant sources, and to do so consistently over a period of time' (Smith and Xie 2010: 5). As far as its relations with Mercosur are concerned, the EU must be able to allocate resources for the development of its strategy towards Mercosur over time. 'It must show that it is possible to relate these resources to agreed medium and long term objectives and to act positively in line with those objectives' (Smith and Xie 2010: 5). I will argue that the EU needs to develop long-term objectives towards Mercosur and then use those resources for that specific policy. 'It must demonstrate that it is capable of generating a strategic narrative that shapes the expectations of both its Member States and other EU bodies and also its key international interlocutors' (Smith and Xie 2010: 5). In its policy towards Mercosur, the EU must be able to create a strategy that has an impact on all the actors involved in EU policy-making and EU decision-making. 'It must be able to adapt its aims, its resource allocations and its strategic narrative to changes in the global context and to challenges that emerge from its developing international activities' (Smith and Xie 2010: 5). The EU must be flexible to accommodate international changes and be able to orientate its strategy towards Mercosur according to the international scene at each stage.

To sum up, in general terms, the EU strategy towards Mercosur must have a plan, an objective(s), the resources to reach that objective, the capability to become a 'EU' plan in the sense that it involves all the EU actors. Also, it must have a strategy that is flexible enough to adapt to changes in the international scene. This book will show that the EU fails to do so.

However, this definition does not cover all the aspects of 'strategic' actor. Part of the definition should be dedicated to the 'intentionality' behind the strategy. The actor holding a strategy needs to undertake consistently intentional actions. This volume will try to make a conceptual contribution to Smith and Xie's definition, discussing the importance of 'intentionality'.

When considering the different definitions of 'strategy' in the dictionary or those used by academics, 'intentionality' is central. According to the *Oxford English dictionary*, a strategy is: 'In (theoretical) circumstances of competition or conflict, as in the theory of games, decision theory, business administration, etc., a plan for successful action based on the rationality and interdependence of the moves of the opposing participants'. It is worth noting that this definition uses the words 'successful action', meaning that the person expects certain consequences from their actions. 'Strategy' comes from the Greek word *strategos*. Evered explains how its strict meaning is 'a general in command of an army: "stratos" = army, and "ag" = to lead' (Evered 1983: 58, cited in Mintzberg 1987).

The area of social sciences where the concept of strategy is most developed fully is in business. Mintzberg continues:

> To almost anyone you care to ask, *strategy is a plan* – some sort of *consciously intended* course of action, a guideline (or set of guidelines) to deal with a situation ... By this definition, strategies have two essential characteristics: they are made in advance of the actions to which they apply, and they are developed consciously and purposefully. (Mintzberg 1987: 11, original emphasis)

Mintzberg himself highlights the part of the definition that Smith and Xie do not develop, 'consciously intended'. As he says, it has to be developed consciously and purposefully. He uses the work of Drucker (1974) on 'purposeful action' and Moore (1959) on 'design for action' to emphasize this point. It is important to locate the intentionality behind the action in order for it to be considered a strategy; otherwise, accidental actions would be considered strategies. This would mean that some actors would appear to be strategic players when they were not.

It is necessary to explain that the development of patterns of behaviour without previous preconceptions should not be considered strategies; this would contradict Mintzberg's argument: 'Thus, the definition of strategy as plan and pattern can be quite independent of each other: plans may go unrealized, while patterns may appear without preconceptions. To paraphrase Hume, strategies may result from human actions but not human designs' (Mintzberg 1987: 13).

Without getting into philosophical debates, strategies that are a result of human actions could arguably come from strategies that the human was not conscious of having. In other words, humans can develop some actions and strategies of which they had not previously been aware (which does not mean that the strategies did not exist).

I asked an official from the Commission (interview 14) who was closely involved in EU–Mercosur relations the central question of this monograph: Why did the European Union develop a policy towards Mercosur? The interviewee replied that there is no answer to that question. This was the same reply that I received from somebody else (interview 1). If the people developing the policy believe there is not a reason behind it, it can hardly be said that there is a strategy. This does not mean that the policy was developed for no reason, rather that the people involved in it did not have a strategy and were more likely responding to somebody else's motivation/ interest/strategy.

Moreover, in the opposite case, inaction should not be considered a strategy either. This book argues explicitly that ignoring Mercosur, or not giving Mercosur the attention that would be expected from a global actor such as the EU, should not automatically be considered a strategy – the strategy of indifference. If the EU was doing so deliberately, it would have reasons, and a plan that explained that indifference was the strategy. But for us to be able to present this as a strategy, the EU would have to have known everything about Mercosur and have had reasons that supported its planned indifference. This point will be developed further in Chapter 7.

In terms of 'interest', the actor does not need to have interest in the object affected by its strategy since it could be part of a bigger plan. In other words, the EU could develop a strategy towards Mercosur as part of a global EU strategy and have no interest whatsoever in Mercosur per se. Mercosur could be the pathway to achieve something, not the end in itself. Therefore, 'interest' is not a necessary part of the definition.

This section has examined the wider debates that focus on the EU's status as a global actor and its potential as a strategic player. The discussion has outlined what is understood by the term 'global actor', and what is expected of the EU in order for it to be considered a global actor in terms of presence, capability and opportunity. In relation to the strategic aspects of the EU behaviour towards Mercosur, the necessity of plans and objectives and the resources to achieve those aims have been stated. The repercussion in the external sphere, such as changes in international politics, on that strategy must also be considered.

Contextualizing the case study: historical review of regional politics

This section provides the historical background to the emergence of Mercosur. Since Mercosur involves most of South America, a general understanding of regional politics is crucial to comprehend the importance of some parts of the EU policy towards Mercosur. This region has been influenced historically by three countries, Spain, Portugal and the US. After this outline of how these have influenced politics in South America, the next section will focus on a discussion of Mercosur's institutions. This will enable us to see not only how Mercosur institutions have evolved but also the way in which their evolution has been affected by their dialogue with the EU.

The shadow of Spain and Portugal over Latin America

Relations between these two regions date from the late fifteenth century, when Christopher Columbus arrived in the Caribbean region on 12 October 1492. He first arrived at Watling Island (nowadays known as the Bahamas group), which Columbus later called El Salvador. Columbus kept sailing for a few days towards Cuba, which he 'identified' as Japan or China in search of the palaces covered in gold that Marco Polo had publicized many years before (Pendle 1963: 33–34). Leaving aside the incredible way these two continents encountered each other, it is crucial to understand that from that moment a conquest of Latin America was begun by Spain. Spain was soon followed by Portugal, and other European states. Due to the competitiveness between the Portuguese and Spanish kings at that time for 'ownership' of the land in the region, Pope Alexander VI established a geographical line that divided the Spanish territory from the Portuguese territory (Pendle 1963). This line has been crucial for the development of both regions, with Brazil on one side and the rest of Latin America on the other. It precipitated a different evolution in the Spanish colonies from that of the Portuguese, to the point where there was little interaction between them until very recently. In fact, Brazil was until the late 1970s in frontier disputes with its neighbours. This also demonstrates the power of the Catholic Church in Europe which was translated to Latin America, particularly in terms of other Portuguese and Spanish invasions of Latin America. Those three centuries of colonial dominance by Portugal and Spain meant the imposition of their languages and their religion, and the creation of a clear demarcation between the two colonies which would affect America in the long term – so much so that Furtado argues that the 'essential features of what was to become the social structure of the Latin American countries originated in the Spanish conquest itself and in the institutions established by the Spanish and Portuguese to create an economic base which would consolidate their conquest of the new lands' (Furtado 1976: 14).

When these territories gained independence in the eighteenth century and figures such as Simon Bolivar inspired the revolutions that led to the independence of Latin American countries, the direction of Spanish and Portuguese territories again progressed in different ways. The Portuguese territories, through a transition without revolutions, became independent and created one nation that became Brazil. Spanish territories experienced revolution and were eventually divided into thirteen republics. According to Murilo de Carvalho (1987: 55–56), this was partly a consequence of education policy. The Portuguese did not want universities to be created in Brazil. Therefore, the elite would have to come to Portugal to study, which led to a generation of graduates from the same university who both knew and trusted each other and would eventually lead to this group gaining control of the Brazilian government. In contrast, Spain modelled the universities in Latin America to resemble the organization of Spanish universities. More specifically, the royal universities replicated the Spanish University of Salamanca, whilst the religious universities were modelled on the Spanish University of Alcala. Thus, according to Murilo de Carvalho, the 'twenty-three universities were scattered in what eventually would become thirteen different countries' (1987: 56). The influence of Spain and Portugal also continued in other ways following de-colonialization.

In terms of regional politics, Brazil did not start to cooperate with its neighbours until the early 1980s. In fact, during the Malvinas/Falklands conflict in 1982, Brazil reacted in a very positive way towards Argentina in response to the wider international reaction to the conflict (Gomez Saraiva and Tedesco 2003). Furthermore, in 1985, Argentina and Brazil, which until that point were clear adversaries and competitors for the leadership of South America and therefore Latin America, started to develop a project of regional integration which would be known later as Mercosur. In many ways this development was unexpected, especially when we consider that centuries of rivalry had ended only recently.

North America comes along and demands its 'backyard'

Just a few years after achieving independence in Latin America from the European countries (with the exception of Cuba), another great power in the making came along and had a dramatic impact on Latin America. The US was reaching the size that it is today when it started to influence Latin American countries internal politics. By the 1890s, the US reached from Maine to California and was intent on further territorial increases. In 1898, after the short (three-month) Spanish–American War, Cuba came to be under US military rule, which lasted until 1902, whilst Puerto Rico passed into the hands of the US (Pendle 1963). The US had strategic interests in Latin America and was not shy in its attempts to achieve these objectives. The 'creation' of Panama in just a few weeks through the US's implicit intervention and the following 'concession' to the US only two weeks later by Panama of the right to create the Panama Canal encouraged Roosevelt further: 'In the western hemisphere the adherence of the United States to the Monroe Doctrine may force the United States, however reluctantly, in flagrant cases of such wrongdoing or impotence, to the exercise of an international policy power' (Pendle 1963: 177).

The various actions of the US in Latin America during the twentieth century provoked the accusation of imperialist behaviour. There is abundant literature which highlights that issue in US–Latin America relations in the twentieth century. The most influential example of that time was *Ariel* by Jose Enrique Rodo (1922, first published 1900), but for more contemporary issues see Chomsky (1992), for example. The Cold War and the fear of

Latin American countries following Cuba's example, after Castro led the revolution in 1959 and made it into a communist state, gave the US the perfect excuse for adopting an even more interventionist approach. This is somewhat evident in the case of the 1980s Central American crisis. At that point the EU intervened in the region for the first time, opening the door to different types of relationships between Europe and Latin America, among them EU–Mercosur relations.

An introduction to Mercosur: the golden boy of regionalism in Latin America

There have been many attempts to develop regional groups in Latin America: for example, the Organization of Central American States in 1951, the Latin American Free Trade Association in 1960 and the Andean Pact in 1969. However, none of these groups was ever able to achieve the same degree of integration as Mercosur. Mercosur has been considered to be not only the most integrated regional group in Latin America, but also one of the most integrated regional groups in the world after the EU. This section will begin by introducing each of the countries that are members of the Mercosur, followed by an explanation of the Mercosur institutions which are central to the discussion and analysis offered in this case study.

Mercosur countries

Brazil
Brazil is by far the largest of all Mercosur countries, covering roughly 75% of the Mercosur geographical territory. Due to both its colonial past and the way that it gained independence from Portugal, Brazil's socio-economic profile can be described as a system of oligarchies. This system has had a direct impact on the question of land distribution/re-distribution, which in turn has had both a continuous and direct impact upon the Brazilian political landscape. In the area of politics, there have been a series of shifts from democratic to dictatorial governments over time. In very broad terms, one period could be seen as running from 1930 to 1964, an era characterized at the outset by a quasi-democratic government, but due to economic instability the country started to experience social turmoil in the late 1940s. Skidmore (1967) provides a comprehensive discussion of Brazilian politics during this period. Skidmore also outlines the nature of the US's involvement in the *coup d'état* that resulted in a military regime from 1964 until 1985. At the same time that democracy returned to Brazil, Mercosur was beginning to be designed. In political terms, the Brazilian dictatorship cannot be compared to the dictatorships of Videla in Argentina and Pinochet in Chile because in the Brazilian case it was not a personal dictatorship. Rather it was a succession of presidents chosen and installed by the military.

Moreover, although it was a dictatorship, it was a government which was recognized internationally – unlike Videla's or Pinochet's, which were subject to international criticism.

The elections of 1985 were not open; instead a very constrained electoral team selected the president, but the first non-military president was chosen, Tancredo Neves. He died of natural causes shortly after being elected and was subsequently replaced by José Sarney, who was not so far from the previous regime in political terms. Sarney was involved in ethically questionable deals, but they did not affect him politically in the same way as some of the deals of the next president, Collor de Mello (1990–1992), who was accused by his own brother of corruption and consequently resigned after two years (Weyland 1993). The level of corruption and the lack of full democracy were the defining features of Brazil at the time of the creation of Mercosur.

Argentina

In Argentina, the twentieth century saw a switch both from military regimes to democratic governments and from democratic governments to military dictatorships. 'Since the 1940s Argentina's political history has been dominated by the military and Peronism, a populist movement with its own political party, the Partido Justicialista (PJ), whose corporatist and statist tendencies are hard to characterise on a left/right continuum' (Waylen 2000: 775).

In 1976, the last military regime and the most repressive in the history of Argentina began when Jorge Rafael Videla instigated a *coup d'état* which brought about his own personal dictatorship. Videla adopted an extremely repressive political line. The Malvinas/Falkland conflict brought international attention to the political situation in Argentina and condemned Videla's dictatorship.

In 1983 democracy returned to Argentina and Raul Alfonsin consolidated the democratic institutions. Alfonsin's victory was possible 'because (unlike the Peronists) it was untainted by the repression and failures of the outgoing military regime' (Waylen 2000: 775). Although Alfonsin enjoyed a good reputation thanks to his efforts towards the democratization of Argentina, economically his policies failed and the next government under a 'Peronist', Carlos Menem, won elections in 1989. Menem was the president for ten years, but just a few years later he was accused of high levels of corruption, like his colleague Collor de Mello in Brazil. Menem was the president who would sign the Treaty of Asunción that created Mercosur in 1991 on behalf of Argentina.

Uruguay

Although Uruguay also experienced dictatorial rule, from 1973 to 1985, it has always been seen as one of the most economically and politically stable countries in South America, to the point that it has been called the Switzerland of Latin America. Apart from the authoritarian government between 1973 and 1985, Uruguay enjoyed democracy during the whole of the twentieth century, and is the Latin America country that has had the longest democracy (Cason 2000).

Uruguay's dictatorship was not as ruthless as that in Argentina but a bit more restrictive than in Brazil in relation to the repression of left-wing ideology and activism. It was not a personal dictatorship and during its twelve years there were different individuals in power. In 1980 the referendum for the constitution proposed by the military was rejected, but it marked the beginning of the transition to democracy because this incident forced a programme of elections and in 1984 the Naval Club Agreement between the leaders of the political parties and the military made possible the elections of 1984 (Chasquetti and Buquet 2004). With Julio Maria Sanguinetti (1985–1990) first, and Luis Alberto Lacalle later (1990–1995), democratic institutions were re-established. The military were afforded an amnesty – considered the price for a stable government in a period of transition. This was the situation in Uruguay when it accepted the invitation of Brazil and Argentina to join the project in 1990: a brand new democracy, in a country considered to be one of the most stable in political and economic terms, and the most democratically advanced in Latin America.

Paraguay

In 1947 a civil war exploded in Paraguay due to huge social inequality. From 1947 to 1962 there was only one legal political party, the Partido Colorado. The first eight years of this period saw a civilian government, but in 1954 there was a *coup d'état* by Alfredo Stroessner Matiauda, who became the dictator until 1989. This was 'only the latest in Paraguay's long and violent history of dictators, international wars, and army intervention in politics' (Sondrol 1992: 128). This dictatorship, known as the '*stronato*', was a personal dictatorship, and although the military had helped Stroessner with the *coup d'état* the military were not the institution ruling the country but the dictator kept a close relation with the military (Sondrol 1992). However, in 1989 another member of the military, Andrés Rodriguez Pedotti, and his supporters challenged Stroessner, who at that time was in his seventies, and negotiated his surrender. The *stronato* was by then weak and with internal divisions which were only increased when Stroessner tried to impose his son Gustavo as his successor. Rodriguez called for elections months after the coup and presented himself as a candidate (Valenzuela 1997). The first elections were suspected of being fraudulent, but they were a first step towards full democratic elections, which finally happened in 1993, when civilian Juan Carlos Wasmosy was chosen in free and direct elections (Valenzuela 1997).

Of the four Mercosur members, Paraguay was the state with the lowest level of democratization at the time of the Treaty of Asunción. Furthermore, it is the most economically dependent of all the Mercosur countries. Therefore, for Paraguay, the development of Mercosur was crucial.

Mercosur

In 1985, the Argentina–Brazil Integration and Economics Cooperation Programme was established. The first important agreement of this programme was the Act of Cooperation and Integration, signed by Argentina and Brazil on 29 July 1986. The objective of this programme was to create economic cooperation between the biggest countries in South America. On 29 November 1988, two years after the Act of Cooperation and Integration, the same countries signed the Treaty of Cooperation, Integration and Development. This treaty was designed to reduce internal tariffs on some goods within ten years (Alvarez 1995; Simancas 1999). On 6 July 1990, the Act of Buenos Aires was signed, with the intention of establishing a common market by 31 December 1994 (Laporte Galli 1995). In the second semester of 1990 Brazil and Argentina invited Uruguay, Paraguay and Chile to join; Chile declined the invitation (Manzetti 1994). On 26 March 1991, the Republic of Argentina, the Federal Republic of Brazil, the Republic of Paraguay and the Oriental Republic of Uruguay subscribed to the Treaty of Asunción. This treaty created the Common Market of the South. Despite consisting of a mere twenty-five pages, the treaty outlined a basic set of objectives and the methods by which these objectives would be achieved (Bouzas and Soltz 2001). One of the main aims was the reduction of the tariffs for Brazil and Argentina by 31 December 1994 and the reduction of the tariffs for Paraguay and Uruguay exactly one year later. In order to achieve this objective, there was an attempt to develop a free circulation of goods and services, in addition to the introduction of a common external tariff, adoption of a common commercial policy, the coordination of macro-economics and sectorial policies and the harmonization of the necessary legislation to strength the process of integration (Bouzas and Soltz 2001; see also www.mercosur.int).

At the end of June 1992, the institutional structure was established. However, it was not until December 1994 that the four members of Mercosur signed the Ouro Preto Protocol (OPP). As a result of this protocol, on 1 January 1995, Mercosur received its international legal powers at the same time that it signed the Europe–Mercosur Inter-regional Framework for Cooperation Agreement (EMIFCA) with the EU.

The institutions of Mercosur

The institutions of Mercosur have been in a state of continuous change since the Treaty of Asunción, which is not surprising since the treaty only had twenty-four articles. The North American Free Trade Agreement (NAFTA) did not have the same political aspirations of integration, yet had more than 1,100 pages with 245 articles (Bouzas and Soltz 2001). Figures 1.1 and 1.2 provide a timeline and an outline of the organization of the Mercosur institutions. As it shows, the decision-making bodies are

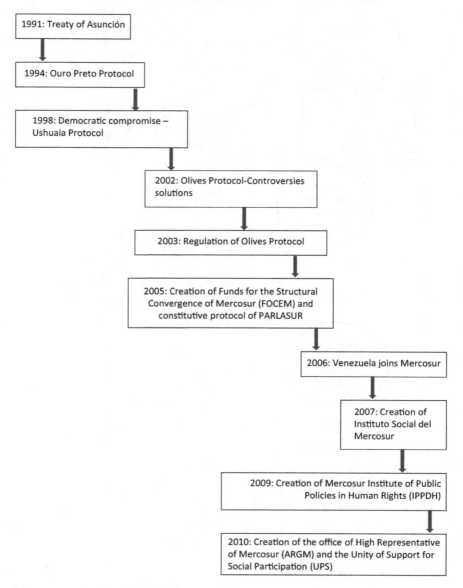

Figure 1.1 Timeline of development of Mercosur

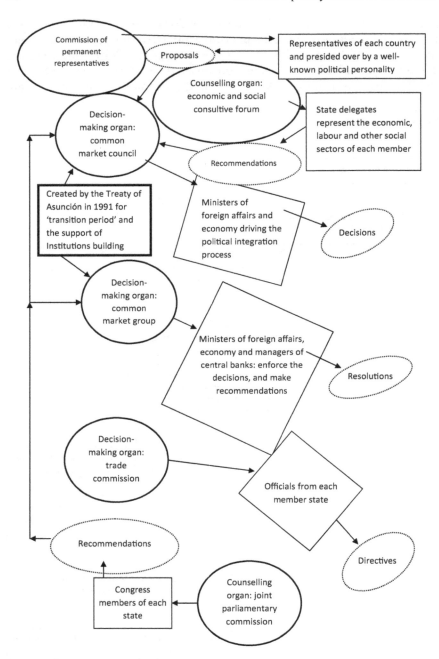

Figure 1.2 Mercosur institutions

completely inter-governmental, with the ministers of economy and foreign affairs the main actors.

Three of Mercosur's decision-making bodies, the Common Market Council (CMC), the Common Market Group (CMG) and the Trade Commission (TC), meet periodically. The first two were created after the Treaty of Asunción and the latter was created at the time of the Ouro Preto Protocol. The CMC was responsible for the process of integration, and the results of its work are decisions. The heads of states are present at CMC meetings at least once per year. The CMG is the executive body and is responsible for executing the decisions of the CMC through resolutions. In addition to this, the CMG is responsible for negotiations with third parties in the name of Mercosur. The third decision-making body, the TC, supports the CMG and produces directives (Bouzas and Soltz 2001).

Mercosur also has three counselling groups: the Joint Parliamentary Commission, the Economic and Social Consultative Forum, and the Commission of Permanent Representatives. These groups were created in 2003 and are very similar to the European Commission in that they are in charge of proposals from the CMC regarding the integration of Mercosur. Mercosur only has one permanent institution, the Administrative Secretariat, which is located in Montevideo (Uruguay). The main function of the Administrative Secretariat is to provide the relevant documents and information to Mercosur members in relation to the protocols and agreements agreed by members (Manzetti 1994; Bouzas and Soltz 2001). The Administrative Secretariat was created by the Treaty of Asunción in 1991 but was improved in the OPP in 1995. The legal sources of Mercosur were defined in the OPP as the following: the Treaty of Asunción, its protocols, related instruments and the agreements reached in the context of the Treaty of Asunción and other related instruments and the decisions, resolutions and directives issued by Mercosur competent organs (see www.mercosur.int).

Conclusion

In order to uncover these reasons behind the EU policy towards Mercosur, the focus of the analysis will be the level of engagement shown by the EU policy towards the South American region. This engagement will be measured by looking at the relation between commitment and ambition. The former is related to the EU's will in achieving its objectives. The latter is related to the EU's status quo and its efforts at moving away from that position. This study will also challenge the value of existing explanations in the literature relating to this topic.

This case study of EU–Mercosur relations is important since EU–Mercosur relations were the first case of inter-regionalism in history and as such this is a crucial moment in the debate regarding the EU's global 'actorness' (or lack thereof), one of the most keenly contested topics in discussions related to EU foreign policy.

This chapter has focused on the introduction of all the aspects of this volume, establishing a broad framework for the case study. First, it has conceptualized the EU's global 'actorness' and linked this concept to the discussion of the EU as a strategic actor since the debate about the existence of an EU strategy towards Mercosur is key for the argument. The discussion then moved on to give some background on Mercosur, starting with a review of regional politics in South America and the three main countries that influenced regional politics, Spain, Portugal and the US. The description finishes in the mid-1980s with the Central American crisis, when the EU became involved in Latin America for the first time. This EU involvement marked the beginning of EU–Mercosur relations, and therefore the discussion is focused on the situation of Mercosur countries in the 1980s. Finally, there is a description of the Mercosur institutions. The next chapter will move to a concise literature review of this topic.

Chapter 2 will critically examine the existing literature in relation to EU–Mercosur relations. In doing so, it will outline the six main arguments offered to explain the development of EU policy towards Mercosur. In addition to this, Chapter 2 will briefly consider those explanations given in relation to the development of EU foreign policy more generally, and how these explanations correspond with the arguments given in relation to the development of EU policy towards Mercosur. Chapter 2 will also provide an account of the methodological approach employed in this study. The discussion in Chapter 3 will focus on outlining the various features of EU policy-making and decision-making that may have influenced the development of EU policy towards Mercosur. Building on this, Chapters 4, 5, 6 and 7 will analyse the different stages of the policy's development.

In the following chapters it will be argued that the EU developed its policy towards Mercosur in a responsive way. More specifically, it will be argued that the EU responded to Mercosur demands that were advanced with the intermediation of Spain and Portugal when they became members of the EU in 1986. Therefore, the argument put forward here will also make a contribution to the general debate about the Europeanization of national foreign policies. In addition to this, it will suggest that there has been a clear response by the EU in relation to promoting regional integration, albeit to a lesser extent. In doing so, this monograph will, therefore, complement existing contributions by critiquing the various arguments presented in the literature which seek to explain the development of EU policy towards Mercosur. Here the discussion will critically examine those arguments concerning Europeanization and the external federator perspective that see it as a proactive process, not reactive as this monograph claims. The other arguments are: counterbalancing the US, global aspiration, long-standing economic and cultural ties and economic interdependence.

2

Analytical framework: relations between the European Union and Mercosur

Introduction

This chapter establishes the analytical framework that will be used to examine EU–Mercosur relations. It begins by offering a critical review of the existing literature. Until now, the literature on EU–Mercosur has been very descriptive but not very analytical. It has tended to cover specific moments of the relations and as a consequence it has forgotten to look at the bigger picture. Most authors have chosen to explain EU–Mercosur relations by using more than one argument at a time without choosing one as the most representative. Furthermore, some authors explicitly say that until the end of the negotiations of the association agreement there cannot be a final answer. This is hardly a clear and strong debate on a policy.

The different arguments presented in the literature will be reviewed in this chapter and will also be considered throughout the monograph in order to understand to what extent they can offer an explanation of the evolution of different stages of the policy. All of the arguments given in the literature suggest that the EU has been proactive in terms of developing this policy and that the EU has more or less acted in a strategic manner. This study questions the proactive perspective by analysing the role of the EU during each of the three key stages of policy development outlined above. Nevertheless, the existing arguments shed some light on the extent to which the EU has behaved as a global actor, which is also one of the most important debates in the area of EU foreign policy. These points will be discussed in more detail below.

The chapter is divided into the following sections. The first section will critically examine the reasons given in the existing literature which seek to explain the development of EU policy towards Mercosur. This section will also consider those arguments which link the EU's role in EU–Mercosur relations to the more general arguments which claim that the EU is a global actor. As Grugel points out, the link between EU–Mercosur relations and the global 'actorness' debate is clear: 'New regionalism thus offers the EU a chance of reaffirming its role as a global actor; in creating a relationship with Mercosur, the EU also remakes itself' Grugel (2004: 622). In the second section the discussion moves on to the methodology used, and the structure of this book in terms of empirical chapters.

Literature review of EU foreign policy towards Mercosur

This section will focus on examining previous attempts to explain the development of EU policy towards Mercosur from the mid-1980s onwards. Since the external relations of the EU have arguably been the last area to be developed, there is a shortage of both theoretical and empirical literature analysing the actions of the EU abroad in the 1980s.

Most of the work on EU–Mercosur, unfortunately, is descriptive (for example, see Sanahuja 2000a; 2003; Kinoshita 2001; Cienfuegos 2006). In this category has to be placed most of the work produced by the Mercosur Chair at the University of Sciences Po, Paris, as well as other studies such as Kirkpatrick et al.'s (2006) work on the Sustainability Impact Assessment. Nevertheless, academic work related to EU–Mercosur relations has grown at different times, which also happen to coincide with successes in EU–Mercosur relations, such as the period around 1995 after the signature of EMIFCA; circa 1999 after the launch of the negotiations for an association agreement, which included an FTA; and circa 2004 when there was a high expectation that there would be a successful end to the negotiations for the association agreement. The way that the literature has developed in terms of analysing EU–Mercosur relations – that is, by focusing on specific successful moments – tends to avoid a detailed discussion of unsuccessful moments. More specifically, the existing literature does not focus on the lack of agreement or progress or on the reasons for those failures, which are just as important to our understanding of the EU–Mercosur relations. They are especially important if we are to fully understand the arguments which suggest that the EU has behaved as a global actor. Another noticeable feature of the existing academic work is the short temporal framework that is used. As already mentioned, there is a clear emphasis on studying EU–Mercosur relations around the time of the 2004 negotiations. This lack of long-term analysis fails to engage with discussions of those explanations which examine other periods of EU–Mercosur relations.

Nevertheless, those works that do look at the situation of the earlier relations between the EU and Latin America in general and Mercosur in particular agree that there has been a clear change in EU–Latin America relations since the mid- to late 1980s (e.g. Aldecoa Luzarraga 1995; Laporte Galli 1995; Anacoreta Correia 1996; Ayuso 1996; Dauster 1996; Piening 1997; Cepal 1999; Hoste 1999; Freres 2000; Youngs 2000; Vasconcelos 2001; Sanahuja 2003; Smith 2003; Cienfuegos 2006). In contrast, other authors (Camino Munoz and Nieto Solis 1992; Bizzozero 1995; Smith

1998; Dinan 1999; Sanchez Bajo 1999; Santander 2005) suggest that it was the early 1990s that marked the change in EU–Latin American relations.

The change in relations at some point between the 1980s and 1990s tends to be explained by several issues. Firstly, it has been suggested that there was a wave of democratization in South American countries. Secondly, it has also been argued that there has been a shift from old regionalism to new regionalism across Latin America which has led to a greater degree of economic openness in the Latin American markets. Thirdly, others have suggested that the change in relations between the EU and Latin America came as a direct result of the EU's involvement in Central America. Furthermore, some authors have argued that the membership of Spain and Portugal of the European Union instigated a change in EU–Latin America relations. Finally, the end of the Cold War and the changes in the international balance of power have also been cited by those who claim that the change in EU–Latin American relations began in the early 1990s. On the surface, all these explanations seem plausible. Nevertheless, although they are not incompatible, the fact that they are treated with the same importance in terms of explaining the development of EU relations with Mercosur demonstrates a degree of ambiguity. Some could claim that EU involvement in Central America was a result of Iberian membership of the EU. It is unclear, though, why the end of the Cold War would be so significant in a region that was already democratic and opening its markets – which did not have links with the Soviet Union – and was also so geographically far from both Europe and Asia. In addition to this, it is remarkable that the change in relations was so dramatic, yet it has attracted so little academic attention. It is important to highlight that the mid-1980s were a pivotal moment and caused a turning point which changed the trajectory of EU policy towards Latin America, a region which had been so blatantly neglected in the previous three decades. Therefore, this period requires further academic analysis in order to clarify our understanding of the development of the relations between the EU and Mercosur.

It should be noted that for most of the period up to 1995, EU policy towards Latin America was synonymous with EU policy towards Mercosur (Aldecoa Luzarraga 1995). In the period after 1995, the EU developed relations with other regional groups and countries. In the existing literature it is common to find scholars using the same reasons to explain both EU policy towards Mercosur and EU policy towards Latin America more generally. These explanations can be grouped into six distinct categories. The remainder of this section examines each of these six explanations.

This monograph seeks to examine the compatibility of each of these arguments across the three distinct periods of policy development. The first possible explanation in the literature suggests that over a period of time the EU sought to counterbalance the influence of the US in the region. It proposes that if the US increased its involvement in Latin America, the EU's involvement would also increase as a direct response. The second explanation that is offered is based on the EU's global aspirations. Here it is suggested that if the EU increased its involvement in international affairs, it would be expected that the EU would become further involved in Latin America. The third way of explaining the development of EU policy towards Latin America is related to the promotion of regional integration abroad. This argument suggests that if there is greater regional integration *within* Latin America, then it is likely that the EU's involvement in the region will also increase. The fourth explanation that is offered in the literature relates to the EU's long-standing, economic and cultural ties with Latin America. This argues that it is to be expected that there will be an increase in the EU's involvement in Latin America as a result of there being an increase in shared values between both regions. The fifth explanation given in the literature, the interdependence debate, is related to the increasing levels of globalization. This argument predicts that if there are increasing levels of trade and foreign direct investment (FDI) in Latin America, the EU's involvement in the region will also increase. Finally, the sixth explanation is that the Iberian membership of the EU will result in an increase in the EU's involvement in Latin America over time.

Counterbalancing the US

The most common argument that can be found in the existing literature focuses on the notion of competition between the EU and the US over Latin America. It suggests that the EU has sought to counterbalance the power and strong levels of influence that the US exerts in the region (Smith 1998; Bulmer-Thomas 2000; Crawley 2000; Giordano 2002; Holland 2002; Santander 2002, 2003; Smith 2003: 80; Torrelli 2003). This literature tends to focus on the last stage of the policy, which takes place from the mid-1990s onwards. Latin America has been considered the 'US's backyard', and the influence of the US in the entire region was important throughout the course of the twentieth century. This argument suggests that, for normative and economic reasons, the EU is trying to achieve the same degree of influence in the regions. In relation to economic issues, this argument is evidenced by the supposed reaction of the EU to the Free Trade Area of Americas project. This US-led project sought to establish economic agreements between the Mercosur and individual Latin American countries. It is suggested that the US and the EU would compete to exert higher levels of influence in Latin America by trying to increase import and export trade levels (Sanahuja 2000b; Arenas 2002; Alecu de Flers and Regelsberger 2005). Santander (2005), for example, specifically refers to the EU's *strategy* against the US.

For Crawley (2000), the strategy is sustained by the timing of events on both sides of the Atlantic. Crawley suggests that the EU was dealing with

Mercosur and trying to get Chile involved in Mercosur, whilst the US was trying to get Chile to join NAFTA. The literature suggests that initiating an FTA has the same level of impact as the negotiations since it demonstrates the 'intentions' of the actor offering the trade agreement. In fact, Crawley (2000) suggests that something similar happened at the Asia–Pacific Economic Cooperation meeting in 1995, where discussions were also held regarding FTAs. Therefore, it could be argued that the EU and the US were fighting for access to markets around the world and not just in Latin America. Similarly, Holland (2002) also argues that the EU was competing with the US in different fields at the same time, continuing the EU's global policy of free trade:

> For the EU, the proposed Latin American FTA does not signify any departure from the dominant economic philosophy of the 1990s: free trade is consistent with its global approach and international rivalry with the United States for trading dominance. Indeed, the prospect of a USA-led Free Trade Area of the Americas (FTAA) composed of a 34-country group from north to south proposed for the year 2005 was an additional motivation for the Europeans. (Holland 2002: 59)

A similar argument is put forward by Claudia Torrelli (2003), who shares Holland's view that the EU and the US were competing for access to the markets of developing countries through the use of FTAs. For some scholars this only partially explains the nature of EU policy development in that there are also other reasons which explain EU policy towards this region (for example, see Smith 1995, 1998). This view is also held by Bulmer-Thomas (2000), who contends that as well as competing with the US, the EU's interest in Latin America emerged as a result of an increase in Mercosur imports, in addition to the EU seeking better access to the automobile sector in Latin America.

The notion that there is a growing political competitiveness between the EU and the US is advanced by Grugel (2004). Grugel argues, 'New regionalism thus offers the EU a chance of reaffirming its role as a global actor; in creating a relationship with Mercosur, the EU also remakes itself' (Grugel 2004: 622). Furthermore, Grugel suggests that the EU has a very specific way of dealing with Mercosur which is more in line with the EU's project on regional integration. The EU is 'attempting to establish new and deeper regional relationships in order to cope with and mitigate the impact of US power' (Cienfuegos 2006: 81). In a way, the 'confrontation' between the EU and the US would be on the normative side, since the EU and the US would be presenting different images and presence to Mercosur. And for a change Mercosur would be in a position where it would be possible to deal with a powerful global actor other than the US. Some writers explicitly disagree with the 'competing' argument. For example, Sanchez Bajo (1999) contends that the EU is trying to integrate developing countries into the world economy. In contrast to the EU–US competition perspective, Klom (2000) argues that regional integration offers a better explanation for the development of EU–Mercosur relations.

This argument on EU–Mercosur can be linked to other general discussions of EU external relations, such as the discussion on EU trade power. Meunier and Nicolaidis argue that:

> The EU is a formidable power in trade. If it is considered as one single economic unit, there is little doubt that it has become, since the last enlargement, the biggest trading bloc in the world. As a result, its potential hegemonic power, based on the capacity to grant or withhold access to its internal market, has become as strong as the US. (Meunier and Nicolaidis 2005: 265)

If the EU is such a powerful actor that it is comparable to the US, then we must consider whether the EU will compete with the US. This is a central question in the debate and the answer seems clear in the literature. For example, Soderbaum and Van Langenhove (2005) argue that the EU is already competing with the US and Japan.

The fact that the EU does not have a military capacity similar to that of the US is a main objection in the debate about whether the EU is a great power. However, this does not seem to be a problem:

> The EU is also becoming a power through trade. Increasingly, it uses market access as a bargaining chip to obtain changes in the domestic arena of its trading partners, from labour standards to development policies. Indeed, one of the central objectives of EU trade policy under trade commissioner Pascal Lamy has been to 'harness globalization' and spread, through the negotiations of trade agreements, the European model of society to the rest of the world. (Meunier and Nicolaidis 2005: 266)

In many ways, this has led to the suggestion that the EU has something in common with the US in that the EU is trying to replicate the US's hegemonic type of behaviour. The EU is taking the US example in promoting trade agreements with regions that are in a weaker position than the EU (Aggarwal and Fogarty 2004).

Hardacre (2009) goes further and draws explicitly on concepts which tend to be found in debates on realism such as 'balancing' and 'bandwagoning' in the area of trade competition. Drawing upon the work of Rüland (2002a: 3), Hardacre outlines the motivation behind seeking further interregionalism between the EU and Mercosur:

> Power balancing is thus now increasingly linked to mercantilist ideas of commercial advance and competition as well as control over international institutions ... In this view, power balancing is pursued for purely commercial reasons, to gain extra preferences, to protect from preference erosion and to open new markets. (Hardacre 2009: 37)

In the case of EU–Mercosur, it is argued that the pursuit of inter-regionalism would be motivated by the EU's desire to counterbalance the influence of the US in Latin America. Aggarwal and Fogarty (2004) contend that such a motivation clearly emanates from a desire to counteract American hegemony by promoting the EU as a political and economic power, able to guarantee security in the international arena by pursuing a 'hub and spoke' strategy, a reply to the American approach to the Free Trade Area of the Americas (FTAA).

Hardacre writes, 'Closely linked to the balancing is the concept of bandwagoning, a related realist concept which describes the joining of regional or inter-regional initiatives so as not to be left out, or behind' (Hardacre 2009: 37). In this instance, EU–Mercosur inter-regionalism would be activated on the EU side in order that the EU is not left out of the potential success of the FTAA. Furthermore, Hardacre contends that 'Balancing and bandwagoning are closely related concepts and can be related to inter-regionalism' (Hardacre 2009: 38) and uses Rüland's work (2002b) to explain that by being flexible with each other, regional players could help each other if the occasion necessitated it. With the help of Rüland's work, Hardacre tries to further extend the debate on the motivations underlying the EU's interactions with other regions by focusing on the EU's foreign policy.

Leaving aside the debate on EU foreign policy, this section has discussed the argument that the EU has sought to counterbalance US influence in Latin America. The discussion above has suggested that the EU has interacted with Mercosur by adopting a 'hub and spoke' tactic, trying to develop agreements with regions in a weaker position to gain influence in the region as a whole since the EU will be the one setting the agenda. All the authors mentioned above who advanced this argument take for granted the notion that the EU is a strategic actor. This argument will be critically examined in more detail in the following chapters.

Affinity

Another set of scholars cite the affinity between the EU and Latin America as the main reason for both the development of relations and for the two regions becoming 'natural' partners (for example, see Aldecoa Luzarraga 1995; Sanahuja 2004; Freres 2000; Freres and Sanahuja 2005). According to Dinan (1999), since 1960 the traditional relations between the EU and Latin America were the result of the close socio-historical and cultural links between the two regions. This perspective also suggests that this relationship would become even closer as a direct consequence of the Iberian membership of the EU. However, this did not happen, mainly as a result of both the levels of debt and the political instability in Latin American countries. This suggests that there are limitations to the 'affinity' argument and the notion that the EU and Latin America would become more intimate. In other words, increased levels of closeness were hindered by the debilitated state of the economies in Latin America and also as a result of the political instability which stems back to the 1960s. This, perhaps, demonstrates that concrete events and issues prevented the natural course of events predicted by those advocating the 'affinity' perspective from taking place when Spain and Portugal joined the EU.

Sanahuja (2004) also shares the view that convergent objectives and values would determine the EU's increasing involvement in Latin America. However, he does not offer a further explanation for why this would occur. Nevertheless, Sanahuja does provide important information which gives insights into the main obstacles that prevented the EU from developing a more intimate relationship with Mercosur. He cites the EU's protectionist approach to its agricultural markets which were in direct competition with the very competitive South American agricultural products, particularly in negotiations at the World Trade Organization (WTO). Furthermore, Freres (2000: 63) interestingly points out that despite the affinity that is said to exist between the EU and Latin America, and although a policy of inter-regional integration would in fact be in keeping with the EU's wider international agenda, such a policy did not emerge because of the ambivalent way that the EU has behaved towards Latin America.

Other authors have further elaborated on the notion that there are natural links between the EU and Latin America. For example, Aldecoa Luzarraga (1995) argues that the structural factors that strengthen the links between the two regions are the historical and cultural links of the last five centuries. For Aldecoa Luzarraga, these links are evidenced by similarities in legal principles, written constitutions and a common patrimony, in addition to similar social models, patterns of democratization, regional integration and the improved competitiveness of Latin American economies. Aldecoa Luzarraga also suggests that the development of relations between the EU and Latin America follows a cause-and-effect mechanism.

Drawing upon the work of Dromi and Molina del Pozo (1996), Kanner (2002) also argues that the EU and Mercosur are 'natural' partners due to a series of factors, including the following: a common culture as a result of colonialism and a process of immigration between both regions; common political values; process of democratization; the development of open market economies; and, finally, both share a similar respect for individual rights and freedoms, the rule of law and have a common model of integration. However, in contrast to Kanner, Smith (1998) argues that it is the US, not the EU, that is the 'natural' partner of Latin America. More specifically, Smith argues that this is a result of 'simple geographic proximity, increasingly a common culture with Latin American elites being trained in the United States and Spanish-speaking Latin Americans forming a growing part of the workforce and social landscape of the United States' (Smith 1998: 165–166).

There is, however, a glaring omission in Smith's argument. She does not discuss whether individual Latin American countries actually want to be partners with the US due to the historically difficult relationship the region has had with the US throughout the course of the twentieth century. Without getting into the debate about 'anti-Americanism' in Latin America, it is, however, important to examine to what extent Mercosur was keen to develop its relations with the EU – whether doing so was a result of 'anti-Americanism' or whether the Mercosur was looking to place itself in a stronger position when it came to future negotiations of the FTAA. The progress that Mercosur had been able to achieve in terms of creating intra-regional integration also appears to be the best method of advancing cooperation with the EU (Laporte Galli 1995: 12). Nevertheless, if it was Mercosur's intention to make it easy for the EU to establish the first inter-regional agreement in history, it is also plausible that this could have had an effect on the EU's policy towards Mercosur. In this case, it could be argued that inter-regionalism was in fact an aim in itself rather than the means to achieve something else.

Regionalism

In contrast to the 'counterbalancing' and 'affinity' perspectives discussed above, some authors suggest that in general the EU's role as external federator in Latin America and Mercosur in particular provide the main explanation for the development of the EU's policy agenda towards Latin America (e.g. Hoste 1999; Sanchez Bajo 1999; Klom 2000; Kanner 2002; Carranza 2004; Grugel 2004; Botto 2007). However, much of this work is largely descriptive and fails to offer a satisfactory analysis of what the EU was actually trying to achieve by promoting regionalism (i.e. EU civilian power) (Hoste 1999; Kanner 2002). Here it should be noted that there is a fine line between EU actions and EU intentions. In other words, Latin America may in fact choose to imitate the EU as a model of regional integration, but this does not mean that it is the EU that is pushing Latin America/Mercosur to follow the EU model.

Interestingly, the article by Andy Klom (2000), who was, at that time, the desk officer for Mercosur at the External Relations Directorate General of the European Commission in Brussels, confirms how important the EU model of integration was in terms of how Mercosur was constructed. Klom also confirms that the explanation of promoting regionalism explains EU–Mercosur relations more clearly. However, what is not clear is whether this is in fact the view of the desk officer or indeed the position of the European Commission as a whole, particularly when taking into

consideration just how powerful the director general is within the Commission. Botto (2007) brings a more Eurocentric view to the discussion of
regional cooperation and the promotion of regionalism. According to
Botto, the move towards regional integration was a consequence of advantages to be gained by dealing with an entire group of countries at the same
time rather than dealing with each country individually. Furthermore, this
would also help to ensure that each member state remained committed to
the group as a whole. In addition to this, Sanchez Bajo (1999) suggests
that the EU is actually behaving in accordance with its institutional design,
which prioritizes regional integration in Mercosur over and above its own
trade interests. However, Smith (2003) is opposed to this position, arguing
that EU support for regional integration is not the actual aim but in fact
the means to achieve another goal – a competitive advantage over the US,
particularly in relation to the FTAA. For Smith (1998), regional integration is supported but at the same time ensures that the EU had greater
access to the economic markets of Latin America.

Carranza (2004) and Grugel (2004) both discuss the promotion of
regionalism within a wider discussion of the distinctiveness of the EU's
civilian power in contrast to the US's approach to the region. According to
Carranza, the difference between the approaches can be found in the fact
that the US approach has a military component, whereas the EU approach
is more orientated towards economic development. In contrast, Grugel
argues that the difference between the EU and the US is that the EU treats
Mercosur as a partner and respects the latter's wish to pursue regional
integration. Grugel supports the argument and cites the promotion of
regional integration through normative values. However, there is a lack of
supporting evidence for the argument that the EU prioritizes the promotion
of regional integration.

The argument of promoting regionalism abroad can be linked to the
general debate about EU normative power. There is some discussion which
argues that the EU is a normative power, and he normative approach is
related to the idea that the EU model is an example for other regions. This
argument suggests that the European project has set both an example and
a standard of regional integration project and stability that promote the
consolidation of universal values with other regions, especially regional
integration.

The evolution of the EU project has also been linked to Kantian philosophy. Dunne (2008) argues that the EU's identity has been shaped by cos-
mopolitan values. Regarding international relations, the development of the
EU has also been analysed using the concepts of civilian and normative
power in terms of the way that the EU behaves in the international context
(for example, see Manners 2002). However, Duchene (1972: 9) has used
the concept of 'normative power' in relation to civilian power in order to
understand the way in which the EU has tried to exert its influence in

international relations. In his article which develops the idea of EU normative power, Manners (2002) has become one of the strongest defenders of
the idea of EU normative power. Here Manners argues that the European
project has challenged the traditional Westphalia system of states and set
an example to others by behaving as a normative power. More recently,
Manners (2008) has argued that the notion of the EU as a normative power
is linked to the following nine substantive normative principles which the
EU promotes in international politics: sustainable peace, freedom, democracy, human rights, the rule of law, equality, social solidarity, sustainable
development and good governance. Manners (2008) contends that this form
of EU normative power is based on a further three primary principles: living
by example, being reasonable and doing least harm (Manners 2008).
However, it could be argued that this is a list of what the EU is not rather
than a checklist of what the EU actually does.

In terms of the economic attraction of Latin America to other countries,
the existing literature questions whether the EU's involvement is related to
what the EU is capable of doing or to what it has actually done. For
example, it is argued that the EU's power comes from the size of its markets,
its levels of capital and technological resources and the soft power that it
can operationalize diplomatically (Maull 2005). The membership perspective, however, is the strongest evidence of European influence. This
perspective:

> generally rests on its track records in sustaining peace and creating wealth,
> and in the ideas on which its civilization model is built, its most important
> specific source of influence is the perspective of EU membership [...] Yet it
> needs to be borne in mind that this source of European influence mostly rests
> on what the EU has and is, rather than what it can do. (Maull 2005: 782)

In addition to the socio-economic weight of the EU, which is used in
order to exert the EU's influence in terms of international relations through
association agreements, including the use of diplomacy, financial offers and
the potential to threaten sanctions. However, the most important factor is
'the EU's post-modern conceptualization of sovereignty, which has allowed
it to evolve superior forms of governance of considerable attraction to
others, and its ability to engage other regions in dialogue and cooperation
and thus to catalyse regionalism elsewhere' (Maull 2005: 784).

This brings us to the third point advanced by Maull: that the EU has
tried to influence the political interaction of states by promoting regional
cooperation through dialogue or cooperation, or by trying to install the EU
model as an example which can civilize international relations. This leads
us to the following question: what has the EU actually done in terms of
promoting and establishing regional integration?

It is generally accepted that the EU is the most integrated regional group
in the world and is very much a pioneer in doing so. Moreover, the EU

actively tries to promote regional integration across the world and promotes inter-regionalism. For example, as Soderbaum and Van Langenhove (2005) highlighted, in September 2001 the president of the European Council of Ministers, Belgian prime minister, Guy Verhofstat, proposed that the G8 should be replaced by a forum where the EU, the African Union, Mercosur, the Association of South East Asian Nations (ASEAN) and NAFTA are able to speak at the same political level. Therefore it is not surprising that the EU has been a prominent actor in most cases of inter-regionalism, such as the EU–ASEAN, EU–Mercosur and the EU–Central American Common Market (CACM) partnerships. The EU has also developed more than twenty groups of states through which trade, aid and political dialogue are coordinated (Marsh and Mackenstein 2005). There are examples of inter-regional agreements under different EU treaty articles. The EU agreement with the European Free Trade Association was made under Article 113 for the 1972 and 1973 agreements, under Article 235 (the most popular for inter-regional agreements) the joint European Community–Council for Mutual Economic Assistance Declaration and under Article 238 the agreement with the African, Caribbean and Pacific Group of States (ACP) (Flaesch-Mougin 1990). Arguably the starting point of the EU's inter-regionalism strategy is the association agreement of Yaounde I in 1963 and Yaounde II in 1969. These were soon followed by the Euro-Arab Dialogue and negotiations for agreements with ASEAN in the 1970s and in the 1980s with discussions with Latin America through the Group of Latin American Ambassadors, which met in Brussels (Regelsberger 1990).

In terms of examining the different types of inter-regional projects, some work has been done by Aggarwal and Fogarty (2004) and Hardacre (2009). However, there has been little debate about these in recent years. The discussion is somewhat hindered by the fact that there is not a sufficient amount of information available about when and why inter-regional projects have developed as a constituent part of the EU's foreign policy (Soderbaum and Van Langenhove 2005). In fact, 'There is no consensus on the main concept in the study of regionalism, and there is even greater disagreement in the conceptualization of inter-regionalism' (Soderbaum and Van Langenhove 2005: 257).

In relation to the suggestion that there is little agreement amongst academics regarding the 'conceptualization of inter-regionalism', an excellent book edited by Edwards and Regelsberger (1990: 9–10) laid out the initial arguments, suggesting that it started some time ago and explaining the specific reasoning regarding the development of inter-regionalism. Christopher Hill, for example, argued in 1988 that there is a need for an empirical study of the EU's involvement in other regions if we are to truly understand the notion of EU civilian power. Jorg Monar's (1997) work is another of the best works focusing on the early years of inter-regionalism.

Nevertheless, Regelsberger argues that group-to-group relations are the result of the EU's internal logic in that this:

Adds another dimension to the existing multi-faceted picture of a European foreign policy. It does not develop in a linear and precisely defined manner, but more in an accidental and pragmatic dialogue – ... the posture of the EC/ Twelve in it ... will be determined by similar factors inherent in the complex system of intra-European decision-making in general. (Regelsberger 1990: 10)

According to Regelsberger, group-to-group relations are the outcome of complex and difficult intra-European bargaining processes which may have different goals but in the end positions converge.

The issue of multilateralism versus regionalism is also important because the EU publicly promotes the former and at the same time continues to develop inter-regional agreements. Smith (2006) points out that according to several scholars (Aggarwal and Fogarty 2004; Young 2004; Meunier and Nicolaidis 2005), the EU could end up in a difficult position as a result of the WTO's stipulations. Aggarwal and Fogarty (2004) argue that an analysis of inter-regionalism as a process or an outcome is also useful. However, Soderbaum and Van Langenhove (2005) see this approach as a policy strategy. Soderbaum and Van Langenhove (2005) contend that inter-regionalism itself is the aim and should also be linked to the development of the EU's role as a global actor. In this sense, the EU aims to develop inter-regionalism as part of its global strategy, which is not designed to achieve defined outcomes in those regions which are partners in projects of inter-regionalism. However, Monar (1997) offers an alternative explanation: he argues that the dialogues are not set up as a specific policy strategy, although he agrees that they are without an intended consequence:

Seen from a historical perspective, the main reason for setting up dialogues has been a strong demand from third countries to enter into somewhat more structured relations with the emerging political actor, European Political Cooperation ... This 'reactive' component of the dialogues' origins does not mean, however, that there were and are not other good reasons for engaging in dialogues on the European side. (Monar 1997: 266)

Monar also outlines the characteristics of dialogues with groups: 'Dialogues are very flexible instruments that can be either precede or complement economic relations' (Monar 1997: 266). He suggests that dialogues can show no clear plan or strategy towards a specific region. Instead, he argues that relations between the EU and regions develop through more of a 'learn by doing' approach. The level of 'commitment is not high with decisions on meetings according to time and interest constraints, and even freeze the dialogues altogether' (Monar 1997: 272). Thanks to the lack of precision, the EU can play a powerful game with the third parties since in most of the cases it is the bigger player: 'They can be useful when pursuing mid or long-term political strategies' (Monar 1997: 272). Monar's argument also reinforces the suggestion that there are multiple possibilities in terms of dialogues between the EU and 'third parties' which are continually ongoing and display a lack of precise or coherent strategy. Monar also argues that the reactive nature of the EU can have unexpected consequences: 'It hardly seems an exaggeration to say that many third countries are competing for "upgrading" of their dialogues with the Union, asking for higher levels of meetings and/or more frequent meetings. There is a serious risk that the dialogue system will become the victim of its own success' (Monar 1997: 272).

This section has examined the various arguments which suggest that it is the EU that has promoted regional integration. The discussion began by examining the existing literature that focuses on EU–Mercosur relations, before moving on to discuss the more general debate relating to whether or not the EU has actively promoted regional integration. In doing so, it was argued that there needs to be a distinction made between what the EU is and what the EU actually does. It has also been suggested that there needs to be a distinction between what the EU has actually done and what the EU is capable of doing. Finally, this section has also outlined another key theme in debates relating to the promotion of regionalism – the possibility of the EU undertaking a reactive role in promoting regionalism, particularly in terms of acting as an external federator in wider international affairs.

The European Union's global aspirations

Another argument in the literature is related to the EU's global aspirations. It could be argued that discussions relating to EU policy towards Mercosur should be placed within a broader examination of the EU's agenda regarding external relations. If it is accepted that the EU is developing a global agenda, then the case of Latin America, and Mercosur in particular, must be included as part of that agenda. This is certainly the view of some scholars (for example, see Laporte Galli 1995; Galinsoga 1995; Smith 1998; Freres 2000; Santander 2005). The intention of the EU is to play a greater role at the international level through inter-regional agreements and that is why these arrangements have emerged (Santander 2005).

It has been argued by some scholars that the EU's global pretensions are not completely separate from the way that the US has sought to influence international politics (see Galinsoga 1995; Smith 1998). However, it could be claimed that this is, in part, a result of the unipolar system that has been created following the end of the Cold War, which has seen the US adopt the role of the most dominant global political power. Therefore, in order to promote its own global agenda, the EU has to respond to the US position. As Smith explains, the EU and the US have come together in order to pursue their shared interests:

The end of the Cold War allowed the Clinton administration to pursue a global foreign policy with proactive emphasis on promoting US economic security through opening into dynamic regional trading blocs. For its part, the EU was compelled to reconsider the adequacy of its economic and political strategy vis-à-vis Latin America. The EU and the US share the same economic objectives in terms of wanting to create and maintain open markets. (Smith 1998: 165)

In summary, it could be argued that the end of the Cold War and a wider discussion about processes of globalization can partly explain developments in inter-regional dialogue between the EU and Mercosur (see Doctor 2007).

The work of Giordano (2002) in this area is somewhat ambiguous and fails to present reasons for why the global strategy occurred. Giordano focuses only on the reasons behind the negotiation for the inter-regional association agreement EMIFCA and presents the explanation for why the EU sought to create such an agreement. Firstly, Giordano claims, this agreement would allow both regions to deal with a multi-polar global governance system. Secondly, this agreement would set an example for the European Commission on how to develop trade and cooperation relations with other countries and regions. In addition to this, Giordano argues that the inter-regional association agreement would also strengthen the historical links between Latin America/Mercosur, Spain and Portugal. However, more importantly, this agreement would secure a regulatory framework for the EU's FDI in the region.

Laporte Galli (1995) is also somewhat ambiguous in terms of providing reasons. According to Laporte Galli, the European Commission wants to develop an external policy independent of the individual member states; Laporte Galli also suggests that the development of an ambitious external policy could not ignore a region of the size and economic weight of Latin America, and points also to the importance of the roles of Spain and Portugal even before they were members. In addition to this, Freres (2000) adopts an approach which focuses on a more civilian perspective, particularly the notion of 'world responsibility'. Here, Freres argues that it is imperative that the EU consider the development of policy frameworks with Latin America if the EU really has global 'ambitions'. There are, however, gaps in Freres' argument. For example, almost since its creation, the EU has developed inter-regional dialogues. This is evidenced by examples such as dialogues with the ACP, Mediterranean and ASEAN countries. If the EU has developed a new impetus following the end of the Cold War, Freres does not offer a rationale which explains dialogues with the other groups such as Mercosur and the intimacy of the dialogues between the EU and Latin America more generally, which started in the 1980s while the Cold War was still ongoing. Furthermore, these dialogues did not dramatically alter during the course of the 1990s.

Trade

Less common in the existing literature are discussions focusing on globalization processes and the impact that these would have on trade relations between the EU and Latin America, and whether this would lead to an increase in the EU's interest in Mercosur, especially in terms of the FTAs. Nevertheless, Holland (2002) contends that the free trade agreement is part of 'the proposed Latin American FTA [that] does not signify any departure from the dominant economic philosophy of the 1990s: free trade is consistent with its [EU] global approach' (Holland 2002: 59). Holland argues that this is of potential benefit to European companies. The existing studies diverge on this, with some suggesting that the FTA would discourage European FDI (see Robles 2008), whilst others claim that the FTA would encourage European FDI in Latin America/Mercosur (Cienfuegos 2006).

Some of the most analytical work has been carried out by Faust (2004) and Doctor (2007). These works are particularly important, bearing in mind that in other studies it is common to find a somewhat superficial analysis of both the nature of and the motives for the way that the EU developed its policy towards Mercosur. Faust (2004) tries to explain the EU trade strategy using a multi-causal research strategy. He examines the interplay of economic interest between groups and political actors and how this relates to the wider international context. This leads Faust to classify the EU–Mercosur case as an example of the EU's inter-regional trade strategy and he concludes that 'the empirical evidence demonstrates that there is no single variable with sufficient explanatory power to clarify the course of EU–Mercosur trade relations' (Faust 2004: 20). Doctor (2007) builds upon Faust's attempts to develop a multi-causal framework analysis which focuses on international, regional/national and societal/sub-national factors in order to understand the processes of EU–Mercosur inter-regionalism. In doing so, he links the international factors to processes of globalization and the end of the Cold War bipolarity and also links the strategic interests of political actors in both the EU and Mercosur with the interests of other economic and societal actors (Doctor 2007: 289). From this, Doctor outlines the reasons as to why the FTA between the EU and Mercosur was not completed, particular after 2004. It could be argued that Doctor has developed a conceptual framework based on inter-regionalism which is, to a certain extent, close to a complex interdependence approach. This differs from the perspective developed in this study, which aims to analyse the actions of the EU, whereas Doctor's work focuses on analysing the relationship between the EU and Mercosur rather than the individual parties.

There is a comprehensive range of data in the existing literature which highlights levels of exports, imports and overall trade between the EU and Latin America or between the EU and a specific country in the region, or on levels of exports, imports and overall trade between the EU and Mercosur. Each of these cases tends to emphasize the economic importance of relations with the EU, particularly to what extent trade between the two regions is important for Latin America, but they do not highlight the small importance for the EU in relative terms. Cienfuegos (2006: 275) does mention the percentage increase of imports to the EU from Mercosur in relative terms, but does not mention the actual volume of that trade. More importantly, it ignores the point of how important an increase of 0.023–0.027% of all the EU imports can be. They are different relative gains rather than absolute gains for analytical purposes, as is explained in this monograph. This is particularly important in terms of understanding the real economic interest of the EU in this region.

The influence of Spain and Portugal after they joined the EU

The importance of the Iberian countries becoming members of the EU is another factor that is cited in attempts to explain the development of EU policy towards Mercosur. Across the literature on this topic this argument is granted different degrees of importance. The significance of the Iberian membership of the EU also tends to be explained alongside other factors and not as the principal factor that explains the development of EU policy towards Mercosur. It is also clear that those who employ this argument tend to refer to the cultural, historical and social links between Spain and Portugal and Latin America which are the product of the Iberian countries' role as colonizing powers in the region.

Aldecoa Luzarraga (1995) mentions the issue of EU membership and without further explanation affirms how important it was that Spain held the presidency of the EU in 1995, in terms of improving relations between the EU and Mercosur. In contrast, Ayuso (1996) discusses the importance of Spain and Portugal becoming members of the EU in 1986 and Spain's aims of becoming a bridge between both regions. Ayuso (1996) argues that this was somewhat unsuccessful due to the opposition from both the UK and France, which had their own vested interests in their own former colonies. Crucially, Ayuso also claims that Latin America has always been a secondary area of interest compared with the Mediterranean and the Eastern and European countries. Unfortunately, however, Ayuso does not provide a detailed discussion of these points or detailed research on this topic. Therefore, there is a lack of evidence to support the argument.

Grabendorff (1987), an expert in EU–Latin America relations since the 1970s, wrote about the importance of the role of Spain and Portugal as early as 1987. He explains that the EU did not fully support Spain and Portugal's efforts to develop their interests in Latin America. In doing so, Grabendorff argues that Spain and Portugal would require an alliance of countries if they were to achieve substantial progress:

> Biregional relations have not have not displayed any substantial change up
> to now. Spain has distinguished itself within the Community by focusing
> greater attention on the problems of Latin America, functioning not so much
> as a broker who acts as an advocate or, at the least, critic, but more as a
> defender of the region within the EC, a role previously played – to a certain
> extent – by Italy, and by the FRG [Federal Republic of Germany]. (Graben-
> dorff 1987: 70)

It is extremely interesting just how clear and precise Grabendorff's predic-
tions were at such an early stage. It is also unfortunate that Grabendorff's
study only takes us up to 1987.

Piening (1997) argues that it is not a surprise that there is a link with
Latin America after Spain and, to a lesser extent, Portugal joined the EU.
In fact, Piening suggests that this is typical for the EU to try and develop
links with the former colonies of its member states. This also provides
reasons as to why the EU intervened in the Central American peace process
since 1984. 'Above all, the return to Latin America of democracy and a
measure of political stability, along with the attractions of an emerging
market, combined to make the consolidation of relations irresistible'
(Piening 1997: 123).

Sanahuja (2003) also explains how the EU's interest in Latin America
has varied over time. According to Sanahuja, since the 1970s there has been
a network of economic and political relations which has been given new
impetus following the Iberian membership of the EU. The extent to which
this network of relations is important is somewhat debatable as it has not
been discussed by other authors studying EU–Latin American relations
prior to Spain and Portugal joining the EU.

Sanahuja argues that the EU became a strong counterweight for Latin
America in the latter's dealings with the US, which is something of an
exaggeration. According to Sanahuja, in the 1990s the EU developed a
strategy towards Latin America which displayed a clear emphasis on trade.
Hoste (1999) argues that, in addition to the economic reasons, there were
also political motivations for the EU to develop a new policy agenda towards
Latin America. For example, Hoste makes reference to the end of the Cold
War and, in particular, Spain and Portugal becoming members of the EU,
which, as already mentioned, was consistent with the EU's traditional focus
on developing relations with the former colonies of EU member states.

In relation to this, Baklanoff (1996) makes two very interesting points
when analysing relations between Spain and Latin America during the
1980s and early 1990s. Firstly, Baklanoff argues that the massive FDI in
Latin America during this period should be understood as a 'reconquest'.
Crucially, he suggests how Spain's membership did improve the relations of
Latin America with the EU as well as how the membership had an effect
on Spain, since membership automatically halted any economic preferential
agreements with Latin America.

One of the richest studies on the relationship between Spain, Latin America and the EU was carried out by Richard Youngs (2000). In his article 'Spain, Latin America and Europe: the complex interaction of regionalism and cultural identification', Youngs also questions the idea that Spain has benefited from EU membership in relation to its policies towards Latin America. Although this is not the primary focus of this monograph, Youngs's study does unearth important empirical data and confirms the importance of Spain and Portugal joining the EU. This data will be used in this book to explore relations between the EU and Mercosur. Kennedy (2000) also confirms the strategic importance of Latin America for Spain and the way that this has enabled Spain to try and exert a greater degree of influence within the EU since becoming a member state in 1986. He also argues that Spain was unsuccessful in influencing the EU, but a lack of empirical data undermines this claim. Furthermore, unlike this study, Kennedy's work focuses on Latin America rather than trying to explain how Spain and Portugal played a role in developing EU policy towards Mercosur.

By far the most comprehensive empirical study in this area has been conducted by Klaus Dykmann (2006) in his book *Perceptions and politics: the foreign relations of the European Union with Latin America*. This extraordinary piece of work analyses a vast amount of empirical data. Dykmann examines Spain's role in developing EU foreign policy towards Latin America, as well as demonstrating that there were other countries involved in developing the EU's foreign policy in the region. Unfortunately, his study only focuses on the last few years of policy development and therefore fails to examine the role that Spain has played since the 1980s. Furthermore, Dykmann uses very few documents or written statements and there is a degree of bias in that the evidence is mostly based on the information gathered from the interviews conducted. For example, the discussion of the shutdown of the Institute of European–Latin American Relations (IRELA) is not completely convincing. In addition to this, his study would have benefited from comparing the development of EU foreign policy towards Mercosur with other contexts in the international system, such as the WTO and the development of external relations between the EU and other regions similar to Latin America.

Vasconcelos's (2001) work is also very persuasive and develops a clear understanding of the differences in terms of the preference of the EU member states and institutions in relation to Latin America. According to Vasconcelos, historical factors explain why Spain, Portugal and Italy prioritized Mercosur, while the potential of investments in the region explained Germany's prioritization of Mercosur in EU foreign policy. Vasconcelos (2001: 146) suggests that France has an incoherent political line due to its position in the agricultural sector, its particular view of Mexico, and its acceptance that Mercosur has a place in a multi-polar world. Vasconcelos also argues that the interest of other EU countries in Mercosur only relates to trade. Therefore, when Spain and Portugal became members of the EU it gave new impetus to EU–Latin America relations at the same time as the wave of democratization in the region and the establishment of regional groups. However, it is not clear why wealthier and more power-ful nations within the EU such as Italy and Germany did not previously develop relations with Latin America at an earlier stage. Once again, the issue of trade interest does not seem very definitive if attention is given to the lack of importance for the EU trading with Latin America in relative terms.

In contrast to those who support the idea that EU–Latin America rela-tions developed when the Iberian countries joined the EU, Smith argues that Spanish and Portuguese membership of the EU did not impact on EU policy towards Latin America:

> The Latin American states were not reassured by the entrance of Spain and Portugal into the EC [European Community] in 1986. There was concern that the Iberian accession would mean more difficulties for Latin American agri-cultural exporters … Neither has Spain evolved as a significant political interlocutor for Latin America as had been predicted by some sectors of European and Latin American opinion. (Smith 1998: 166)

Similarly, Ribeiro Hoffmann (2004) also questions the degree of importance that can be attached to the influence of Spain and Portugal, particularly in the area of FDI since Spain and Portugal would deal with this at a national level.

In broader debates relating to the influence of individual member states on EU policies, the discussion also refers to the Europeanization of national foreign policies of EU member states.

Historical institutionalism and Europeanization

The concept that 'history matters' is the starting point of historical institu-tional approaches emphasizing the importance of the Europeanization of national foreign policies. Initial decisions about the way that an institution is created will affect the future but decisions taken at a particular moment of history by an institution can also be a factor that can determine the future of the protagonists of those events. By transporting the idea that 'history matters' into the framework of historical institutionalism, the concept is used to follow the idea that historical events can produce institutional change. In order to chart the evolution of certain events within institutions, this approach starts from an explanation of the historical event. Here it is argued that the historical event will create a path dependence as explained in Chapter 1, relying on the work of Pierson (2000) and Sewell (1996).

More generally, 'Institution-based approaches emphasise the role of existing institutional configurations as independent explanatory factors in the analysis of political outcomes and institutional development' (Knill 2001: 21). This means that the explanation of a policy outcome – for example, the outcome of an EU policy towards a region – needs to be linked to the way that the EU institutions are configured. In other words, the way EU institutions work helps to explain the processes which are directly linked to the outcome of a particular policy. In the case of historical intuitionalism, time and timing are key. Drawing upon the work of Skocpol (1992) and King (1995), Peters explains, 'the policy choices made when an institution is being formed, or when a policy is initiated, will have a continuing and largely determinate influence over the policy far into the future' (Peters 2001: 63).

The link between historical institutionalism and the concept of Europeanization is based on the idea that Europeanization, broadly speaking, is related to the influence of or influence in EU institutions. As a consequence of this 'influence', EU institutions upload a national idea/policy and 'institutionalize' the idea/policy to the point that it is taken up by other EU member states. Nevertheless, whether it is through a process of downloading or uploading, EU institutions provide the framework in which a policy is developed. In other words, EU institutions 'matter' in terms of the way this policy is taken up or downloaded. EU institutions are also an independent variable during the development of a policy. More specifically, understanding the nature of EU institutions helps to explain why the policy is created and the way that it is either downloaded at the national level or uploaded at the EU level. And finally, EU institutions matter in terms of historical context, particularly the way that it takes a historical event to initiate a policy or a process of path dependency. However, the historical event does not need to be something unusual or totally unexpected but rather a critical juncture where the success of a policy is determined by being in the right place at the right time. In other words, if the policy had emerged at a different time and place, the nature of the policy would be quite different.

Europeanization is certainly not a new concept; it has been used in many studies. However, very few scholars have tried to provide an exact definition of Europeanization (Featherstone and Radaelli 2003). In the area of foreign policy, Wong (2008) argues that the notion of there being a Europeanization of foreign policy was initiated by Ben Tonra (2001). Therefore, the definition of Europeanization will echo the definition used in the area of foreign policy. Tonra defines Europeanization as: 'A transformation in the way in which national foreign policies are constructed, in the ways in which professional roles are defined and pursued and in the consequent internationalisation of norms and expectations arising from a complex system of collective European policy making' (Tonra 2001: 229, in Wong 2008: 323).

A key question in the study of European foreign policy relates to the concept of 'movement'. The concept of Europeanization itself is about movement, particularly when speaking of 'transformation'. When examining the issue of transformation, it is important to ask what is actually transforming. In other words, what is changing and what are the mechanisms and direction of change (top-down from the EU to the member states, bottom-up, or socialization)? (Wong 2008: 323). In relation to 'what is changing', the discussion is about the changing of either procedures or the substance of the foreign policies of individual members states (Wong 2008). In line with the discussion above, this relates to the idea of a member state trying to influence EU foreign policy in a particular area and, as a result, the EU uploading the policy.

Finally, the last aspect of the Europeanization approach to consider is the different processes of Europeanization within the EU. This is outlined in Table 2.1 Firstly, the national projection relates to the foreign policy of member states. In this instance, EU countries will try to upload their own foreign policies to the EU level and as a consequence their influence within the EU will increase. In addition to this, the country initiating the policy will be able to influence other EU countries, especially those countries that

Table 2.1 The Europeanization process in an EU member state's foreign policy

Aspects of Europeanization	National foreign policy indicators
1. Adaptation and policy • Harmonization and transformation of a member state to the needs and requirements over of EU membership ('downloading').	a) Increasing salience of European political agenda. b) Adherence to common objectives. c) Common policy outputs taking priority over national domain's reserves. d) Internationalization of EU members and its integration process ('EU-ization').
2. National projection[1] • **National foreign policy of a member state affects and contributes to the development of a common European foreign policy ('uploading').**	a) **State attempts to increase national influence in the world.** b) **State attempts to influence foreign policies of other member states.** c) **State uses the EU as a cover/umbrella.** d) **Externalization of national foreign policy positions onto the EU level.**
3. Identity reconstruction • A result of above two dimensions. Harmonization process tending towards middle position; common EU interests are promoted ('crossloading').	a) Emergence of norms among policy-making elites. b) Shared definitions of European and national interests. c) Coordination reflex and 'pendulum effect' where 'extreme' national and EU positions are reconciled over time.

Source: Wong (2008: 326).
Note: [1]Emphasis added.

have not yet formed a coherent or strong policy towards a region or country. This can enable a country to hide behind the EU's umbrella, which can, therefore, allow that country to feel more powerful.

There is a more extensive literature dedicated to the topic of EU–Mercosur relations. This part of the literature is not relevant to the questions that will be addressed in the following chapters, but nevertheless, before discussing the methodological approach that will be taken to address these questions, a brief overview of this literature is appropriate. Firstly, Cuadros Ramos et al. (1999) analysed the commercial relations between the EU and Mercosur by looking at exports from the EU to Mercosur between 1967 and 1995. In doing so, Cuadros Ramos et al. concluded that the dynamic period of the early 1990s can be linked to the process of liberalization between the two regions thanks to EMIFCA. Other works describe the difficulties that occurred during the negotiations for the FTAA (for example, see Sanahuja 2000b; Bizzozero 2001; Cienfuegos 2006). In addition to this, the EU and Mercosur blocs have also been compared from an economic-institutional perspective (see Bologna 2003 and Martinez 2005). In fact, Martinez dedicates a whole book to the study of Mercosur institutions and at times compares these institutions to EU institutions (2005: 61). There is also a discussion in the existing literature which focuses on the Mercosur point of view of EU–Mercosur relations. For example, Alemany (2004) focuses on the importance of the diplomatic efforts of Mercosur in terms of developing the EU–Mercosur relationship whilst others have focused on the EU in the sense that it has acted as a model of integration for Mercosur to follow (for example, see Sanchez Bajo 1999; Vasconcelos 2001; Kanner 2002).

In summary, this section critically examined the main arguments in the existing literature which attempt to explain the evolution of the relationship between the EU and Mercosur. The discussion above has also linked these debates to the more general literature which focuses on other more general EU external policy debates. In doing so, the discussion has identified and critiqued six potential arguments which have been used to explain the developing relation between the EU and the Mercosur, as well as examining those previous efforts which attempted to explain the way in which the EU has developed a policy towards Mercosur. The discussion will now turn to outlining the methodological approach that will be undertaken in order to investigate the ability of these perspectives to explain the development of the EU's policy towards the Mercosur during the course of the three distinct stages of policy development discussed above.

Methodology

Having looked closely at the existing literature, it is clear that there was a 'boom' in publications between 1995 and 2004. It could be argued that this is a consequence of the two key moments in policy development which occurred at this time. By focusing only on policy outcomes, key questions have been ignored, particularly: what could have happened but did not take place due to opposition? Why did it take so long for those events to happen? More crucially, however, by concentrating on the outcomes, studies have failed to develop a more indepth analysis of how everything started between the EU and Mercosur countries; therefore, key issues that affected the development of the policy are not covered. This has led to overly simplistic and misleading attempts to explain the relationship. Therefore, it is necessary to take a long-term approach which examines the nature of policy development.

A review of events in the 1980s between the EU and Mercosur countries is key. A regional group like the one in South America could not have suddenly been created in 1991 out of nowhere. Neglecting the study of the lead-up to the creation of Mercosur in 1991 misdirects the study of EU policy towards Mercosur. In 1985, Argentina and Brazil started to create the project that would later become Mercosur. The fact that the EU policy towards Mercosur started a month after its creation (1991) makes it difficult to believe that nothing relevant to the EU–Mercosur relationship occurred prior to 1991. In other words, the EU did not suddenly begin to develop a policy towards Mercosur for the first time in 1991. This study also covers the two launches of the negotiations of EMIFCA, in 2001 and 2010.

The analysis of the dependent variable

In order to investigate the motivations (or lack of motivations), this monograph will examine the contribution of the main policy- and decision-makers, the European Commission and the Council of Ministers, as well as the different contributions within the two institutions. This will make it possible to show the degree of 'involvement'/'engagement' reflected in the EU's policy towards Mercosur, which is the dependent variable in this study. Similar measures are implication, participation and contribution, to explain the same issues: what the EU has really done and not done in relation to Mercosur.

In order to assess this concept, two criteria which characterize involvement have been chosen: 'ambition' and 'commitment'. I have already suggested that EU policies should be explained in relative terms rather than absolute. Therefore, these two criteria should be measured in relative terms – top, high, medium, low and none – instead of absolute terms – yes or no.

Ambition is related to aspiration, desire, and purpose. It is, in other words, related to what an actor wants to do. In this case, it concerns how far the EU is trying to shift from the status quo. In order to assess the level of ambition at the different stages, it is necessary to contrast with the status quo: EU policy pronouncements; negotiating mandates; plans for the future of the relationship; promises to Mercosur. The link between ambition and engagement is that if ambition is present, it is easier to measure engagement, even if the policy fails. If there is ambition, there is intention in the policy, there is interest, and if the policy does not advance then it could not be concluded erroneously that it was because the EU did not care, but rather because the policy was not possible. On the other side, if there is no ambition and only low involvement, it will be easy to understand the lack of interest of the EU in Mercosur.

Once the level of ambition has been measured, the analysis will move to the second criterion, commitment. 'Commitment', in general terms, is synonymous with obligation and intention. It is related to what an actor has promised to do or say, and a revision of what is promised and what is delivered is essential. In this case it reflects how hard the EU is willing to try to realize its objectives, and how much it is willing to pay in order to achieve those objectives. In order to assess the level of commitment it is necessary to pay attention to different indicators: the frequency of meetings and the importance of those meetings given by the EU (official, ministerial or head of state level); the amount of aid or funding provided by the EU for the different aspects that compound the relationship; and the willingness to compromise during the negotiations.

The link between commitment and engagement is that you need the first one to have the second. This is especially the case in an area such as South America which has been ignored for decades. The more concise and less abstract the commitments, the more verifiable they are, which helps to assess engagement. If there is no commitment, the involvement will come as a reaction to the other players or as an unintentional action. It is important to note the existence or absence of strategy.

Ambition

In relation to ambition the different levels are as follows:

Top:
- Offers of negotiations mandates or agreements
- EU official policy pronouncements
- Promises to Mercosur
- Plans for a potential relationship.

High:
- EU official policy pronouncements
- Promises to Mercosur
- Plans for a potential relationship.

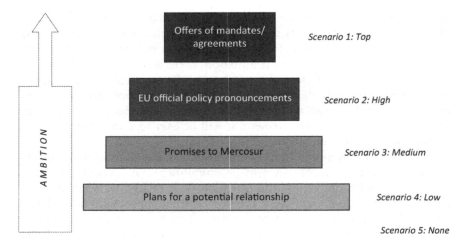

Figure 2.1 Levels of ambition

Medium:
- Promises to Mercosur
- Plans for a potential relationship.

Low:
- Plans for a potential relationship.

None:
- The EU does not have any intention to do anything for Mercosur, the EU will not shift from its status quo.

Once ambition has been measured, the analysis will move to the second criterion, commitment.

Commitment

The same clarification is necessary for commitment, the indicators of the different levels of this criterion are as follows:

Top:
- Independence, prioritization of negotiations over other agreements/ negotiations
- Substantial content of agreements and of offers during the negotiations
- Aid, funding, or technical help provided by the EU
- Meetings either official or unofficial at any level: civil servant level, ministerial level and/or head of state level.

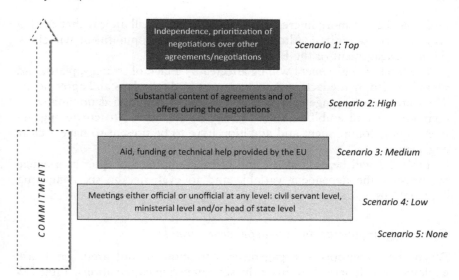

Figure 2.2 Levels of commitment

High:
- Substantial content of agreements and of offers during the negotiations
- Aid, funding or technical help provided by the EU
- Meetings either official or unofficial at any level: civil servant level, ministerial level and/or head of state level.

Medium:
- Aid, funding or technical help provided by the EU
- Meetings either official or unofficial at any level: civil servant level, ministerial level and/or head of state level.

Low:
- Meetings either official or unofficial at any level: civil servant level, ministerial level and/or heads of state level.

None:
- The EU does nothing for Mercosur; there are no or almost no meetings and/or funding.

If there is more ambition than commitment, the EU's behaviour could be described as having more strategy than interest, or pretending to be more interested than it really is. If there is more commitment than ambition, it indicates there is more interest than strategy and it will appear that the EU was not very organized. Altogether, ambition and commitment will show the real engagement of the EU.

The level of engagement will be affected by a lack of strategy, plans, and ideas but also by the lack of actual content in those plans and agreements. The outcome of engagement will be the lowest common denominator of commitment and ambition since both parts are needed to create engagement. Both, commitment and ambition have to be present to have a clear engagement.

Table 2.2 will be used at the end of each empirical chapter as a gauge to measure the dependent variable and to evaluate the six competing explanations.

Competing arguments and the dependent variable

When these concepts – engagement, commitment and ambition – are explained it will help to evaluate the six competing explanations. Table 2.3 demonstrates how measuring EU policy will help to show if the six competing explanations can explain the different stages of the policy.

Sources

The information has been gathered following an exhaustive collection of primary and secondary resources in both Spanish and English, together with interviews conducted in Spanish or English in both Europe (Belgium, France and Spain) and Latin America (Uruguay and Argentina). It is important to understand the different perceptions on either side of the Atlantic about several issues in general and the fact that the author is of Spanish nationality

Table 2.2 Measurement of the dependent variable: engagement

		Ambition				
		Top	*High*	*Medium*	*Low*	*None*
Commitment	*Top*	Excellent				
	High		High			
	Medium			Medium		
	Low				Low	
	None					Status quo

Table 2.3 Competing arguments (independent variables) and the dependent variable

Independent variable	Expectation	Independent variable value	Expectation value	Met/ confronted
Counterbalancing the US	If the US increases its involvement in LA, the EU should increase its involvement. ↑US = ↑EU in LA			
Global aspirations	If the EU increases its presence in international affairs, the EU's involvement in LA should also increase. ↑EU in the world = ↑EU in LA			
External federator	If LA becomes more integrated, the EU will increase its relations with LA. ↑LA integration = ↑EU in LA			
Affinity	An increase of shared values between the regions should develop EU policy. ↑LA shared values = ↑EU in LA			
Interdependence	If trade and investment between the EU and LA increase, EU policy should also increase. ↑LA trade = ↑EU in LA			
Iberia	If the influence of Spain and Portugal increase within the EU, then the EU's involvement in LA should increase. ↑SP + PT influence = ↑EU in LA			

Notes: LA = Latin America; PT = Portugal; SP = Spain.

based in a different European country, which can have an impact on the way interviewees interact with the interviewer.

Conclusion

This chapter has provided both a comprehensive overview and critique of the existing literature that focuses on EU–Mercosur relations and policy development. It has been argued that this literature can be characterized as superficial and fails to reach any firm conclusions. In addition to this, it has been suggested that explanations provided in previous studies are limited because they have failed to undertake a longitudinal analysis in relation to EU–Mercosur relations and the development of EU policy towards Mercosur.

This chapter has also established the analytical framework needed to undertake a longitudinal study of the motivations behind EU policy towards Mercosur. By outlining the different arguments in the EU–Mercosur litera-ture, as well as linking these arguments to the more general discussions focusing on the EU role in external relations, this investigation aims to contribute to several important debates. The contribution of this monograph is clearly linked to more than one debate, particularly the following: EU policy towards Mercosur, EU external relations, and the EU as a global and strategic actor and the Europeanization of foreign policies. In order to examine the real explanatory potential over time, this chapter has also outlined the six key arguments that will be analysed in the following chapters. The next chapter will outline the necessary concepts relating to EU policy-making, therefore making it easier to understand the evolution of EU policy towards Mercosur.

3

European Union policy-making towards Mercosur

Introduction

The EU is not a state and is not a traditional international organization. It is common to characterize it as a hybrid system with a federal component, but nothing comparable exists at this point in time. To understand EU policy-making towards Mercosur it is important to understand the internal system of the EU, its internal policy-making and the internal system of Mercosur, particularly given that Mercosur has tried to replicate the institutional design of the EU.

Since its creation in 1957 in the Treaty of Rome, the EU has changed dramatically in a variety of ways in a short period of time. The discussion here will examine these changes over the period between 1985 and 2015. It is also important to note that the number of EU member states has quadrupled since it was created in 1957. It could be argued that this has resulted in a decline in the power held by each individual member state. In 1986 Spain and, to a lesser extent, Portugal brought a Mediterranean influence into EU politics. This was later balanced out by further enlargement in 1995 which saw Austria, Finland and Sweden joining the EU. However, the single largest enlargement in the history of the EU took place in 2004 when ten Central and Eastern Europe countries became EU members. From 1989 until the enlargement in 2004, the end of the Cold War and the breakup of the Soviet Union into several independent republics had been the main focus EU external relations, to the point that it had an effect on other external relations, including external relations with Latin America. The enlargement of the EU in 2007 is not discussed in any detail here because it did not have an impact on the EU policy towards Mercosur.

The Treaty of Rome introduced legal frameworks that would inform the creation of EU policies. Since then, the EU has introduced further new treaties which have modified these legal foundations. These changes will be discussed here because they have played a crucial role in terms of affecting policy-making and/or decision-making procedures. The Single European Act of 1986 was crucial because it brought changes to policy-making in the area of EU external relations. However, it was the Treaty of Maastricht in 1992 that brought some of the most important policy changes in external relations. In contrast, changes incorporated by the 1997 Treaty of Amsterdam, the 2001 Treaty of Nice and the 2009 Treaty of Lisbon did not alter EU policy-making towards Mercosur. It should be noted that the term EU is used consistently throughout, in an attempt to avoid the confusion that would arise from the use of European Community or European Union, depending on whether the discussion concerns pre- or post-Maastricht events.

EU policy-making towards Mercosur

EU policy towards Mercosur is a key part of the EU's more general policy towards Latin America. It could be argued that for many years EU policy towards Mercosur was in fact the most important part of EU policy in the region, and the following section contextualizes this by briefly discussing EU policy towards Latin America. At this point, however, it should be acknowledged that EU policy towards Mercosur involves a mixture of trade, cooperation and association agreements. Therefore, it is important to start this study by looking at those agreements, especially since they provide the legal framework, and consequently the internal rules, for both policy-making and decision-making. This outline of the introduction of the legal framework is followed by a discussion of policy-making processes. This will enable us to develop a greater understanding of the sequence of events which occurred during the course of those agreements. The final section of the first part of this chapter will provide an analytical account of the various roles of the actors involved in the creation of trade, cooperation and association agreements, particularly the nature of their interactions with one another. This will help us to understand how different actors have different types of room for manoeuvre, whilst acknowledging that the EU Commission and the EU Council are the most important actors because they have most of the power when developing these types of policies.

First, however, it is necessary to explain why the EU prioritized Mercosur for a period of time, particularly since the study of EU–Latin American relations overlaps the study of EU–Mercosur relations for some of the time-frame. Until 1995, the overlapping of EU–Latin American relations and EU–Mercosur relations was so significant that it could be considered to be the interchangeable, or at least the most important feature of EU–Latin America relations, as explained in the previous chapter.

During the 1980s, the EU was an exceptional witness through the EU–Rio Group meetings of Mercosur advances in regional integration which gained momentum in 1985 with Argentina and Brazil signing their first agreement.

With that agreement, Argentina and Brazil played a fundamental role in terms of developing a project that would promote regional integration in Latin America. The first EU–Mercosur inter-institutional cooperation agreement was reached in 1992. Through this agreement the EU provided technical help such as know-how. The following year, the EU and Mercosur considered a further upgrading of their relations once Mercosur was a customs union, and in 1995 the framework for the negotiation of an association agreement between the EU and Mercosur came into force as Mercosur became such a union (albeit an imperfect one). Basically, EU policy-making increased over time and through these different agreements.

Political process

EU policy, according to Wallace and Young, is:

> a kaleidoscope of changing patterns of participation in the collective process of European policy-making on issues of market regulation and policies for industry. Participation in the European arena constitutes a shift in two dimensions. First, the European policy model marks a distinct departure from patterns of policy-making in national arenas. Second, the European policy process is in flux, varying between policy areas and over time. (Wallace and Young 1997: 235)

In order to explain the different aspects of this kaleidoscope, it is useful to look at the political system in both its horizontal and vertical aspects. In terms of the vertical separation of powers, it was noted at the beginning of this chapter that the EU could be described as a form of federal system. At the time of its creation, the transfer of power from individual nation states to the European 'government' was carried out in a series of phases rather than in one single transfer. This was designed to minimize the opposition from the national governments that Jean Monnet had anticipated (Pollack 2005: 28). Trading policy was transferred to the EU straightaway. In contrast, powers that related to international security policy remained in the hands of individual member states. The fact that this is still the case today explains why certain agreements with Mercosur are negotiated by the Commission – who have been responsible for dealing with matters of trade policy since the Treaty of Rome – and why other matters are negotiated by the Commission and the national states' representatives. The distribution of power between the EU and its member states resembles a federal system in many ways (Pollack 2005). However, Pollack (2005) argues that the way that this is expressed in such vague language implies that most policy areas are dealt with at both the national and the supranational levels. The vague nature of this institutional arrangement enables the European Court of Justice to clarify the limitations that are not established in the Treaties. Consequently, whenever there is disagreement, the European Court of

Justice will decide who – according to the treaties – should have a further increase in their competence in that specific area. In other words, when there is a disagreement between the states and the Commission, the European Court of Justice will have the final say.

As well as the vertical separation of powers in the EU, there is the horizontal separation of powers in the EU. The legislative system is often referred to as a bicameral system. The agenda-setter in this system is the Commission, although the legislative powers of the European Parliament (EP) have been growing since the 1980s (Pollack 2005). However, as will be demonstrated in the discussion below, the EP has no real powers in terms of influencing EU–Mercosur relations and policy development. In relation to these matters, the most significant institutional arrangement is the relationship between the Commission and the Council, especially if the Commission is seen as an agenda-setter: 'Deciding what to decide is a crucial part of the policy-making process and one that often takes place in a context where there is a great deal of uncertainty. Deciding what to decide actually involves two steps in the policy cycle: agenda-setting and policy formation' (Young 2010: 115).

The agenda is set through a series of pre-selection of issues or debate about alternatives before a particular policy is chosen and before the discussion moves on to the actual formulation of policy. This is crucial in terms of understanding not only how some policies actually go ahead, but also why some policies are not taken forward. To a certain extent, this can also be influenced by hidden political reasons. During the process of pre-selection, the Commission has considerable power. In October 1994, the Commission produced a document which elaborated on the possible scenarios and options that were available to the EU in relation to upgrading EU–Mercosur relations. At that particular moment in time, the Commission could have included other issues: for example, the Commission could have developed other major and/or more specific ways in which it could have become involved in the political side of EU–Mercosur relations. This, however, was not the case, possibly because the Commission was aware that this could lead to future problems in terms of the relations between the Commission and the Council of Ministers further down the road. In summary, the Commission does not have absolute power in relation to preparation of documents and proposals, and therefore the Commission must consider in advance how its proposals will be received by the Council.

Policy formulation also attracts other actors who are not involved in the agenda-setting (Young 2010). This is interesting in the sense that it demonstrates just how influential the Commission has been when preparing the policy-making agenda. Irene Bellier contends that:

> European civil servants are the first to recognize the influence of pressure groups over certain items of European legislation (notably directives), but they tend to be most conscious of the role of national negotiators and the way

they are able to promote the preferences of large national consortia from farming, industry, and financial services. It is a hard distinction to pin down if we want to assess the patterns of influence; it requires us to distinguish between the factors that belong to the policy process and those which arise from the operation of markets. (Bellier 1997: 108)

The European business associations with interests in Mercosur were in favour of the association agreement between the EU and Mercosur and asked for a liberalization of the markets of both Mercosur and the EU. What is not clear is whether the Commission considered the liberalization of the markets in its October 1994 proposal to upgrade EU–Mercosur relations as a result of any pressure from the business associations or whether this was simply due to the EU's general support of opening up markets in other countries. It could be argued that the Commission was influenced by the business associations because the 1995 agreement included a free trade agreement. However, it should be noted that the Commission's general agenda also promoted free trade. Interestingly, other sectors such as agriculture also lobbied the Commission in order to express their opposition to a free trade agreement and in the end words such as 'free trade' were taken out of the Council directives passed to the Commission for the negotiation of the agreement. The claim that the Commission was influenced needs substantive evidence in order to carry any weight. Furthermore, Bellier claims that

There is a fine line between giving out information on its plans, to which the Commission puts up little resistance, and allowing influence over which options are chosen: but it is here than the distinction is drawn between a decision to promote an overall European interest and the satisfaction of narrower concern, whether national or private. (Bellier 1997: 108)

The bottom line is that the Commission has a key role to play, both in setting the policy-making agenda and in the actual process of policy formulation. This gives the Commission a great deal of power in terms of shaping EU policies (Young 2010). In the area of executive politics, the rational-choice and principal-agent analyses are the dominant approaches in the existing literature (Pollack 2005; Young 2010).

The Commission can take a different course of action from that expected by member states. This was already suggested above when discussing whether or not the Commission can be influenced by other actors when creating a policy agenda. Obviously the Commission may have its own 'ambitions' or ideas that it might try to develop within the region. In relation to EU–Mercosur relations, the Commission has demonstrated a degree of interest in Mercosur and has, therefore, tried to reach an agreement with the Council. It is also clear that not all members of the Commission or the Council agreed with the policy towards Mercosur. Nevertheless, an agreement was reached. However, some states felt that the

Commission had gone too far and there was a discussion about the Commission's proposal in the Council at the time when the directives were being prepared in the Council for the Commission.

The EU's legal basis

In relation to the legal basis for EU agreements with other regions or countries, the use of one or other article implies a different division of power in the areas of policy and decision-making. This does not mean that different types of EU agreements are completely separate from each other and cover entirely different policies in practice. They are different mainly in the sense that different legal frameworks are used according to the type of agreement. The main types of agreements are trade, cooperation or development cooperation and association (Nugent 2003; Smith 2003). The Common Commercial Policy (CCP) since the Treaty of Rome provides the basis for economic agreements. Article 133 is the first legal framework involved when developing economic agreements. However, the creation of trade agreements in isolation from other types of agreement is in fact quite rare because simple economic agreements are somewhat limited and there are other types of agreements which tend to be favoured by third parties (Smith 2003). Therefore, Article 133 tends to be used in conjunction with other articles in order to reach a combination of trade and economic cooperation agreements or association agreements.

It is also common for trade and economic cooperation agreements to be developed under Articles 133 (CCP) and others such as Article 181 (ex 130y) and 300 (ex 228): 'For example, in the case of trade agreements with developing countries, Articles 177 and 181, which are related to development matters, could be employed as part of the legal basis of trade negotiations which are designed to create preferential trade agreements' (Aggarwal and Fogarty 2004: 28).

As this study focuses on policy development between 1985 and 2007, it tends to be the 1992 Maastricht Treaty, alongside other subsequent changes in the EU's legal framework, which form the legal basis for developing agreements. For example, the 1995 EMIFCA continues to be the basis for EU–Mercosur relations today. This agreement was formulated after the Maastricht Treaty. Boxes 3.1 and 3.2 provide an overview of the official text related to the articles that are involved when developing EU agreements with Mercosur. Boxes 3.1 and 3.2 also include changes that emerged when developing new treaties.

In the case of EU–Mercosur policy, the legal basis for the agreement signed in 1995 was Articles 133, 181 and 300. Furthermore, association agreements are covered by Article 310 (ex 238). These are outlined in Boxes 3.1, 3.2 and 3.3. Since different agreements create different divisions of labour in terms of policy-making and decision-making, the various actors

---

Box 3.1 Article 133 (ex Article 113)

1. The common commercial policy shall be based on uniform principles, particularly in regard to changes in tariff rates, the conclusion of tariff and trade agreements, the achievement of uniformity in measures of liberalisation, export policy and measures to protect trade such as those to be taken in the event of dumping or subsidies.
2. The Commission shall submit proposals to the Council for implementing the common commercial policy.
3. Where agreements with one or more States or international organisations need to be negotiated, the Commission shall make recommendations to the Council, which shall authorise the Commission to open the necessary negotiations.

The Commission shall conduct these negotiations in consultation with a special committee appointed by the Council to assist the Commission in this task and within the framework of such directives as the Council may issue to it.

The relevant provisions of Article 300 shall apply.

4. In exercising the powers conferred upon it by this Article, the Council shall act by a qualified majority.
5. The Council, acting unanimously on a proposal from the Commission and after consulting the European Parliament, may extend the application of paragraphs 1 to 4 to international negotiations and agreements on services and intellectual property insofar as they are not covered by these paragraphs.

Amendments included in the Treaty of Nice:
This article was amended by the Nice Treaty to extend the scope of commercial policy and, as a result, of qualified majority voting for agreements in the fields of trade in services and the commercial aspects of intellectual property. There are still, however, some exceptions to this principle:

- The Council may not conclude agreements which entail harmonisation of national legislation in fields such as culture, education or human health (fields in which the Community does not have internal powers of harmonisation);
- The Council must act unanimously where the agreement includes provisions for which unanimity is required for the adoption of internal rules (parallelism) or where it relates to a field in which the Community has not yet exercised its internal powers;
- This article does not apply to the field of transport.

Source: European Communities (2002).

Box 3.2 Article 181 (ex Article 130y)

Within their respective spheres of competence, the Community and
the Member States shall cooperate with third countries and with the
competent international organisations. The arrangements for Community cooperation may be the subject of agreements between the
Community and the third parties concerned, which shall be negotiated and concluded in accordance with Article 300.

The previous paragraph shall be without prejudice to Member
States' competence to negotiate in international bodies and to conclude international agreements.

Source: European Communities (2001).

Box 3.3 Article 300 (ex Article 228)

1. Where this Treaty provides for the conclusion of agreements
   between the Community and one or more States or international
   organisations, the Commission shall make recommendations to
   the Council, which shall authorise the Commission to open the
   necessary negotiations. The Commission shall conduct these
   negotiations in consultation with special committees appointed by
   the Council to assist it in this task and within the framework of
   such directives as the Council may issue to it.

In exercising the powers conferred upon it by this paragraph, the
Council shall act by a qualified majority, except in the cases where
the first subparagraph of paragraph 2 provides that the Council shall
act unanimously.

2. Subject to the powers vested in the Commission in this field, the
   signing, which may be accompanied by a decision on provisional
   application before entry into force, and the conclusion of the
   agreements shall be decided on by the Council, acting by a qualified majority on a proposal from the Commission. The Council
   shall act unanimously when the agreement covers a field for which
   unanimity is required for the adoption of internal rules and for
   the agreements referred to in Article 310.

Box 3.3 Article 300 (ex Article 228)—cont'd

By way of derogation from the rules laid down in paragraph 3, the same procedures shall apply for a decision to suspend the application of an agreement, and for the purpose of establishing the positions to be adopted on behalf of the Community in a body set up by an agreement based on Article 310, when that body is called upon to adopt decisions having legal effects, with the exception of decisions supplementing or amending the institutional framework of the agreement.

The European Parliament shall be immediately and fully informed on any decision under this paragraph concerning the provisional application or the suspension of agreements, or the establishment of the Community position in a body set up by an agreement based on Article 310.

3. The Council shall conclude agreements after consulting the European Parliament, except for the agreements referred to in Article 133(3), including cases where the agreement covers a field for which the procedure referred to in Article 251 or that referred to in Article 252 is required for the adoption of internal rules. The European Parliament shall deliver its opinion within a time-limit which the Council may lay down according to the urgency of the matter. In the absence of an opinion within that time-limit, the Council may act.

By way of derogation from the previous subparagraph, agreements referred to in Article 310, other agreements establishing a specific institutional framework by organising cooperation procedures, agreements having important budgetary implications for the Community and agreements entailing amendment of an act adopted under the procedure referred to in Article 251 shall be concluded after the assent of the European Parliament has been obtained. The Council and the European Parliament may, in an urgent situation, agree upon a time-limit for the assent.

4. When concluding an agreement, the Council may, by way of derogation from paragraph 2, authorise the Commission to approve modifications on behalf of the Community where the agreement provides for them to be adopted by a simplified procedure or by a body set up by the agreement; it may attach specific conditions to such authorisation.

Continued

Box 3.3 Article 300 (ex Article 228)—cont'd

5. When the Council envisages concluding an agreement which calls for amendments to this Treaty, the amendments must first be adopted in accordance with the procedure laid down in Article 48 of the Treaty on European Union.

6. The Council, the Commission or a Member State may obtain the opinion of the Court of Justice as to whether an agreement envisaged is compatible with the provisions of this Treaty. Where the opinion of the Court of Justice is adverse, the agreement may enter into force only in accordance with Article 48 of the Treaty on European Union.

7. Agreements concluded under the conditions set out in this Article shall be binding on the institutions of the Community and on Member States.

Source: European Communities (1997).

hold different levels of power, reflected in the types of decision rules that apply to each of them, according to the different potential scenarios.

Over the years, there have been several changes to the treaties in relation to the EU's legal framework and there have also been corresponding modifications to the division of powers. In relation to the CCP, further legal specification was necessary over the years in response to the development of trade in different areas such as services or intellectual property and their importance at international level. In other words, trade became more interconnected. In the 1990s, the Commission started to put pressure on individual EU member states to expand the framework of Article 133 to include the trade of services and intellectual property (Nugent 2003: 410). In 1994, the European Court of Justice decided that there should be a degree of shared responsibility between the EU and the member states. This matter was not resolved by the Treaty of Amsterdam in 1997 but was, to a certain extent, addressed in the Treaty of Nice. As a result of this treaty, trade in services became an exclusive competence of the Commission, although in some areas it required unanimity and some issues were excepted (Nugent 2003: 410). However, trade issues continued to produce a degree of controversy, particularly issues that were related to environmental and labour standards (Smith 2003: 34–35).

With regard to external agreements, it is also common for Article 300 to be used. In addition to this, there is a tendency for Article 181 to be used because it is specifically designed for matters relating to the development of cooperation (Nugent 2003). Over time, trade and cooperation agreements can include many issues which have previously not been thought possible either because of the lack of development of EU external relations or because of the situation of the third parties. Therefore, it is common for policy development to begin with a simple agreement that is subsequently further developed or upgraded with the intention of developing free trade agreements, or to include, for example, certain political conditions such as human rights, which has been the case since the 1980s (Nugent 2003).

In terms of association agreements, it has already been noted that different types of political agreements bring different conditions. Association agreements are a specific kind of agreement that is produced with particular countries or regions in mind. In some cases they are produced in regard to those preferred countries that will become members of the EU in the future. These agreements are developed in relation to Article 310 (ex Article 238). This was noted by Nugent, who claims that 'The Community may conclude with one or more states or international organisations agreements establishing an association involving reciprocal rights and obligations, common action and reciprocal procedure' (Nugent 2003: 411).

In the case of EU–Mercosur relations, the ongoing negotiations, which include a free trade agreement, are part of an association agreement that was launched in 1999. As will be explained in the next section, association agreements require unanimity among the member states, and the approval of the EP granted by a majority vote before they can become official (Woolcock 2005). Association agreements also include trade issues and in some cases they can encompass aid from the EU and loans from the European Investment Bank (EIB). In these instances, agreements will establish an association council consisting of a minister from either side who will come together to discuss common issues (Smith 2004: 55). This demonstrates that association agreements have a different, if not higher, level of political meaning from agreements which are designed to facilitate interregional cooperation. The different decision-making procedures are explained in the following section.

Policy processes

The policy process for creating trade agreements under Article 133 is different from the policy process that is followed when creating association agreements. The Commission considers the option of a trade agreement with a third party; then the Commission seeks to receive a mandate from the Council. This is done by gaining a recommendation from the General Affairs and External Relations Council. After that, the Committee of Permanent Representatives (COREPER) of the Council works on this recommendation and passes it to the Council. At this point, the Council can modify the directives or guidelines with the help of COREPER, and if the Council fails to reach an agreement a decision is reached using the qualified majority voting (QMV) rule. Once a mandate has been secured, the Commission will lead the negotiations. Different members such as commissioners and director generals can intervene in the negotiations. For example, the commissioners and director generals of agriculture, development and/or trade can intervene in these negotiations. The degree of freedom that the Commission has to negotiate on behalf of the EU depends on each case, linked to the different positions of different member states on that issue (Nugent 2003: 413). Some countries will favour protectionism, whilst others will favour free trade, and therefore the Commission's flexibility is limited. However, the Commission can use this situation as a spur for negotiation and can blame the Council for deals that they do not want to accept (Nugent 2003: 413). Moreover, the Council monitors the negotiations through a committee, as specified in Article 133. This committee is composed of officials from individual EU member states and ministries and meets frequently. The committee can even modify the mandate, but if the mandate relates to a sensitive issue the final decision will be made by the COREPER or the Council (Nugent 2003: 413). Once the agreement has been fully negotiated with the third party, the next step is to pass it to the Council for approval or rejection.

Therefore, it is important to examine why the Council, as part of an association agreement, would delegate the negotiation of an FTA with Mercosur to the Commission. In relation to this agreement we should also consider whether these directives were ambitious. In this instance, it is possible that the Commission would try to go further than the Council wanted in terms of developing agreements with Latin American in general and with Mercosur in particular. It is also possible that the Commission would use trade agreements in order to gain the support of the Council and, in doing so, achieve its own particular goals – such as increasing the Commission's power to negotiate agreements with third parties. On the other hand, it is also possible that the Commission was following not just its own agenda, but was in fact promoting Mercosur's agenda.

It also seems that – depending on the sensitivity of the topic, for example, agriculture – the Council will seek to have more power than the Commission. However, if the issue is somewhat less sensitive – for example, the issue of cooperation with a region like Latin America – then the Council tends to be more likely to give the Commission more autonomy to negotiate agreements and policies.

Qualified majority voting

By the 1980s, the EU consisted of twelve member states. With a view to increasing the number of decisions accepted avoiding vetos, the Single European Act (1986) started to introduce changes such as QMV in relation to issues such as trade in goods. With each enlargement of the EU, more countries are involved and as a result, the level of power held by each individual member state is diluted. However, due to the fact that mixed agreements are very common and they require ratification by each government, the QMV rule is less relevant in relation to issues of cooperation and association agreements. According to Aggarwal and Fogarty (2004), QMV works in favour of those countries which are more pro-free trade than those countries who favour a more protectionist position. However, 'the prevailing status of unanimity vis-à-vis QMV shapes trade policy by determining the extent to which interest groups and member governments have the scope to bend voting outcomes in the Council to their will – whether towards free trade or protectionism' (Aggarwal and Fogarty 2004).

It has already been noted that association agreements tend to be offered to preferred partners. Association agreements are considered to be more important than trade and cooperation agreements. Over the course of the last few years, association agreements have become increasingly common.

Articles 310, 133 (ex 113), 130W and 300 (ex 228(3)) relate to different areas of the decision-making process. Wessels (1997) outlines the following:

- Article 310 (ex 238): according to the EEC Treaty, association requires unanimity in the Council and in the EP assent with absolute majority of members;
- Article 133 (ex 113(3)): according to the EEC Treaty, trade agreements require a qualified majority from the Council and there is not active participation of the EP;
- Article 130W: according to the Maastricht Treaty, development cooperation requires a qualified majority from the Council and cooperation 189c from the EP;
- Article 300 (ex 228(3)): according to the Maastricht Treaty, agreements with third countries require a qualified majority from the Council and a simple majority of votes cast from the EP.

Regarding the process of reaching an agreement with Mercosur, the EU pointed out that although there were three areas which had to be negotiated – trade, cooperation and political dialogue – no individual agreements would be reached until agreements had been reached for all three areas. The interconnection of the three areas implies that there would be higher levels of interaction between negotiators from the Commission and from the member states.

EU institutions

Now that the 'what' and 'how' of the EU policy process has been explained, it is essential to explain issues related to 'who'. There are several actors from various EU institutions that are involved in the development of EU trade policy, such as the Commission, the Council of Ministers and the EP. This section aims to analyse how these different institutions interact. Here the discussion will focus on how much room each institution has for manoeuvre in terms of their powers and the role they play in the development of trade, cooperation and association agreements. The debate will be framed in terms of who has the most power. It has already been suggested that the Council is the most powerful of all the EU institutions (for example, see Westlake 1995; Cini 1996; Hayes-Renshaw and Wallace 1997; Thomson and Hosli 2004; Schalk et al. 2007). However, this is contested by Meunier (2000), who claims that the Council is the central institution in this policy process because it manages to aggregate the preferences of the member states, whilst the Commission is responsible for acting as the negotiating agent of the Council. In addition to this, Thomson and Hosli (2004) contend that there is also a perception that the Commission and the EP have more power than they really have.

The most important relationship in terms of policy development is that between the Council and the Commission. This is due to the fact that these two EU institutions are more involved in the process of policy development than other EU institutions. The power balance between the Commission and the Council is not the most settled (Nugent 2003). On the one hand, the Council tries to control the Commission. On the other hand, the Commission tries to play its role in the development of policy by gaining as much autonomy from the Council as possible (Nugent 2003). On occasion this can produce negative outcomes for the EU, particularly when negotiating with third parties. Paemen and Bensch (1995) suggest that there are three problems in the policy process: firstly, the so-called 'lowest common denominator', as the way the EU agrees on issues in its internal negotiations, takes power away from the EU; secondly, because internal EU negotiations are conducted in public they can give information to third parties about the various positions being adopted within the EU; thirdly, the control of the Council versus the Commission does not allow the Commission negotiators to take instant decisions. In reference to this third point raised by Paemen and Bensch (1995), the Council can slow the momentum of negotiations when there is difficulty in terms of developing a clear and coherent position in relation to a particular policy.

Leaving aside the issue of which EU institution is the most powerful for the moment, there are additional issues related to how the Commission and the Council manage to exercise power. It is crucial that this is understood if we are to comprehend how the EU develops trade policies. Understanding the relative power of the Council, Commission and EP is useful for this (Thomson and Hosli 2004). The Commission, being in charge of developing and putting forward draft proposals, is able to influence the content of proposals. However, these proposals can also be amended by the Council. According to Nugent (1999), the Commission tried to expand its power under Article 133 by citing the changes in EU trade that have occurred since the Treaty of Rome was introduced in 1957. It could be said that the Commission has tried to develop as many negotiations as possible in order to expand its levels of influence both inside and outside the EU (Aggarwal and Fogarty 2004). Aggarwal and Fogarty also suggest that the Commission tries to exert its influence by having a close relationship with interest groups which will participate in the development of EU policies. According to Thomson and Hosli (2004), research has been done on the procedural rules in terms of the opportunities or obstacles faced by institutions and the different outcomes they produced. Thomson and Hosli claim that this is due to the different ways that procedural rules have been interpreted. Therefore, even when informal institutions are included in the analysis of the balance of power between the Commission, the Council and EP, different conclusions have been drawn (Thomson and Hosli 2004). In addition to this, the power/role of informal institutions must be considered if we are to understand the different levels of power held by different actors within the context of EU policy development (Thomson and Hosli 2004).

The European Commission
The Commission is the institution that deals with most of the day-to-day trade relations with third parties. In other words, the Commission is the 'face' of the EU when third parties deal with the EU on a frequent basis (Smith 2003). The internal organization of the Commission has changed over time. There are also different directorate generals which can intervene in international trade issues. For example, there is a directorate general responsible for external relations which works closely with the high representative of the common foreign and security policy since it was created in 2003 following the Treaty of Nice. This is yet another reason why the Commission and the Council have to work closely to make international agreements possible. With regard to the Council's relationship with the Commission, it can be said that, over time, the Commission has developed more political influence, especially during the Delors Commission (Aggarwal and Fogarty 2004). This had an effect on the balance of power within the EU. For example, the presidents of the Commission can produce key changes in the EU general integration project, as well as providing more power to the Commission. Furthermore, a strong president can lead to a stronger, more unified Commission. However, this does not necessarily result in members of the Commission having or sharing a united policy agenda (Nugent 2003; Aggarwal and Fogarty 2004). The Commission is composed of different commissioners and director generals which intervene to varying degrees in the development of international agreements. These

commissioners and director generals may indeed have their own individual agendas and aims, shaped by the specific national interests of the country which they represent (Aggarwal and Fogarty 2004).

Individual commissioners can also have their own particular reasons for the way that they try to influence agenda-setting. For example, a commissioner could have his or her own personal political ambition which has led them to bring a certain issue or policy to the table (Peters 2001). National pressure could also be a reason why an individual commissioner may give special emphasis to a particular policy (Peters 2001). The informal rule of commissioners supporting each other's ideas and portfolios in front of other institutions or in the general public domain is another feature of the way the commissioners highlight certain issues when trying to set the policy-making agenda (Christiansen 2001). In order to bring those issues to the fore, the Commission relies upon expert knowledge on many different issues (Christiansen 2001; Smith 2006), whilst being aware of the political nature of trying to influence agenda-setting. It is not an easy task for the Commission to influence the policy-making agenda when it does not have sufficient resources to do so (Christiansen 2001). This is further complicated by issues such as access to administrative expertise and political preference (Christiansen 2001).

The question of national interest also has to be carefully considered in an institution where European and not national vision has been established on the remit of civil servants. However, on some occasions this is not always the case. For example, Bellier argues that

> In 1992–3 few Spanish firms were selected in the tendering procedures of DG VIII (Co-operation and Development), in contrast to British, German, French, and Italian firms, all coming from countries marked as former colonial powers. Thanks to the commissioner in charge of this sector, the Spanish set about extending Community co-operation to Latin American countries, a shift which fuelled the debate on the philosophy of development aid. (Bellier 1997: 108)

This brought into the open the question of whether national biases, promoted by the nationalities of those responsible for calls for tender, were the cause of a weakness, known in Euro-jargon as the 'rate of return'. This is calculated in relation to member states' financial contribution to a particular budget line, in this case the European Development Fund. According to Commission officials and the Spanish Secretariat of State for European Affairs, enquiries showed that Spanish firms, cushioned by their national markets in the run-up to the Olympic Games and the World Fair, were not competitive (Bellier 1997: 108).

The Council of Ministers
The different Councils are composed of different ministers emanating from the respective member states in charge of a particular area. In the case of

EU external relations, the General Affairs Council was created in 2002 by the European Council in order to increase cohesion. When it comes to international agreements, the different enlargements have contributed to different countries bringing very varied ideas to the table. This is something that can be seen in discussions in the Council. For example, Nugent (2003) contends that countries such as Spain, Italy and France are more protectionist than the UK, whilst countries such as the Netherlands, Denmark, Finland and Germany have a somewhat ambiguous position (Woolcock 2005: 390). According to Woolcock this can be dependent upon the topic under discussion. For example, 'Ireland is liberal on trade in manufacturing, investment, but protectionist on agriculture ... Germany is liberal on trade in goods, but less so on the liberalization of agricultural or services' (Woolcock 2005: 390).

In terms of enlargement, when it became a member of the EU in 1973, the UK came to the table with a very liberal view. In contrast, when the Iberian countries became members of the EU in 1986, Spain and Portugal came to the table advocating a more protectionist agenda (Woolcock 2005). This was further complicated when the Nordic countries became members of the EU in 1995, although this was somewhat neutralized when the EU enlarged further in 2004. More specifically, the countries that joined in 2004 tended to advocate a less liberal position compared to the Nordic countries (Woolcock 2005). Therefore, it can be argued that the more countries that have joined the EU the more complicated it has become to develop a clear and coherent policy agenda (Woolcock 2005). Finally, special interest has been identified by sectors. More specifically, EU trade policy is affected by those interests, and the work of lobby groups in the area of business or agriculture is important because they are strongly organized and are able to exert pressure at both the national and supranational (Commission) level (Woolcock 2005).

Other sources of power

A way of achieving extra power within the EU is when a member state holds the presidency of the EU. The presidency of the Council is based on a rotational system whereby member states take turns in holding the EU presidency for six-month periods. The Council also needs to be represented when interacting with the other institutions and organizations such as the media or bodies outside the EU. In part, this was why the presidency was created (Westlake and Galloway 2004). The EU presidency has a wide remit. For example, the president of the EU is 'at one and the same time manager, promoter of political initiatives, package-broker, honest broker, representative to and from the other Community institutions, spokesman for the Council and for the Union, and an international actor' (Westlake and Galloway 2004: 46). In sum, the EU president has many responsibilities without having a great deal of power (Westlake and Galloway 2004). In EU foreign affairs, the president of the Council plays a key role. This has had a significant impact in terms of dealing with other institutions in relation to external issues. Helen Wallace contends that 'Often the Council and the Commission presidencies have to work closely together, for example in external negotiations where policy powers are divided between the EU and the national levels' (Wallace 2000: 19).

Wallace also demonstrates that the Commission and the presidency have a close and interactive relationship. The level of interdependence is also related to the country that holds the presidency, further complicated by the fact that each country has different needs, agendas or approaches (Johnston 1994). For example, older and larger powerful member states might not need so much interaction since they are used to holding the presidency and have the resources to carry out this role more effectively and also produce more coherent and popular proposals in contrast to the Commission. The different interests of the country that is holding the presidency are also reflected, letting the Commission be more or less active, depending on whether it is in favour of the country holding the presidency (Johnston 1994).

Since the president is responsible for preparing the agenda for the meetings of ministers, there is a fear that the presidency could be used to promote national interests rather than European interests. Wallace argues that:

> In the legislative field it is the Council and EP presidencies that have to work together to reconcile Council and parliamentary legislative amendments. A recurrent question is how far individual governments try to impose their national preferences during the presidency or whether the experience pushes them towards identifying with collective EU interests. (Wallace 2000: 19)

Although, the country holding the presidency is expected to be impartial (Talberg 2006 cited in Schalk et al. 2007), holding this position can impart some extra influence. The role is particularly important for smaller EU member states (Smith 2003), and the extra influence that can be gained is useful in terms of developing the policy agenda and also in having access to information (Warntjen 2008). However, the pressure that these countries face from other member states can often lead to the smaller member states making concessions (Warntjen 2008). The president, in theory, is supposed to be able to broker deals and facilitate negotiations, which is the opposite of being able to use this position in order to pursue specific national interests. Some authors also contend that countries holding the presidency have a low success rate in terms of pursuing their own domestic agendas (for example, Cini 1996; Hayes-Renshaw and Wallace 1997). In contrast, others consider holding the presidency to be an opportunity to influence decision-making (for example, see Westlake 1995; Peterson and Bomberg 1999). In addition, it is also argued that the stage of policy development determines whether the president is able to have any influence, it being more beneficial to receive the policy at the voting stage instead of at the beginning of the policy (Schalk et al. 2007).

As far as EU–Mercosur relations are concerned, arguably the most important moment in the development of this relationship occurred during the course of the Spanish and Portuguese presidencies. For example, in 1992, the first cooperation agreement was negotiated and agreed during the Portuguese presidency. In 1995 the EMIFCA was signed during the Spanish presidency. In addition to this, during the course of the Spanish presidency in 2002 a final calendar was agreed in terms of developing EU–Mercosur relations, and in 2004, during the Portuguese presidency, the negotiations between the EU and Mercosur were planned to end. During the Spanish presidency of 2010 the negotiations were launched again.

Conclusion

This chapter has discussed many of the different aspects that need to be considered when examining the development of EU policy-making towards Mercosur. It has demonstrated that the political process within the EU involves different delegations of power which can have varying degrees of impact at different points during the course of the three distinct stages of policy development. In this sense, the delegation of power from the Council to the Commission was necessary in order to develop policies which Mercosur had officially started in the second stage (1991–1995).

Different agreements between the EU and Mercosur have to be negotiated within different legal frameworks. This suggests that there are different processes in terms of decision-making in the course of policy development. This is particularly relevant in relation to developing the association agreement between the EU and Mercosur, which required unanimous support from the Council. This left little room for disagreements between EU member states. Having outlined the institutional structure of the EU, I have shown that the Commission and the member states are the main actors involved in shaping EU policy towards Mercosur. Attention will now turn to the first of three empirical chapters that will examine the non-institutionalized relation of the EU and Mercosur between 1985 and 1990.

4

Non-institutionalized relations between the EU and Mercosur

Introduction

This chapter covers the first stage of EU–Mercosur policy relations by focusing on the period 1985 to 1990. At this stage, policy relations were not institutionalized. Policy relations began in 1985 for several reasons. Firstly, the EU signed the Treaty of Accession of Spain and Portugal which marked the beginning of a new direction in policy towards Latin America, including the Mercosur countries; this is a clear reflection of the creation of a 'commitment' towards Latin America, although at a very low level due to the low 'ambition' towards the region. Secondly, in 1985, Mercosur countries also started their own regional integration programme. This stage proved to be key in the development of EU–Mercosur relations because it established a new emphasis on EU policy towards Latin America by establishing channels for communication between the two regions, particularly through the development of the annual EU–Rio Group meetings; without this engagement, the EU and Mercosur would not have developed their relationship, and the fact that it came at this point helps to explain the events of the following stages. By the time Mercosur was officially launched in 1991, the EU was fully aware of the integration movement in South America thanks to these years of EU–Latin America relations. The outcome of the engagement of the EU towards Mercosur results from low ambition and commitment on the European side. This stage of the policy shows the lowest engagement of the three stages, but the level of engagement is certainly superior to the pre-Iberian membership era.

The accession of Spain and Portugal to the EU marked the emergence of a new EU attitude towards Latin America, creating a path which was followed until 2007. This was a critical juncture. A decision taken (an Iberian emphasis on Latin America) at a particular moment in the history (Iberian membership) of an institution (the EU) can be a factor that determines the future of the protagonists (EU, Iberian countries and Mercosur) and of those events (the policy). The Iberian countries already had an official declaration in support of improving EU–Latin America relations. New cooperation guidelines for Latin America were discussed and elaborated as Felipe Gonzalez, president of Spain at that time, had demanded in 1986. The EP then held a series of meetings with the Rio Group in 1987, a regional group which at that time covered mainly South American countries, whereas now this group includes virtually the whole of Latin America. Created in Brazil in 1986, the Rio Group consisted of eight members: Argentina, Brazil, Colombia, Mexico, Panama, Peru, Uruguay and Venezuela. Today the Rio Group includes twenty-three Latin American countries, including Cuba. In 1990, the EU acceded to another set of Latin American demands which sought the institutionalization of the EU–Rio Group meetings. The 'critical juncture' is part of the historical institutionalism discussion, as is Europeanization, since the latter represents historical institutionalism in a very specific institution, the EU. The term 'Europeanization' relates to the influence of or in the EU. At this stage of the policy, the influence of the Iberian membership in the EU policy towards Mercosur is clear.

The already-mentioned path dependence created in 1986 is often overlooked by authors who study EU–Mercosur relations. Sewell explained the concept concisely when he claimed that 'what happened at an earlier point in time will affect the possible outcomes of a sequence of events occurring at a later point in time' (Sewell 1996: 262–263, cited in Pierson 2000). And continuing the analysis of Sewell's work, Pierson claims that Sewell's 'definition involves no necessary suggestion that a particular path is difficult to exit. Rather, the claim is that we cannot understand the significance of a particular social variable without understanding "how it got there" – the path it took' (Pierson 2000: 252). The explanations in the existing literature for this stage of EU–Latin America relations are quite poor and inconsistent in that the majority of studies tend to focus on the period after 1991. Few works focus on the new EU attitude towards Latin America as a result of the Iberian membership of the EU, the democratization of Latin American countries and the way that Latin America embraced open economies. This monograph argues that without the study of this stage of EU–Mercosur relations, many scholars have underplayed the influence of the Iberian countries in changing the EU's mentality towards the region. Previous studies have also overlooked how Mercosur was initiated in 1985 and why this has had a profound effect on the policy from that point onwards; it is clear that Mercosur has undertaken a proactive role, whilst the EU has played a reactive role.

Finally, this chapter also explains how the EU finally developed a continued channel of communication with Latin America at this stage in the development of EU–Mercosur relations. This has proved to be critical in terms of the first stages of EU–Mercosur agreements. In this stage, the basis for the development of EU–Mercosur relations was established, and this ensured that the agreements in the second stage were achieved more quickly.

In other words, if this stage had never existed, it would have taken longer to develop these agreements because those trying to develop EU–Mercosur relations would have had to start from scratch.

This chapter is divided into different sections. The first section discusses the impact of Spain and Portugal becoming members of the EU and the consequences of this for both the EU and the new EU member states. It will be argued that policy development and developments in EU–Mercosur relations were very much a bottom-up process because it can be demonstrated that the Iberian countries were a progressive influence in the years that followed their membership. Finally, although the tendency in the literature is to suggest that Spain and Portugal have shown similar actions, influences and preferences towards Latin America, it has also been argued that it was Spain rather than Portugal that showed the most interest in developing relations and policies with Latin America (Gomez Saraiva 2004; Dykmann 2006). In other words, it was Spain rather than Portugal that wanted to continue the special relationship with the region. Even in the case of Brazil, a former colony of Portugal, the political and economic ties with Spain were much stronger than with Portugal (Wiarda 1989) – so much so that Spain also became a credit-lender for Brazil (Baklanoff 1985).

The relationship of the EU and Latin America before and after 1985

The central discussion in this section will focus on the change in the relations between the EU and Latin America after 1985 when the Iberian countries joined the EU. This is crucial for the discussion of the critical juncture created with the Spanish and Portuguese membership which will help in the analysis of the degree of Europeanization. In order to appreciate the degree of change it is crucial to compare EU relations with the region before 1985 with EU relations with the region after 1985 and see how deep (or not) the path created is.

There are different potential outcomes in this analysis. If it is the case that there was a high degree of change after the Iberian countries joined the EU, it will support the argument that Iberian countries were the main reason for the changes in the attitude within the EU. On the other hand, a low degree of change would support the argument which claims that the membership was just one of many reasons behind the EU's new policies towards Latin America and that there are also other more important factors such as access to the markets. An intermediate degree of change would support the argument that suggests that the Iberian countries' membership of the EU was crucial for the new policies but that policy development also needed something else in order to make this process possible. For example, these changes would not have been possible had Mercosur not had its own set of demands. This will be the central argument advanced in this monograph. However, none of these three outcomes denies the importance of the

Iberian membership, which can confirm the creation of the path at this point.

This section will also explain the degree of progress in the relationship between the EU and Latin America over time in order to assess the progress after the Iberian membership of the EU. In order to do so, EU–Latin American relations will be compared before and after 1985. The analysis below will also consider changes in terms of policy-makers, agreements and the outcomes of important areas of political dialogue, cooperation and trade which are the key dimensions of EU–Latin American relations and EU–Mercosur relations.

EU–Latin American relations before the Iberian membership

Throughout the course of this chapter there will be a discussion of why the EU did not displayed any sort of interest towards Latin America prior to 1985. The lack of interest in the region prior to the Iberian membership can be seen in the poor relations between the EU institutions and Latin America. The increase of Commission offices in Latin America after the membership (Aldecoa Luzarraga 1995) is just one of many examples of how basic logistic tools necessary for a fluent relationship were not yet in place. Another example was the fact that the EU documents relating to Latin America were either in English or French until 1986 (IRELA 1996) in an area where Spanish and Portuguese are the predominant languages. It is true that English and French are the official languages of the EU, and even today much information that is considered important for the relations between both regions is in French (Freres and Sanahuja 2005: 46), when this information could also be easily translated into Spanish and Portuguese now that the Iberian countries are members of the EU. Without overestimating the importance of these examples, they do suggest that there was an overall lack of real effort or interest in progressing relations with Latin America both before the membership in 1986, and to a certain extent after Spain and Portugal became members of the EU, although it changed to some extent after it.

The lack of interest in Latin America also comes from the asymmetrical relations of the EU and Latin America due to both regions having different interests and different geopolitical priorities, rather than because the EU showed differing degrees of preference in favour of Africa and Asia in the area of development (Grabendorff 1987; Hoste 1999). Moreover, the protectionism that the EU showed towards the European agricultural sector was also a serious component of political relations (Grabendorff 1987; Hoste 1999). In addition to this, the presence of the US did not help the potential EU–Latin American relations because an alliance with this North American country was also considered to be of more importance than developing a new policy towards Latin America (Grabendorff 1987).

Furthermore, developing EU–Latin America relations was hindered by a lack of the necessary resources to facilitate cooperation, and the limitations placed on imports into the EU (Hoste 1999). It has also been suggested that a lack of relations between both regions was a consequence of the complexity of the EU's internal institutional framework. For example, Grabendorff contends that 'When the Community uses the argument of lack of adequate Latin American intermediaries, the Latin Americans frequently respond by citing a lack of interest by the EC and the complexity of the latter's decision-making apparatus' (Grabendorff 1987: 78).

It is unclear whether the complexity of the EU's institutional framework, especially its policy-making and decision-making mechanisms, made it difficult for other regions such as Latin America and other countries to be able to get the most out of these relations. It could be argued that this is something of an exaggeration and that Latin American countries used it as way of defending themselves from the accusations of the EU. This could have affected the EU policy towards the regions.

With regard to political dialogue, the Commission's report to the Community Council on 'Relations with the Latin American countries' in July 1969 was its first significant action towards Latin America since its conception. This is important in the sense that this was the first time that 'relations' with Latin America were recognized at an official level. However, it should also be acknowledged that this report is purely a diplomatic document. Nevertheless, it did have an effect on the other EU institutions. For example, the first resolution from the EP came one month after the first Council of Ministers' Declaration about the region in November 1969, and six months after the Commission's original report to the Community Council (EP 1969). One year after the Commission's report to the Council, Latin America responded to these political statements through the Declaration of Buenos Aires. Exactly one year later the Council responded positively and as a consequence this was followed by regular contact between the Latin American ambassadors to the EU and officials from the Commission (Ribeiro Hoffmann 2004).

The EP is the EU institution that has traditionally shown the most political interest towards the region and has in fact produced many declarations in favour of collaboration with the region. The EP acknowledged that the EU did not consider Latin America to be particularly important in terms of the EU's interests in a resolution that was signed the day after Spain and Portugal signed their Act of Accession, 12 June 1985. This resolution said that the EP: 'Deplores the low priority that LA [Latin America] has been for the EU having in mind the necessities of the region and the traditional links with the continent' (EP 1985).

The first document from an EU institution related to Latin America was the maritime report from the EP in 1964. However, this can hardly be considered to be a significant political statement about the region, even though it does prove that the EP was one of the first EU institutions to enter dialogue with the region. This argument is further supported by the EP's support for the region through the inter-parliamentary conferences between the EP and the Parliament Latino (Parlatin – Latin American Parliament). These conferences were first held in 1974 and have been held every two years since 1975. They were suspended during the Malvinas/Falklands conflict before being resumed a couple of years later. Ayuso (1996) claims that these conferences had little influence on the EU since the EP itself did not have much influence in those early days and in the 1980s had none. The resolutions of the EP–Parlatin meetings showed which topics were discussed and that the discussion was not very different from the resolutions the EP passed to the Council and the Commission in support of developing relations with Latin America. This is demonstrated in the following quotation: the EP 'Invites the Community to stimulate the efforts of regional integration and congratulate the creation of the Latin American Economic System (SELA) the 18th of October of 1975 with the purpose of creating economic and commercial cooperation among Latin-American and Caribbean countries' (EP 1976).

Nevertheless, integration in Latin America seems to have been a significant issue for the EU. As mentioned, the EU's lack of involvement in the region had been justified by the lack of appropriate intermediaries on the Latin American side (Grabendorff 1987). However, at this time there was at least one intermediary: there were discussions in the EP–Parlatin, which was a forum for biregional discussions (see Boxes 4.1 and 4.2). Therefore, it could be argued that the EP was the bridge between Latin America and the EU since no other EU institution had such permanent contact and discussion with the region.

In relation to aid, the first time that the EU created a programme for financial and technical cooperation with Asia and Latin America was on 15 March 1976 (Anacoreta Correia 1996; Ayuso 1996). This programme lasted for a period of four years and focused on non-associated developing countries and the distribution of funding, which was set around 75% for Asia, 20% for Latin America and 5% for African countries. When Denmark, the UK and Ireland became members of the EU in 1973, it prompted discussions about the EU's external relations which had previously been ignored due to French pressure (Ayuso 1996; De Pablo Valenciano and Carretero Gomez 1999). However, pressure from the UK blocked the decision on the budget for ACP countries until a programme for financial and technical cooperation with Asia and Latin America was decided (Ayuso 1996: 5). In many ways it was this move that led to the change in direction of EU policy towards Latin America (Ayuso 1996: 5). It will be demonstrated later in this section that this strategy was later copied by Spain. In 1981 this programme for financial and technical cooperation with Asia and Latin America was renewed. It was the first piece of legislation to be dedicated to

---

Box 4.1 The European Parliament's support for links with Mercosur at the political and economic level

At the political/diplomatic level

Support for the regular contacts started between tge regions (EP 1976).

Support for the creation of institutions that will help the promotion and the provision of information about the potential of these countries (EP 1976). Support for the creation of an institute that promotes the relations between the regions with two headquarters, one in Latin America and one in the EU.

Support for cooperation between the two regions, keeping in mind the major economic, political and social differences among the Latin American countries; therefore a differentiated policy towards Latin America adjusted to the real needs of the different problems of the region will let the EU appreciate the Latin American reality (EP 1983, 1985).

At the economic level

Support for the generalized system preferences (GSP) for Latin America which would help the increase of exports from Latin America to Europe at the same time as regional integration (EP 1976, 1982). The EP points out the decreased participation in the GSP and asks for an improvement in the system for Latin American countries (EP 1983, 1985).

Support for help with external debt (EP 1983). Ask the Commission and IRELA to study the solutions to the external debt (EP 1985).

Source: EP (1976, 1983, 1985).

non-associated countries (Birochi 1999). 'The Council's guidelines prioritised agriculture sectors and humanitarian aid. However, this was not considered to be very innovative or even significant when looking at the amount of aid offered by the EU' (Hoste 1999).

It is crucial to look at the EU and individual countries in Latin America before Spain and Portugal joined the EU. The most important aspect of the relations between the EU and individual countries in Latin America was the creation of a few short-reaching trade agreements – the 'first generation agreement'. In addition to this, the inclusion of some Latin American countries into the generalized system of preferences (GSP) also helped the development of this relationship. The relationship between the EU and

---

Box 4.2 European Parliament resolutions supporting the relations between the EU and Latin America

Regionalism

Support for: a global EU policy towards Central America; the opening of an office in Central America; the use of the EIB in Central America; the acceptance of the international agreement on sugar (EP 1982).

Support for integration and intraregional cooperation in Central America as well as supporting the collaboration of Venezuela and Mexico with Central America in terms of funding for development, provision of energy and industrial cooperation (EP 1982). Support for regional integration and regional groups such as the Latin American Economic System, the Central American Common Market and the Andean Pact and favouring the creation of programmes or projects with those regions (EP 1985).

Cooperation agreements

Support for cooperation agreements with Mexico, Argentina, Brazil and Uruguay and the support for bigger agreements with those countries. Support for cooperation agreements with other Latin American countries that are interested (EP 1976).

Support for the continuation of the relations between Argentina and the EU and the conclusion of a cooperation agreement with that country (EP 1985).

Source: EP (1976, 1982 and 1985).

Brazil started rather sooner thanks to an agreement on the peaceful use of nuclear energy in 1961 (EEC 1961; Smith 2001). In 1973, Brazil achieved the status of 'most favoured nation' by the EU, which gave the South American country preferential treatment on the exports of cocoa butter and soluble coffee (EEC 1973a). 'Although the first cooperation agreement did not happen until 1980 as part of the so-called "first generation agreement", this agreement brought about cooperation between both parties, the EU and Brazil, on the trade and economic areas' (EEC 1980).

In relation to Argentina, a similar agreement to the one with Brazil was reached in 1971. However, when the Malvinas/Falklands conflict started in 1982, relations between the EU and Latin America were affected. Argentina was put under an economic embargo and the inter-parliamentary conferences were suspended for some years. This was the first time that there had been strong disagreement within the EU regarding Latin America but the

EU sided with the UK. It could be argued that this shows that relations with Latin America were not that important to the EU because, even though they disagreed with the behaviour of the UK, the EU did not dare to challenge the embargo. The same kind of agreement was secured with Uruguay in 1973 (EEC 1973b) and Mexico secured a cooperation agreement in 1975 (EEC 1975).

The relationship between the EU and Chile was based on EP resolutions regading the *coup de état* (EP 1973), the anniversary of the coup, opposition to human rights abuses carried out by Pinochet's regime (EP 1983) and in relation to the political situation in the country in 1983 and 1984. Although the European Commission's declarations in opposition to Pinochet's regime were the first political statements made by the EU towards the region, they were nothing more than declarations and not a definitive policy against the Chilean coup (Dykmann 2006). Furthermore, the few agreements with Brazil and Mexico had a minimum impact in the development of these countries (EP 1985).

The discussion so far has shown that there were biregional economic agreements reached with Latin American countries, such as Brazil, Argentina, Uruguay and Mexico, which were considered to be either more developed and/or politically stable. Since the three first countries were part of Mercosur, and Mexico achieved a bilateral agreement with the EU almost at the same time, it seems that over time the EU has shown preference towards developed and politically stable countries in Latin America. This undermines, to a certain extent, the normative view of EU actions towards Latin America.

In summary, prior to Spain and Portugal becoming members of the EU, the EU had virtually no relationship with Latin America. The EU institution involved in developing dialogue was mostly the EP, which in those years had very little power, even in the area of aid, where Latin America drew much attention for traditionally being the region receiving the lowest amount of aid from the EU compared to other regions in the world. It was not until the 1970s that the EU developed official links with Latin America. The EU had very narrow commerce agreements with some Mercosur countries, such as Brazil, which were not considered to be especially important. For most other developed countries in Latin America at this time, particularly in the area of aid, it was not until the 1970s that the EU developed a policy that covered Latin American countries as part of a general approach to the EU's external relations agenda by including Caribbean countries in the Lome Convention that was pursued by the UK when it became a member of the EU. From the creation of the EU until 1985, relations between the EU and Latin America were virtually non-existent.

A new scenario was created for EU–Latin America relations after Spain and Portugal joined the EU. The attempt by Spain and Portugal to influence in the EU in relation to Latin America and the acceptance of such behaviour by the EU was clear even before they officially joined. For example, Spain and Portugal played an important role during the Central American crisis in the mid-1980s. Bilateral relations politicized the relationship, starting with EU actions during the crisis (Grabendorff 1987).

The first institution that showed a new interest in Latin America was the EP. One of the many pieces of evidence that show the creation of a new policy path regarding this region is the development of inter-parliamentary meetingns. Grabendorff argues that 'Besides publishing a considerable series of really constructive reports regarding desirability of improving relations with Latin America it [the EP] clearly indicated a high degree of flexibility, at the inter-parliamentary meetings held in Brasilia in 1985 and in Lisbon in 1987, toward a more positive development of joint relations' (Graben-dorff 1987: 78).

This does not, however, mean that the parliaments were powerful or influential in their respective homelands. Therefore, there was not a direct action–reaction relation during these biregional discussions and/or during the EU's actions to Latin America at this stage. Nevertheless, these inter-parliamentary conferences in 1985 and 1987 welcomed the presence of Spain and Portugal and declared that they expected that with this event the relations between the EU and Latin American would only get stronger. According to Grabendorff (1987), the EU had at least started to show movement towards improving relations between the two regions after the Iberian membership.

Leaving the EP aside for the moment, there are also other issues that showed that the EU was starting to develop a new approach towards Latin America. For example, the opening of the IRELA, funded by the Commission, was an indicator of EU intentions, since it created an instrument for cultural, political, economic and scientific cooperation between both regions. The IRELA was created in Madrid in 1984 with the aim of promoting and strengthening relations between the two regions. This is further evidence of an EU institution following the new path towards Latin America. The Commission was aware of how much change the historical event of the Iberian membership was likely to produce, therefore it developed an institution that would be a source of information on a region that had traditionally been ignored. The institute served as a forum for dialogue and a centre for contact. Its principal functions were: firstly, to provide advice and undertake specific consultancy activities, principally for regional institutions in Europe and Latin America; secondly, to organize conferences, seminars and workshops, and to arrange training programmes on issues of common interest, primarily for European and Latin American politicians, officials, diplomats, academics, journalist and businessmen; thirdly, to promote, coordinate and undertake specific research on relations between Europe and Latin America, and to make information and analysis available to the opinion-formers and decision-makers of both regions.

In the area of aid and cooperation, and on the issue of drugs, there was a change towards Latin America which can be attributed to the creation of this new path. The first credits to fund workshops and seminars in different places were given in 1987 (Blanco Garriga 1992). It seems obvious to say that funding workshops and seminars is not a particularly important policy nor part of a highly developed strategy towards the region. However, it should not be forgotten that in most areas EU–Latin American relations had been non-existent before Spain and Portugal became members of the EU. In other words, although these workshops and seminars do not appear to be very ambitious, these events played an important role in initiating EU policy towards Latin America. This had been an area where there was not much knowledge of either how these issues could potentially be developed or how basic problems could be overcome. In relation to the issue of aid, Dykmann claims

> It is evident that the peninsular authorities and their representatives are very present in institutions concerned with European policy towards Latin America as 'l'Amerique latine occupe dans la politique espagnole de cooperation une place toute aussi centrale que celle occupée en France par l'Afrique' [Latin America is of central importance for the Spanish policy of cooperation in the same way that Africa is for France]... Additionally, some critics say that Spain indeed determines the development cooperation of the EU with Latin America to a large extent, but does not provide proportional contributions to respective EU funds. (Dykmann 2006: 92–93)

In relation to combating drugs, Spain was the leader within the EU. Abel Matutes, the Spanish commissioner in charge of relations with these regions, recognized the benefits of eliminating restrictions on the exports of Colombian goods, which was also extended to Bolivia and Peru (*El País* 13/10/1990). This plan was fully supported by all the governments of the EU apart from France. The president of Colombia considered Spain to be the leader at the EU level with the socio-economic measures proposed (*El País* 13/10/1990).

Another important piece of evidence supporting the argument that an interest had been created towards Latin America was the fact that even the European Council of Dublin Declarations of June 1990 discussed issues related to Latin America. These declarations brought the EU together to discuss environmental issues and to ask the Commission to develop plans for consultation with countries close to the Amazon, giving special attention to Brazil (Blanco Garriga 1992). To what extent these declarations and proposals had any real influence is a matter of debate. For example, when the new programme for cooperation with Latin America and Asia was approved for the period of 1991–1995, it was agreed that the amount of aid given to develop cooperation with Asia and Latin America would be doubled. On this occasion, Latin America would receive 30% of the €2,300 million (*El País* 9/5/1990). Abel Matutes pointed out that there was a fear of 'Eurocentrism' concerning the high levels of attention dedicated to the Eastern European countries (*El País* 9/5/1990). This issue will be discussed in more detail in the following section.

In the area of political dialogue, the level of change has not been as impressive as it could have been, which supports the claims that the changes created with the Iberian membership were necessary but not sufficient: this is the central argument of this monograph. When EU political dialogue with Latin America did not properly take off, both regions tended to blame one another. On the one hand, Latin America criticized the EU for not showing interest in the region, as well as citing the difficulty the Community's institutional framework created for decision-making. On the other hand, the EU tended to cite Latin America's lack of intermediaries for the lack of development of inter-regional relations (Grabendorff 1987). It could be argued that the fact the EU cites the lack of Latin American intermediaries is an indication that the EU was expecting some kind of representation from the entire region. This is interesting because the Rio Group and Mercosur were being created at around the same time as Grabendorff was highlighting the issue. This gives support to the argument that Mercosur countries, and Latin American countries as a whole, tried to develop regional groups which could provide a forum where dialogue with the EU was possible. However, conversely, the EU was not trying as hard to deal with its failures in relation to Latin America. This issue has been developed more fully in more recent research.

In discussing to the interest in the region within the EU, Grabendorff highlights the differences in terms of the degree of interest (or lack of interest) the different institutions have shown. He explains how the EP is by far the most interested in the region, as well as being the most active and showing a great deal of flexibility during the course of the inter-parliamentary meetings. Other than the EP, it would appear that it was only the EU's Council of Ministers that showed any real interest in Latin America (Grabendorff 1987). This illustrates a problem that will affect EU policy towards Mercosur in the long term: the lack of interest of most EU states towards Mercosur.

The third area of EU–Mercosur relations is in trade, where the lack of significant change leads us to underestimate the importance of the Iberian membership in EU trade with Mercosur. Table 4.1 below suggests that levels of trade have, in relative terms, remained very much the same.

To summarize: the three areas of EU policy towards Mercosur show differing degrees of change which helps to explain the medium importance of the Iberian membership in relation to the policy towards Mercosur. As mentioned in the introduction to this chapter, Sewell (1996) claims that the importance of some event in the future is due to the path dependence that was created. In this case, the Iberian membership had an impact that would become apparent in the long-term, not so much immediately.

Table 4.1 EU[1] exports and imports with Mercosur countries, 1980–1990 (values in US$ million)

	1980	1981[2]	1982	1983	1984	1985	1986[3]	1987	1988	1989	1990
EU exp to Arg	2,495.2	2,525.7	1,492.8	2,193.2	1,932.6	1,551.3	1,707.2	1,757.1	1,311.3	1,161.2	1,234.9
EU imp from Arg	2,017.9	2,073.9	2,152.7	2,345.8	3,206.5	3,282.1	2,309.1	1,888.6	2,623.9	2,787.0	3,472.1
EU exp to Braz	2,703.6	2,655.6	2,639.3	2,254.4	2,977.8	2,679.9	3,503.1	3,353.8	3,121.6	3,841.0	3,635.5
EU imp from Braz	4,777.8	5,740.7	6,593.7	7,641.2	9,546.6	10,473.3	7,371.3	7,273.5	9,329.5	10,445.6	9,196.3
EU exp to Par	n/a	n/a	n/a	n/a		92	171	181	160	130	223
EU imp from Par	195.7	127.8	196.4	336.7	323.1	319.9	167.7	252.0	366.5	426.7	445.4
EU exp to Uru	262.6	264.8	186.6	148.3	198.8	190.5	216.3	234.6	214.5	252.0	232.9
EU imp from Uru	205.5	333.5	309.0	263.3	284.8	249.3	299.6	367.7	883.7	658.6	567.2
Total EU exp to Mercosur countries	5,461.4	5,446.1	4,318.7	4,595.9	5,109.2	4,513.7	5,597.6	5,526.5	4,807.4	5,384.2	5,326.3

EU exp to world	753,835	697,195	670,490	654,260	673,050	708,810	871,875	1,050,355	1,166,000	1,243,625	1,508,795
EU exp to Mercosur as % of total	0.72%	0.78%	0.64%	0.70%	0.75%	0.63%	0.64%	0.52%	0.41%	0.43%	0.35%
Total EU imp from Mercosur countries	7,196.9	87,275.9	9,251.8	10587	13,361	14,324.6	10,147.7	9,781.8	13,203.6	14,317.9	13,681
EU imp from world	847,000	754,545	717,955	686,340	696,030	723,545	855,570	1,049,980	118,4730	1,280,750	1,558,035
EU imp from Mercosur as % of total	0.84%	1.15%	1.28%	1.54%	1.91%	1.97%	1.18%	0.93%	1.11%	1.11%	0.87%

Sources: The author's own elaboration with the data from IRELA (1994), WTO's statistics Database and Eurostat Database.
Notes: Figures in bold are percentages for Mercosur imports/exports. Figures in italics are for the years when the EU took on new members.
[1] EU 15.
[2] Greece joined the EU.
[3] Spain and Portugal joined the EU.

So far the evidence has shown a low level of ambition and commitment on the EU's side, implying a low level of engagement. But the fact that there is some ambition, and some commitment – as has been seen with the aid part of the policy especially, and the political dialogue to some extent – means that it would not be accurate to say that there is no engagement. This engagement is critical to the central argument of this book; there was progress due to the Iberian membership and the interest on the part of Latin America in engaging with the EU.

It is important to discuss EU relations with other regional groups in Latin America to understand the position that Mercosur achieved. EU policy towards Mercosur developed out of the EU's more general policy towards Latin America as soon as it was materially possible. During the first stage of Mercosur (1985–1990) there was still very little development that was capable of meriting an individual relationship with the EU. Therefore, any dialogue that did take place tended to occur on an informal basis through the Rio Group. This was made possible thanks to the pressure that Spain exerted in order to get the EU more involved, first, in Central America and then in other areas at a later date. However, the dialogue covered most issues related to Latin America, and under that same umbrella were the dialogues between the EU and the Rio Group.

The hard experience of the Central American conflict of 1979–1985 and the complex redemocratization of the 1980s reshaped the principles of a Latin American politics of cooperation. The creation of the Rio Group and the links with the Contadora group (a group created by Colombia, Mexico, Panama and Venezuela to deal with the Central American crisis) helped the consolidation of the peace process in the region. Those groups created the necessary trust in the new political context which helped to develop a permanent political dialogue between the EU and Latin America and to improve the democratic credibility of the Central American countries (Duran 2009). The approach of Latin American and Caribbean countries to Europe is asymmetrical; the urgency of having access to bigger and more stable markets is on the Latin American and Caribbean side. For the Europeans, trade with Asia, Oceania and the special emphasis on the US is the priority. The fact that this region is not a priority for Europe does not mean that the EU does not accept a move towards Latin America and the Carribbean for strategic reasons (Duran 2009).

It is important to point out that EU–Mercosur dialogues did not officially take place until 1991, only a few years after the process of integration between Brazil and Argentina had started to emerge in 1985. The process was then later extended to Paraguay and Uruguay. Because these states formed the bulk of Mercosur's membership, these relations are referred to as EU–Mercosur dialogues. EU–Mercosur dialogues during this period continued to experience problems primarily as a result of the lack of integration between Mercosur countries. At the end of the 1980s Brazil was still reluctant to advance on a sub-regional agreement with the EU (Bizzozero 1995). It seems that the EU's cooperation on regional integration and the consolidation of Mercosur enabled EU–Mercosur agreements to really take off in the early 1990s (Bizzozero 1995). According to Grabendorff (1987), the obstacles the EU encountered in South America compared with the other EU–Latin American sub-regional groups were not a surprise. They were caused by two main issues: firstly, relations between the EU and Argentina over the Malvinas/Falklands conflict continued to make EU–Mercosur relations difficult; secondly, there was still the long-standing competitive rivalry between Brazil and Argentina in terms of which would be Mercosur's external representative.

The highest profile dialogue between the EU and a regional group was the dialogue between the EU and Central America. The EU's peaceful intervention in the Central American crisis with the development of the San José process was an important step in terms of furthering Central American relations with the EU, but only to a limited extent. Hoste's (1999) argument that this was due to the lack of economic or political interest is understandable. However, what is more difficult to accept is Hoste's contention that the EU developed relations with Central America in order to gain access to Latin America more generally. These Central American countries had very little influence over Latin America and an unstable political situation that had been created by suffering several decades of civil wars, as in the case of El Salvador. Moreover, most of the EU intervention was done through the French, Spanish and German embassies in Central America. In addition to this, Spain and Portugal were part of the San José dialogue even though they were not members of the EU when the dialogues began. They were involved, nevertheless, because of both the interest and the pressure that was expressed in the EU by Spanish President Felipe Gonzalez. 'The cooperation between the EU and Latin America was already one of the most important precedents to understand the project of relations between regions, at the Latin American and Mercosur level' (Caetano et al. 2010: 200).

The more general lack of interest in Latin America did not suddenly change completely after the EU's initial contact with Central America, but the contact did mark the beginning of a sort of relationship between the EU and Latin America. It is more likely that the policy with Central America also happened due to the seriousness of the situation that was being created by the international conflict with the US, which had contributed to destabilizing the region. I would argue that what is also interesting is that the EU had found, quite accidentally, an interlocutor for the region in the shape of the Rio Group. Political dialogue with the Rio Group was then later extended to become political dialogue with the whole of Latin America:

> Political dialogue was also established with the countries which organised to promote peace in the region and created the Contadora Group (in January 1983) and later became known as the Rio Group (in 1986). Those early

meetings were first designed to establish peace and had therefore an agenda focused on democracy, peace, conflict resolution. (Dykmann 2006: 44)

The San José dialogue also brought into being a new set of institutionalized relationships between the EU and other regions (Smith 1995). However, the institutionalized dialogues with the Rio Group became the most successful. By 1989, the Rio Group covered approximately the same geographical territory as the former Latin American Association of Integration and, therefore, became a permanent political forum and the main interlocutor substituting for other broader regional integration groups (Ayuso 1996).

The dialogue between the EU and the Rio Group soon developed to cover more than just political issues. The meeting of March 1986 covered a discussion of the external debt, whilst the 1990 meeting of the Rio Group proposed cooperation between both regions at technological and commercial levels (Hoste 1999). As a consequence of this new dialogue there were now more delegations of the Commission in the region and there was a move from bilateral towards multilateral dialogue between the EU and Latin America (Aldecoa Luzarraga 1995). In the early 1990s, the number of delegations doubled from four to eight (Hoste 1999). There was still a limit to the dialogues between the two regions. According to Dykmann: 'Since the Rio Group has no rigid institutionalised organisational structure, no organic dialogue with the EU evolved and no real negotiations took place' (Dykmann 2006: 45).

At this point, we also need to consider the influence of the long-standing lack of relations between these regions, which affected the speed of the changes in the first stage. Dykmann argues that the real goal of this forum at this particular time was 'to create an atmosphere of trust, which should lead to common positions and harmony between the regions and it strengthened the position of Latin American countries relative to third parties' (Dykmann 2006: 45).

Another sign of the importance of Latin American demands to the EU in order to advance the EU–Latin American relationship was the behaviour of the ambassador of Chile in Brussels regarding the institutionalization of the dialogues with the EU. He played a key role in convincing the other ministers from Latin America to seek a common declaration from the EU. As a result of the Chilean ambassador's efforts, the Declaration of Rome institutionalized a dialogue which meant that the Rio Group would be formally recognized as the EU's main partner in Latin America (Dykmann 2006: 45). This would not be the first time that the EU needed specific demands from Latin America in order to develop policies towards the latter. According to Dykmann, the EU was satisfied with this dialogue because 'the European Union is especially happy about the Rio Group because it enables dialogue among four dozen entities but requires only two voices' (Dykmann 2006: 45). In the following chapter the dialogue between the

EU and the Rio Group, particularly in terms of its importance in the development of EU policy and relations with Mercosur, will be further discussed in relation to the fact that: 'More weight has also been given to development of relations with Latin American regional associations such as the Andean Pact and Mercosur, relations which became autonomous after having been developed unofficially on the margin of the meetings with the Rio Group' (Hoste 1999: 4).

The main point of this section is how important an earlier event – such as the pressure Spain, among other actors, put on the EU to intervene in Central America – became to the blossoming of EU–Latin American regional groups' dialogue, as well as affecting that dialogue, the beginning of the EU policy towards Mercosur. This is absolutely crucial for the development of EU–Mercosur and therefore for the understanding of EU policy towards Mercosur. The link between EU involvement in Central America as a consequence of the Iberian membership which influenced the future EU–Latin American and EU–Mercosur relations has been ignored in the literature that focuses on the EU policy towards Mercosur of the late 1990s and early 2000s.

In terms of ambition and commitment, again this section shows a low degree of both, which produces a low level of engagement. This should not be confused with no engagement, since the EU did have a sort of ambition, as the institutionalization of the EU–Rio Group meetings shows, and a sort of commitment shown by the launching of several political dialogues with the region.

The Iberian countries' membership of the EU

On 1 January 1986, Spain and Portugal joined the EU. This event has proved to be crucial for the development of EU relations with Latin America, becoming a historical event which created a path. It also had effects for Spanish and Portuguese foreign policy towards Latin America. The degree of Europeanization from a bottom-up and top-down perspective happened at the same time as the EU membership of Spain and Portugal. This reinforces the central argument that explains that the membership of Iberian countries was necessary but not sufficient to create the policy, since they did not manage to get the EU uploading the policy. In relation to Spain more specifically, it was a turning point for Spain's own foreign policy from the very moment that Spain's membership of the EU was being considered. Spain was aware that it had to make a choice between belonging to the EU or Latin America, and in the end it chose the former, but that does not mean that it forgot about Latin America.

This section analyses to what extent the EU agreed to incorporate the Spanish foreign policy agenda in relation to Latin America, and to what extent Iberian countries sacrificed their national foreign policy objectives towards Latin America as a result of becoming members of the EU. This analysis considers the work of Reuben Wong (2008) on Europeanization which has been discussed in Chapter 2. In this case, two aspects of Europeanization are considered.

First, 'adaptation and policy' which is considered the 'downloading' aspect: 'Harmonization and transformation of a member state to the needs and requirements of EU membership' (Wong 2008: 326). The most important indicator for the discussion here is: 'Internationalization of EU members and its integration process' (Wong 2008: 326). By looking at the way the EU has downloaded its views on Latin America to Spain and Portugal we can see how much the membership did not achieve in relation to Latin America.

And second, 'national projection' which is considered the uploading aspect: 'National foreign policy of a member state affects and contributes to the development of a common European FP [foreign policy]' (Wong 2008: 326). And the most important indicator for this is 'externalization of national FP positions onto the EU level'. By looking at the way the EU uploaded the views of Spain and Portugal it will be evidenced how much the membership achieved in relation to Latin America.

Reasons for membership

This section will focus on the reasons for membership to see which entity, the EU or Spain and Portugal was in an easier position when negotiating the issue of Latin America. It was clear that the UK was already a very powerful country when it joined the EU, which favoured its demands for its former colonies. The discussion below will consider whether the same can be said in the case of Spain and Portugal.

Spain and Portugal joined the EU for both economic and political reasons. The reasons behind Portugal's desire to join the EU were political. Portugal's aim was to include its former African colonies in the Lome Convention, as well as using the EU to adapt Portugal to the international changes and develop the country (Medeiros Ferreira 1993: 177). In relation to the Lome Convention, Portugal also aimed to have Portuguese recognized as an official language in the Convention, where up until now only English and French were the officially recognized languages (Medeiros Ferreira 1993). Medeiros Ferreira claims that in doing so 'The introduction of linguistic criteria for the promotion of regional cooperation could enable those African countries whose official language is Portuguese to take better advantage of financial assistance under the Lome Convention' (Medeiros Ferreira 1993: 177).

This would also enable Portugal to receive assistance for its former colonies in terms of generating stronger levels of cooperation at the regional level. As a consequence, it would also increase Portugal's influence in the Lome Convention due to Portugal's special relationship with the former colonies. In a way, this made it possible for Portugal to acquire a more powerful position in one of the most developed areas of EU external relations. In other words, thanks to its EU membership and its special membership with the former colonies, Portugal would end up in a more powerful position than would have been possible had it not been a member of the EU. Economically, however, trading with Europe was the most important issue because Portugal, like Spain, had already started to move towards integrating its economy with the European market during the 1960s and 1970s (Wiarda 1989: 192).

Similarly, in terms of political issues, Spain was also pursuing EU membership for many reasons. It is undeniable that the EU provides a model of democracy, liberty and progress to Spain and Portugal and that the modernization of the Iberian countries had to be based on integrating their countries into the European club (Royo 2006: 211). However, this process was more difficult for Spain than for Portugal because Portugal had an easier time than Spain at an international level. Portugal was admitted to the United Nations (UN) earlier than Spain, and even became a NATO member while Spain was being treated as something of an outcast (Wiarda 1989: 192). This was most certainly a product of Spain's recent political history which had generated strong feelings against Spain within the EU (Wiarda 1989: 192). This strong dislike of Spanish politics in the twentieth century was generated by events such as the Spanish Civil War and Franco's alliance with Hitler. It could be argued that this put Spain in a relatively weak position when it was trying to become a member of the EU. The negotiations of Spanish membership with the EU will be discussed below, but the important point to make here is that at the international level Spain was looking to strengthen its historical links with Latin America, as well as its links with the Arab world (Holmes 1983: 165).

In terms of the EU's position in relation to Spain and Portugal becoming members, it is clear that the EU had developed a clear agenda. According to Wiarda (1989), the EU's political agenda was far more developed, although somewhat overblown at times:

> The belief of the German Social Democrats, the French left, British Labour, and Benelux and Scandinavian Socialists that the continuing 'Fascist' regimes of Spain and Portugal were unacceptable in the European community of democratic and social democratic nations ... Much evidence shows that political leaders in France and Germany especially feared the potential for domestic upheaval in their own nations, which the Portuguese revolution seemed to inspire ... Fearing a repeat of the revolutionary events of 1968, or worse, the European leaders sought to moderate Portugal's revolution (and prevent one in Spain) by pushing for their entry into the EEC. Although the fear that France or Germany might explode as Portugal did seems ludicrous in retrospect, at the height of the Portuguese revolution in 1974–1975 the threat of upheaval elsewhere seemed real. (Wiarda 1989: 194)

Fear of political uprisings in other EU member states was not the only reason why EU member states were interested in integrating Spain and Portugal into the EU. For example, there was a belief that by bringing the Iberian countries into the EU, the EU would be able to prevent Spain and Portugal from going 'Communist', and 'who knows about Italy, Greece, and Turkey – perhaps the entire southern flank of Europe' (Wiarda 1989: 194). As the author explains, with even a little of knowledge of the Spanish and Portuguese systems of that time, these fears would seem ridiculous, nevertheless there was discussion of the possibility of a 'red Mediterranean' at many levels, including academic and government ones. The US was also very keen on the Iberian countries becoming members of the EU for similar reasons. This argument is supported by the fact the US transferred funds to European parties (Wiarda 1989: 194). Wiarda also claims that the Iberian membership was used as a mechanism to secure political changes at the national level such as democratization – a crucial point in relation to the issue of EU–Mercosur relations since this is also an indicator of the US's influence in European politics at the time, never mind US influence in its own backyard. This issue will be discussed in more detail later on.

Although there were general political and economic reasons for allowing the Iberian countries to become members of the EU, not all the EU countries were equally in favour of doing so. This is especially the case in relation to economic issues, particularly around the time that it seemed likely that Spain and Portugal would become members of the EU. For example, France was not very excited that the Iberian countries might become members of the EU, principally because of the effect this would have on France's agricultural sector. The focus of the discussion will now turn to examine the actual process of negotiating the Iberian countries' inclusion into the EU.

For both economic and political reasons, the negotiations lasted seven years. During the first years, the political obstacles were the main problem. Interestingly, some EU countries helped or desired concrete political outcomes during this time. Germany, for example, went as far as giving aid to Felipe Gonzalez's political party PSOE (Spanish Socialist Workers' Party) (Holmes 1983), which would go on to win Spanish national elections from 1982 to 1996. However, the EU demanded more than just political changes. Once some form of democracy had been put in place in both countries, Spain and Portugal were denied membership once again. This produced dismay in both countries, especially because it was France's idea to postpone and review their membership (Wiarda 1989: 198). The main problem was the potential effect that the Iberian countries would have on the Common Agricultural Policy (CAP) because both Spain and Portugal's economies were heavily weighted towards producing agricultural products. The UK's rebate only served to further complicate the negotiations (Heywood 1995). The UK's rebate referred to the economic contribution that the UK was providing to the EU which the newly elected British prime minister, Margaret Thatcher, considered too big a contribution. It was linked to the CAP, which would make demands on a high percentage of the EU budget which the UK would not benefit from as much as other countries, such as France. In addition to this, Germany was also unwilling to spend money on olive oil when it could be spent on butter (Holmes 1983: 165). The entrance of Iberian countries would mean a percentage of funding from the CAP would go towards the production of olive oil, instead of subsidizing other agricultural products such as butter. Holmes suggests that other EU member states were cautious about allowing Spain and Portugal to become members of the EU because of its agricultural production. As a result, negotiations relating to the Iberian countries' membership were hard fought. According to Heywood (1995), this is an important issue that tends to be overlooked in the existing literature. Furthermore, he argues that in the end, Spain agreed to:

> Opening its markets to EC competitors and bringing down external tariffs on industrial goods from third countries to the Community average within a period of seven years. In return, it would take ten years for the most competitive sectors of Spanish agricultural output –fresh fruit, vegetables and olive oil – to be phased into the CAP. (Heywood 1995: 270)

The French opposition was also linked to the CAP, particularly the effect that Spanish products would have in this area (Royo 2006). As Wiarda discusses, this event reminded the Iberian countries of the old complexes, prejudices and inferiorities, which made them reconsider being part of Europe and also question their future economic relations with third world countries such as Latin America and Africa (Wiarda 1989: 198). This 'Plan B' (stay with Latin America) was not so attractive, though, and it could be argued that Spain and Portugal were not in a strong enough position to defend their interests during the negotiations in many areas, particularly their special relationship with Latin America. However, Spain did use its relationship with Latin America as a way of exerting some pressure or at least positive influence when making its application to join the EU (Wiarda 1989). As highlighted by Dykmann (2006), though, it is difficult to accept the idea that the Iberian members were accepted into the EU because of their relationship with Latin America. More specifically, Spain had promoted the idea that it could act as a bridge between Europe and Latin America as far as possible. At the same time, Spain was unsuccessful in its attempts to ensure that its former colonies would be elevated to the same status as former British and French colonies (Baklanoff 2001; Dykmann 2006). Baklanoff (2001) claims that Spain was forced to sign a 'pre-nuptial agreement' whereby Spain would enter into a new marriage with the EU, from which Latin America would be excluded. This supports the view of low (if any) uploading by the EU.

It has already been argued in this monograph that Spain had, from the beginning, chosen to prioritize its regional relations in Europe rather than develop inter-regional relations with Latin America. However, this does not mean that Spain completely abandoned developing relations with Latin America. It is even debatable whether Spain did not explore this issue for its own benefit.

Nevertheless, although Spain decided to prioritize its relationship with the EU over Latin America from the very beginning, it did not mean that Spain would give up on Latin America. Wiarda argues that 'While negotiating with the EEC Spain also tried strenuously to resurrect its special relationship with Latin America ... These ties are to be built not on the older bases of Hispanismo implying Spanish paternalism and superiority toward its former colonies but on the basis of a "partnership" whose precise dimensions have never been fully articulated' (Wiarda 1989: 200). Nevertheless, strategic attempts to use the EU to enable Spain to become more influential in Latin America and the other way around – Spain using Latin America to become stronger inside the EU – did not end with the negotiations for membership. In fact, it continues to be an important feature of Spanish foreign policy today. As this section will show, there were some small achievements which show a small but important influence of the Iberian countries, how much they achieved is at the centre of the discussion. The following section will examine just how much Spain and Portugal were, in the end, able to achieve in terms of developing relations and policies that would benefit Latin America. It could be argued that these were only crumbs from the table. Nevertheless, this does not mean that relations and policies with Latin America could not be developed over time. Paraphrasing Sewell one more time, the events at a particular time will affect the events later on.

Sustaining these views are the following examples: two months before the signature of the Act of Accession, Spain and Portugal tried to negotiate their contribution to Lome. One of the issues that Spain highlighted during the negotiations was keeping zero tariffs on some products from Latin America. In fact, Manuel Marin (the chief negotiator for the Spanish team) mentioned that this was an obstacle two months before the signature of the accession treaty (*El País* 27/4/1985). Spain suspended the issue of the tariffs from Latin America on the contribution of €3.6 million to the third Lome Convention (*El País* 23/7/1985).

The discussion below will examine whether Spain and Portugal were able to create enough pressure that there would eventually be improvements in relations between Latin America and the EU once they had become members of the EU.

The outcome of negotiations for Iberian membership

This section will show the low but important level of EU uploading towards Mercosur. Spain and Portugal signed the Treaty of Accession in Madrid on 12 June 1985. The same day, the 'Joint Declaration of Intent on the Development and Intensification of Relations with the Countries of Latin America' was also signed by the EU member states (see below Box 4.3). This joint declaration was the result of Spain and Portugal's attempts to raise the status of their former colonies to the same level as the former colonies of Britain and France, as stated in the Lome Convention (Dykmann

---

Box 4.3 Final Act, Joint Declaration of Intent on the Development and Intensification of Relations with the Countries of Latin America

The Community:

- confirms the importance which it attaches to its traditional links with the countries of Latin America and to the close cooperation which it has developed with those countries;
- recalls in that context the recent ministerial meeting at San José in Costa Rica;
- on the occasion of the accession of Spain and Portugal, reaffirms its resolve to extend and strengthen its economic, commercial and cooperation relations with those countries;
- is determined to step up its activities to exploit all possible ways of achieving this goal, thus contributing, in particular, to the economic and social development of the Latin-American region, and to efforts aimed at the regional integration thereof;
- will endeavour, more specifically, to give concrete form to ways of strengthening the present links, of developing, extending and diversifying trade as far as possible and of implementing cooperation in the various fields of mutual interest on as wide a basis as possible, using the appropriate instruments and frameworks to increase the efficiency of the various forms of cooperation;
- is prepared in this context, in order to promote trade flows, to examine any problems which might arise in the field of trade with a view to finding appropriate solutions, taking into account, in particular, the scope of the generalized system of tariff preferences and the application of the economic cooperation agreements concluded or to be concluded with certain Latin American countries or groups of countries.

Source: EEC (1985).

2006: 87–88; Royo 2006: 45). In this declaration, the EU declared that it was keen to intensify its actions in order to help with the economic and social development of the Latin American region (EEC 1985). From the moment of the Iberian accession to the EU, it was already possible to see that there were problems with the GSP and the cooperation agreements that were created or about to be created in reference to this region. The declaration was strongly promoted by Spain (*El País* 20/2/1985; Dykmann 2006). The EP's resolution of the following day recognizes the fact that Spain's membership would help to consolidate relations with Latin America. Beyond this broad declaration, Spain also managed to keep 40,000 tons of cocoa and coffee under special treatment per year (*El País* 31/12/1986). A Final Act Declaration by Spain on Latin America was made on 15 November 1985 (see Box 4.4).

The emphasis that Spain placed on Latin America had a price; during the reorganization of the Commission, a Spanish official, Juan Prat, was given the job of coordinating relations with Latin America, Asia and the Mediterranean countries, but in the corridors of Berlaymount the president of the Commission Jacques Delors said, 'Prat's post is costly'. To gain this post, Spain lost other 'good positions' (*El País* 7/3/1990). However, Spain's interest in bringing Latin America closer to the European Community, according to the president of Spain at the time, was a product of national interests rather than moral reasons (*El País* 22/11/1985). It is not clear if Spain's position was taken because Spain wanted to become more important and more powerful within the EU by having strong connections with Latin America or whether Spain was trying to gain the benefits of having connections in Latin America by securing the support of the European Community.

Box 4.4 Final Act Declaration by the Kingdom of Spain on Latin America

In order to avoid sudden disturbances in its imports originating in Latin America, Spain has highlighted in the negotiations the problems which arise from the application of the 'acquis communautaire' to certain products. Partial and temporary solutions have been adopted for tobacco, cocoa and coffee.

Spain, in accordance with the principles and criteria set out in the joint declaration adopted by the Conference on Latin America, proposes finding permanent solutions in the context of the generalized system preferences, when next revised, or of other mechanisms existing within the Community.

Source: EEC (1985).

The declaration on EU relations with Latin America was a direct result of Spain and Portugal becoming members of the EU. Furthermore, this declaration provoked a series of chain reactions. On 2 December 1986, the commissioner in charge of Latin American affairs suggested to the Council of Ministers that they should improve Europe's relationship with the region (Grabendorff 1987). In addition to this, a communication from the Commission to the Council on 27 January 1987 relating to the improvement of relations between the EU and Latin America was officially made. This communication talked of improving relations in the areas of macroeconomics, financial dialogue, and that this should be done by establishing relations with the institutions in charge of them (Blanco Garriga 1992). The fact that the intention was to begin by improving relations at an institutional level shows how little engagement there was in terms of developing long-term policies and strategies. The establishment of a dialogue at an economic level tends to be the first dialogue between two regions. That it was absent shows that there was a lack of dialogue in relation to political matters. The Luxembourg European Council in June 1987 approved a document that contained new guidelines for EU–Latin American relations (Blanco Garriga 1992; Gomez Saraiva 2004). It also encouraged further integration between the regions (Gomez Saraiva 2004).

The membership of Spain and Portugal is a crucial point, a critical juncture in the relations between the EU and Latin America. It could be argued that this historical moment created a sort of 'bottom-up' movement (see Figure 4.1). With the declaration, the EU proved that it intended to improve relations with Latin America. It is also clear that Spain expected to develop a greater degree of commitment, which in reality developed at such a slow speed that it often appears that the words were just pure rhetoric. This critical juncture also affected other EU external relations. Spain and Portugal, which were now members of the EU, could influence the future of the ACP by trying to favour Latin America over the latter, provoking a diversification of the EU resources. A path had been created and it would affect future negotiations of aid and GSP; Spain and Portugal would

Figure 4.1 Spain and Portugal's EU membership: bottom-up outcome

ask the EU to be more generous in terms of resources given to Latin America. This was very prominent in the Spanish media. For example, a month before Spain joined the EU, the Spanish president commented that the possibility of increasing collaboration between Latin America and Europe was linked to the relationship between Spain and Latin America (*El País* 22/11/1985). The media also pointed out views from Latin America in relation to the Iberian countries becoming members of the EU. For example, the president of the Chamber of Commerce of Bogota, Mario Suarez Melo, considered Spain and Portugal to be two advocates for Latin America at the EU, which would enable Latin America to gain better treatment from the EU (*El País* 1/11/1985). Within the EU there were also statements recognizing this critical juncture. Cheysson, the commissioner at that time, recognized that the membership of Spain and Portugal would increase the possibilities of intensifying the relations between the EU and Latin America (*El País* 23/6/1987). Furthermore, Helmut Kohl, the chancellor of West Germany, days before the accession of Spain to the EU, mentioned that Spain could be 'an intermediary of exceptional category between Europe and Latin America' (*El País* 28/12/1985).

There was, however, a major impediment to this bottom-up relationship – the lack of interest from the EU. The president of the Institute of Ibero-American Cooperation, Luis Yanez, was worried about the lack of interest the EU showed towards Latin America and the possibility that the EU would not want to give all that attention to Spain (*El País* 23/11/1985). Kramer (1980), for example, discusses the deep effects that Spain and Portugal had on other less developed countries that are not members of the EU and, in particular, the impact on EU development policy of the amount of money that would be transferred to the new members. However, Kramer's work was published so early that it was more predictive than factual. The existing literature is also ambiguous in relation to the effect of the Iberian membership for Latin America. Previous studies do, however, recognize that the Iberian membership did open a path but, initially in terms of trade, it had a negative impact on Latin America. For example, Wiarda contends:

> There is still some possibility that the world's most powerful economic bloc (the EEC) and the world's most dynamic developing region (Latin America) will work out new arrangements or, alternatively, that Spain's historic and recently expanding ties with Latin America will enable Spain to act as a bridge between the EEC and Latin America. But at this point it seems likely that the enlargement of the EEC will prove detrimental to Latin America. (Wiarda 1989: 201)

The lack of interest in that region, and the EU's interest in other regions, such as those who were part of the Lome Convention, brought about a 'top-down' movement at the time of the Iberian membership. The lack of interest must be linked to the low EU ambition and commitment, which shows a low EU engagement with Mercosur countries. In relation to ambition, the 12 June Council declaration in favour of improving its relations with Latin America shows a very low ambition, as it was vague and imprecise. In relation to commitment, these are no more than declarations of intent with the membership.

Figure 4.2 outlines this top-down movement in terms of trade. It shows that there are different elements to this top-down process. First is the EU External Common Tariff for the rest of the world, which means that trade with ACP countries (the former Lome group) is at a preferential rate and that Spain and Portugal would stop preferential trade with Latin America. The other effect would be related to the diversification of Spanish and Portuguese trade towards the EU.

Trade with ACP countries meant the acceptance that the: 'preferential EC tariffs granted to Third World countries and especially those granted to the African, Caribbean and Pacific countries under the Lome Convention and to the Mediterranean countries under cooperation agreements, were to apply from accession except for certain temporarily exempt products' (Nicholson and East 1987: 232). More specifically, 'Typical tropical products (coffee, tea, cocoa, spices) will benefit from enlargement in that the

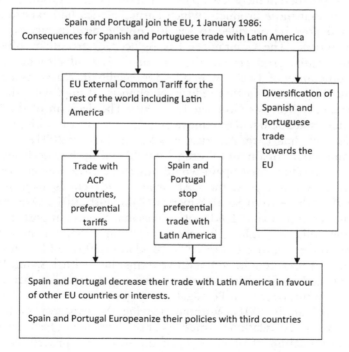

Figure 4.2 Spain and Portugal's EU membership: 'top-down' in relation to trade

three applicant states still levy duties on them, and these will be abolished' (Von der Groeben 1979: 90).

Cocoa and coffee are very important products for Latin America in terms of trade. This change affected Latin America negatively due to the lack of protection these products were given compared with the ACP countries; this is one of the few third world areas that was not protected and one where Spanish products would partly substitute for Latin American products (Wiarda 1989: 201). Essentially, trade with the ACP countries had a negative impact on Latin American interests since they enjoyed a better trade agreement with the EU now that Spain and Portugal were members. The ACP countries are not the only countries that have some trade protection. It seems that Latin America is one of the few areas not protected. More specifically, Spanish imports of tropical products were bought from the ACP countries instead of Latin America because of the preferential agreements (Baklanoff 2001).

The EU External Common Tariff meant that the import of industrial goods from third world countries would be reduced by Spain and Portugal over the course of a seven-year period (Heywood 1995: 270). The new members also had to accept new commercial policies which had a negative impact on exports to Spain from Latin America (Baklanoff 2001). It also seems that the Iberian membership impacted on sensitive products for Latin America in that those products, which Latin America had exported to the EU, would now be provided to the EU by the new members. Von der Groeben writes, 'The Community has reduced or frozen its offers with regard to sensitive products, and there are precisely products where capacity in the Community of Twelve would be appreciably increased as a result of accession. This would further reduce the chances of improving the system of preferences' (Von der Groeben 1979: 90). The decision of the Council of Ministers that Spain had to remove all trade agreements with third world countries, including Latin America, was key (Baklanoff 2001).

To some extent Spain and Portugal would end up buying from the EU agricultural products that Spain would otherwise have bought from Latin America. This was due to the CAP, which made goods such as cereals cheaper than those from South America (Baklanoff 2001). Over time this change has been dramatic. Baklanoff argues that 'Spain's import share from the region collapsed; falling from over 11% in 1985, on the eve of its accession to the EU, to 4.4% in 1999' (Baklanoff 2001: 114). However, it should not be forgotten in comparative terms that neither Spain, Portugal nor the EU had massive levels of trade with Latin America. In fact, in 1985, Spain's trade turnover with Portugal was higher than its trade with Latin America (Baklanoff 2001). Without denying the existence of this 'top-down' movement in relation to trade, its impact should not be overestimated and an examination of other parts of the top-down process is required before we can evaluate the full extent of the degree of the top-down movement.

Top-down in relation to aid

The existing literature discusses how much money would be added to the development budget following the Iberian membership. Kramer examines the opposite possibility but dismisses it:

> It is sometimes feared that the total flows of development aid given by the EEC Member States will stagnate or even decrease. This could happen if the nine old EC countries regarded the net financial flows from the old Community towards the three new members as a form of development aid or at least as payments which could be counted in this category. Such view cannot be regarded as totally unfounded as at least Greece and Spain are still frequently treated as developing countries and Portugal with regard to per capita income ranges behind several other countries which are without question among the LDCs. (Kramer 1980: 96)

More importantly for this section, the existing literature also considers where this money is going to be spent. Kramer argues that:

> This concerns the financial means of the European Development Fund (EDF). The sum to be distributed to the ACP states is laid down in the Agreement of Lome, and the share of the different Member States has been fixed by an internal agreement. It seems politically impossible that the EDF could be reduced on account of an enlargement of the Community. Rather, the increase of the number of Member States will be accompanied by an increase of the EDF, although the contribution of the new Members States might not be very big. (Kramer 1980: 96)

In fact, Kramer discusses how, although this aid might be small, the real effect is not going to be on the ACP countries which will continue to receive their share of the budget. Kramer contends that the real impact will be in other areas, for example where financial aid goes to Latin America (Kramer 1980: 96). Crucially, Kramer points out the idea of Spain reducing its aid to Latin America as a consequence of its contribution to the EDF, only to reject it because:

> More likely is, however, that Spain (and for that matter Portugal) instead of reducing aid to Latin American countries will, on the contrary, try to increase it by way of reorientation of the Community, changing its interest from the heavy preoccupation with Africa a little towards more cooperation with South America. (Kramer 1980: 100)

According to Kramer, this would follow from the history of development aid in the EU in a way that is similar to what has happened with France and the UK in terms of their former colonies.

Top-down political relations

It appears that there have not been major top-down flows in political relations in terms of the development of policy towards Latin America. In fact, it can be said that the political part of the European foreign policy was not very advanced in the 1980s. Therefore the Spanish concessions were related to other areas and one-off events, such as the recognition of Israel (Heywood 1995: 270). It is difficult to say precisely how significant top-down relations were in terms of the Iberian membership, to the point that it is difficult to confirm whether the membership of Spain and Portugal was at this point good or bad for Latin America. This could be justified in relation to the weak position of the Iberian countries in their negotiations, and their strong desire to become members of the EU at any price. However, once they were inside the EU, the pro-Latin American policy increased. This is why the declaration added to the Treaty of Membership is so significant. The critical juncture was 12 June 1985 when it was signed, not so much for the instant changes that this would produce but what would happen in the long term, following the path that this created. It seems, as Wiarda explains, that Spain was not in an easy position when trying to explain its special relationship with Latin America:

> The EEC has said that Spain failed to specify how its special relationship with Latin America will affect its relations with the European Community. The EEC insists that Spain, as a condition of its membership, define the nature of its relations with Latin America and also agree to accept the 'commitments' made by the EEC with the southern Mediterranean nations and with the ACP countries, that are signatories to the Lome treaty. The Europeans are concerned that will all its special Latin American relationships Spain may try to bring in its EEC wake a string of 'miniLomes'. (Wiarda 1989: 200–201)

Therefore, it seems that the EU was constrained somehow by the fear of 'mini-Lomes' and the Iberian membership could have been jeopardized (again) because of this, as well as not forgetting just how important agricultural issues were during these negotiations.

This section has shown how there has been both a top-down and a bottom-up process with the Spanish membership, and a low ambition and commitment which implies a low engagement at that specific point. As has been mentioned, it does not mean events that happened in the past affect the future, and this is the perfect example of how an event did not lay the basis for big and immediate changes, but for later and more moderate ones.

EU engagement with Mercosur

In order to assess the level of ambition at the different stages, it is necessary to contrast the presence of: offers of negotiation mandates or agreements, EU official policy pronouncements, promises to Mercosur, plans for a potential relationship. In relation to ambition the different levels are shown in Figure 4.3.

The level of ambition is low as a consequence of three decades of complete ignorance of the economics and politics of Mercosur countries by the EU. The EU could not develop an ambitious agenda until it had a minimum of knowledge about Mercosur countries, which developed over time, and specifically after the membership of Spain and Portugal. Figure 4.4 shows that the level of commitment at this stage was low as well since nothing was officially agreed between the EU and Mercosur countries.

The EU's level of engagement with Mercosur countries was at its lowest point since all the talks were informal and under the umbrella of the EU–Rio Group annual meetings. The EU did not sign any agreement at this stage with Mercosur itself, or even with the Mercosur countries. As Table 4.2 shows, after measuring the dependent variable, this stage of the policy should be placed at the low/low point of the spectrum.

Although it is clear that there is low ambition and commitment, this should not be confused with 'none', since that would mean there is no involvement. If there is no involvement, there is no policy. To say that there is low involvement does not mean that this is the least important stage of

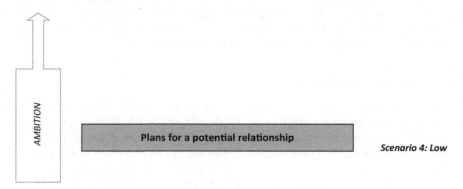

Figure 4.3 Level of ambition: first stage

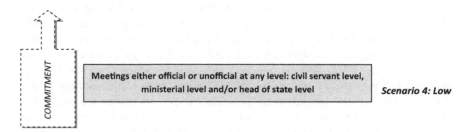

Figure 4.4 Level of commitment: first stage

Table 4.2 Measurement of the dependent variable, engagement: first stage

		Ambition				
		Top	*High*	*Medium*	*Low*	*None*
Commitment	*Top*					
	High					
	Medium					
	Low				First stage: low/low	
	None					

the policy since, thanks to the membership of Spain and Portugal, it provoked a historic moment in EU policy towards Mercosur.

As the introduction to this chapter outlined, the explanations provided in the existing literature for EU–Mercosur relations during this period are almost non-existent. By assessing if the expectations established in Chapter 2 for each argument became a reality or not at this stage, we can uncover the real explanatory potential of each explanation.

Counterbalancing the US

The first explanation given in the literature relates to the US and the EU's aim to counterbalance the power and influence of the US. Here it is expected that the EU would become increasingly involved in Latin America if the US was to increase its own involvement in the region. At this stage of the policy, the EU did, very slowly, increase its involvement in Latin America. The US also continued its involvement in Latin America in different areas, such as external debt. Moreover, in 1988, the first talks regarding the creation of the FTAA also took place. However, to suggest that the EU was trying to counterbalance the US at this stage is an exaggeration. In fact, it seems that the US was influencing Europe at this point. For example, it has already been shown that the US was very keen on the Iberian membership, and this is supported by the fact that the US transferred funds to European parties (Wiarda 1989: 194). Wiarda goes as far as suggesting that the Iberian membership was used to secure political changes such as democracy at the domestic level in the Iberian countries. This shows the influence of the US at that time in Europe, never mind in its own backyard. Therefore the expectation that the EU would look to counterbalance the US is not applicable at this stage of EU–Mercosur relations.

Global aspirations

The global aspirations of the EU as an explanation for the EU's involvement in Latin America also fail to provide a satisfactory explanation of EU–Mercosur relations at this stage. These arguments would expect there to be an increase in EU involvement in Latin America if there was an increase in the EU's involvement in other regions. This, however, was not the case because the EU continued its high involvement in the ACP countries and, more importantly, from 1989, the priority for EU external relations for the next fifteen years was its policy towards Central and Eastern European countries.

External federator

With regard to the role of the EU as a promoter of regional integration abroad, it can be acknowledged that at this stage the expectations proved to be true. It was expected that if Latin America became more integrated, the EU would increase its involvement in the area. Mercosur countries started an integration process in 1985 and from this moment the EU started to increase its involvement in this area. It could also be argued that the EU was impressed by the integration movement in this region, particularly the decision to develop a more open market economy.

Affinity

It also seems that the proposal that an increase in shared values between the regions explains an increase in the EU's involvement does not fit at this stage. At this point, the EU shared more political, economic and cultural values with Latin America than with most of the regions in Asia and Africa. For example, the EU and Latin America share languages, religion and similar political systems. This is due to the large influence of Spain and Portugal over the course of three centuries, and even during the twentieth century. Franco in Spain and Salazar in Portugal were seen as examples of authoritarian regimes for Brazil, Chile, Argentina and Uruguay, which were, at the same time, capable of developing the economy in these countries without necessarily creating a degree of political openness (Wiarda 1989). Wiarda argues that 'Those who lived and worked in Spain and Portugal during the early 1970s were witness to a virtually continuous parade of Latin American heads of state, military officers, and civilian technocrats all eager to learn the Spanish system' (Wiarda 1989: 311). This is not to suggest that the whole of the EU shares dictatorships as a common value with Latin America, but that Latin American countries have continued to develop similar economic and political systems to those in Europe due to the influence of European countries in the Americas for centuries.

Interdependence

The argument based on the complex interdependence of development between both regions is also not applicable in terms of explaining EU–Latin American relations at this stage. This argument would expect the EU to increase its involvement in Latin America if there was an increase in the EU's investment in terms of trade between the EU and Latin America. As this chapter has already shown, the latter's investment in trade did not increase significantly at this time. For Latin America, trade with the EU is important, even if it is not important for the EU: EU trade with Latin America accounts for less than 2% of EU trade.

Iberian influence in the EU

Finally, the EU membership of Spain and Portugal has clearly been an important moment for the EU's relations with Latin America. It would be expected that the EU would increase its involvement in Latin America if Spain and Portugal's influence increased in the EU. In the discussion above, it has already been shown that this was very much the case. Therefore, this argument can indeed be applied in attempts to explain the development of the EU's involvement in Latin America.

This chapter has analysed in detail the historical moment of the membership of Spain and Portugal. It could be said that 'history matters' on this occasion and that the path created by Spain and Portugal, with their emphasis on Latin America, has been followed to some extent. The path dependence in relation to EU policies towards Latin America was also crucial over time, as will be seen in the future. The involvement of the EU in Mercosur will never be as low as it was before the Iberian membership, as will be shown in the following empirical chapters. The main characteristic of the institutionalization of EU policy towards Latin America is that it did not produce profound changes at once, but over time they became more obvious. However, due to the slow speed and power of the Europeanization process, this event alone was not sufficient for the development of an EU policy towards Mercosur. As the central argument of this monograph claims, the proactive behaviour of Mercosur countries was crucial for the development of any policy towards Latin America.

In essence, it could be argued that there has been a degree of Europeanization, with the EU slightly uploading Iberian policies to Latin America. As was explained in Chapter 2, following Reuben Wong (2008), there are several indicators that help to discuss the concept of Europeanization. In the case of the EU downloading policies, 'Internationalization of EU members and its integration process' (Wong 2008: 323) is the most relevant for this study. Spain and Portugal had to give up several agreements with Latin American countries that gave preferential treatment to Latin American products because of the common external tariff. Also, it seems that Spain and Portugal had to accept the distribution of EU aid in a way that did not favour Latin American countries, which initially met resistance from Spain. In the case of the EU uploading policies, the 'Externalization of national foreign policies positions onto the EU level' is the crucial one. Spain and Portugal tried very hard to achieve foreign policy positions towards Latin America at the EU level, as the documents of 12 June 1985 show. They only had limited success.

As this chapter has shown, there is evidence that the changes in EU behaviour towards Mercosur were due to the Iberian countries' accession to the EU. In fact, the central argument of this monograph maintains that the EU developed a policy towards Mercosur thanks to the Iberian interests in the region, although it was not sufficient on its own – Mercosur's proactive behaviour was crucial. The EU locked in the development of a policy towards Mercosur after the Iberian membership. The path-dependence created was followed until the end of the period of time studied here.

The relation between the competing arguments for EU involvement in Mercosur can be seen in Table 4.3 by looking at the value of the independent variables and subsequently the expectation. The value assigned to each argument at this stage makes it easy to see if the argument was met/confronted. It is clear that only in two cases do the competing arguments meet the measure assigned at this stage of the policy.

Conclusion

This chapter has explained the developments in relations between the EU and Mercosur at the first stage of the policy. The central point is that the inclusion of the Iberian countries in the EU was extremely important for both this stage of the policy and the central argument of this monograph.

In addition, this chapter has explained that the first stage of policy development between the EU and Mercosur was not institutionalized. It has explained that at this stage different steps were taken in order to develop higher levels of interaction between the two regions. The desire to do so came from both sides of the Atlantic. On one side, the EU, influenced by Spain and Portugal, which were now members of the EU, took the first steps towards increasing its involvement in Latin America. On the other side, the creation of different groups in Latin America – for example, the Contadora Group, followed by the Rio Group – influenced the level of dialogue between the EU and Latin America. Mercosur countries were a key part of the Rio Group from its creation in 1986. Dialogue with the EU started the following year, becoming institutionalized in 1990, after Latin America demanded a greater degree of commitment from the EU.

This chapter has discussed broadly the level of Europeanization from two points of view, from an 'adaptation and policy' view and from a

Table 4.3 Competing arguments and the independent variables: first stage

Independent variable	Expectation	Independent variable value	Expectation value	Met/confronted
Counterbalancing the US	If the US increases its involvement in LA, the EU should increase its involvement. ↑US = ↑EU in LA	None	None	No
Global aspirations	If the EU increases its presence in international affairs, the EU's involvement in LA should also increase. ↑EU in the world = ↑EU in LA	None	None	No
External federator	If LA becomes more integrated, the EU will increase its relations with LA. ↑LA integration = ↑EU in LA	**Low**	**Low**	**Yes**
Affinity	An increase of shared values between the regions should develop EU policy. ↑LA shared values = ↑EU in LA	High	High	No
Interdependence	If trade and investment between the EU and LA increase, EU policy should also increase. ↑LA trade = ↑EU in LA	**Low**	**Low**	**Yes**
Iberia	If the influence of Spain and Portugal increase within the EU, then the EU's involvement in LA should increase. ↑SP + PT influence = ↑EU in LA	Top	Top	No

Notes: LA = Latin America; PT = Portugal; SP = Spain.

'national projection' view. The historical event of the inclusion of the Iberian countries in the EU has been the starting point of the discussion since it started a path that has been followed by the subsequent development of EU policy towards Mercosur. This chapter has shown how, although Iberian countries were not in a strong position to defend their interest in Latin America – which meant the acceptance of the EU way of dealing with Latin America – they did manage to sow the seeds for a future blossoming of EU–Mercosur relations. Through the work of Pierson (2000) and Sewell (1996) this chapter has discussed the path created, and through the work of Reuben Wong (2008) the discussion continued on Europeanization. This discussion has explained how Europeanization is directly linked to historical institutionalism since the EU institutions are the ones that matter in this case; therefore, the discussion of path dependence fits here.

After discussing to what extent the EU had uploaded and downloaded its policies, this chapter has explained the low engagement shown in the EU policy towards Mercosur due to the low levels of ambition and commitment. In terms of ambition, there were some moves towards the development of new guidelines. The joint declaration of the EU and the Iberian countries independent from the Treaty of Accession – as Spain and Portugal wanted – from a legal standpoint, shows a low level of ambition too. The meetings of the EU with the Rio Group after the San José process are evidence of low but existent commitment, which should not be confused with an absence of commitment. The level of aid distributed is another example of the level of commitment. The final assessment of engagement is 'low'.

5

The most productive years of EU–Mercosur relations

Introduction

This chapter covers a new stage in EU policy towards Mercosur and Latin America. It started with a new framework of policies within which agreements between the EU and Latin American countries, including the Mercosur countries, were made. By explaining EU–Mercosur agreements within the general context of EU–Latin America relations, it is possible to shed light on the level of EU engagement with Mercosur in relative terms, to avoid either over- or underestimating the engagement. The discussion will show how EU–Mercosur relations were the most important ones within the EU–Latin America framework. As has already been established, the level of engagement will be explained by discussing two aspects of it: ambition and commitment. This chapter shows that at this stage there was a medium level of ambition and a high level of commitment, pointing to a medium level of engagement.

In relation to this stage, in the literature it has been accepted that, in 1990, the EU's means of dealing with Latin America changed (Aldecoa Luzarraga 1995; Bizzozero 1995; Laporte Galli 1995; Birochi 1999). Some indicate that these changes were due to wider changes in the international arena. With the end of the Cold War, the EU was given the chance to develop a global vision and a space in which to do it (Aldecoa Luzarraga 1995; Birochi 1999). The internal changes in the EU, especially its increased integration, have also been mentioned in this regard (Aldecoa Luzarraga 1995). For Laporte Galli (1995), the reasons are various: firstly, the Commission had an ambition to develop an external policy with one voice, independent from the individual interests of member states; secondly, the promotion of an ambitious external policy at global level necessarily involved Latin America due to its political and economic importance. There is a certain contradiction in Laporte Galli's explanations: where, in the first place, the importance of an EU independent of state interests is mentioned, later it is Spain's special role in intensifying the relations between the EU and Latin America that is emphasized. The identities of the people behind this notion of the projection of a global, external policy remain mysterious, so too does the identity of the institution(s) involved in this shift of policy.

For Laporte Galli (1995), evidence that the EU's attitude to Latin America had changed can be seen in the intensification of EU relations with Latin America. This reached its peak at the EU–Mercosur agreement of 1995. However, for Aldecoa Luzarraga (1995), the third-generation agreements and the institutionalization of the Rio Group are more compelling evidence. For Bizzozero (1995), the official strategy of the cooperation policy, approved by the European Council in December 1990, is the key evidence. All these points will be discussed, since all explanations of the new stage are related, in some way, to EU–Mercosur relations. EU–Mercosur agreements have to be placed within the framework of these sets of evidence. By looking at these events' influence on the EU–Mercosur relations, the identity of the agent(s) of this policy will become apparent, as will the main driving force of the policy. Additionally, it will also be possible to discount the involvement of certain figures and/or institutions.

This period is relevant because it places the EU–Mercosur relationship, including the cooperation agreement of 1992 and, to some extent, EMIFCA (1995), in the context of the wave of EU agreements with Latin American countries and regions in the early 1990s. Several similarities between these agreements are obvious: they are all third-generation agreements; they took place in (roughly) the same time period; and they had the same form or structure and similar aims. However, Mercosur countries were not the only ones negotiating individual agreements and sub-regional agreements with the EU at this time. All these events help to link the EU policy towards Mercosur with the broader EU policy towards Latin America, which follows the pattern created in the previous phase of the policy. As will be seen, all these advances follow the same path. This path was created in the previous stage, with the membership of Spain and Portugal into the EU, and as explained in Chapter 4.

The limitation of this policy can be seen both in the lack of substance and in the lack of a clear content in those agreements with Latin America – something not typical of other EU agreements with third countries or regions. This supports the idea that there was a fundamental lack of clarity in the EU policy towards the region, its sub-regions and countries, arguably originating from a lack of interest in the region, and/or a changing of aims towards Latin America over time. A contrast of what has been achieved and what could have been achieved (given the limitations) aids the discussion of ambition and commitment in order to analyse EU engagement with Mercosur.

The outcome of this stage fits into the general argument: the development of EU policy was possible thanks mainly to the influence of Spain and Portugal, and the advent of the Iberian membership of the EU that institutionalized EU relations with Latin America; but again, Mercosur countries and other Latin American countries such as Mexico were keen to improve relations with the EU. In short, Latin American countries and Iberian countries collaborated in the development of these agreements. Additionally, the influence of a new political situation at the international level in the area of security should not be forgotten; that is to say, the end of the Cold War and important negotiations in international trade through the WTO. The EU's ultra-protectionist agricultural policy and the end of the Uruguay Round trade negotiations (which created the WTO) were additional obstacles to the development of relations between Latin America and Europe, already characterized by a lack of interest on the EU's part. The facilitation of better relations took place through the approaches to the Commission of European business associations who formed themselves into a lobby.

One might expect that this period would be described differently according to the different arguments put forward in the literature. The argument that suggests that EU strategy was influenced above all by its direct competition for the Latin American market with the US would be supported if a clear link could be shown between relative EU and US involvement in Latin America. The EU role should have increased at the moment the US increased its involvement. Indeed, the US did increase its economic involvement in the region with the development of the FTAA in 1988. The argument suggesting that the EU's involvement in Latin America increases as part of its global strategy has some merit. There was indeed an increase in the EU's involvement at the global level in the post-Cold War era. The argument that defends the EU's actions in Mercosur as part of its external federator role is also plausible since it was at this stage that the Mercosur institutions were created. The argument that it was long-standing political, economic and cultural ties that drove EU policy is difficult to sustain, however. There is no evidence of an increase of those ties in the period. Arguments for the interdependence created between the two regions are also not credible. According to this argument, a higher interdependence between both areas would mean a higher interaction between the regions. The data related to trade between the regions disprove this theory. Another argument incompatible to this stage is that the development of the relationship was due to the Spanish and Portuguese influence, since both countries lacked power within the EU, and this even decreased during the time period in question because of the new membership of wealthier countries.

This chapter is divided into five sections. All the sections help to explain how EU–Mercosur relations were affected by different events which provide evidence for the discussion of the level of engagement. The fact that there were different instances that do not come necessarily from EU actions undermines the notion that there was a strategy behind EU actions towards Mercosur. The first section is focused on the development of the new cooperation guidelines and their influence on EU–Mercosur relations. The second looks at the development of EU agreements with the different countries in Latin America and regional groups such as Mercosur, highlighting the legal commitments that were made by the EU, and those that were not. The third section examines the EU–Rio Group relationship, since Mercosur, from the very beginning, had used it to develop its contacts with the EU. The fourth section discusses the advance of, and the obstacles to, EU–Mercosur relations. Finally, the last section will discuss the various explanations given in the existing literature, and to what extent they provide a satisfactory explanation of EU–Mercosur relations between 1991 and 1995.

New broader cooperation guidelines for Latin America lead to new cooperation guidelines for Mercosur

This section discusses the development of a new framework of EU–Latin America relations through the new EU cooperation guidelines for Latin America. The relations between the EU and Mercosur at this stage were affected by different aspects of the wider, EU–Latin America relationship, of which EU–Mercosur was just one facet. The other aspects – the EU–Rio Group dialogue and the wave of agreements between the EU and individual Latin American states – will be explained in later sections of the chapter.

The document that set up the new guidelines was produced by the Commission (European Commission 1990) at the end of 1990: 'Guidelines for cooperation with the developing countries of Latin America and Asia'. These guidelines proposed to restructure the policy around two areas, 'development aid for the poorest countries and population groups, and economic cooperation with countries or regions which have high growth potential, to the mutual benefit of those countries and of the Community' (European Commission 1990). These new guidelines were an upgrading of the ones set in 1982. The impetus for the new guidelines came from the European Commission and the president, Felipe Gonzalez of Spain, at the Council summit in The Hague in 1986 (see Chapter 4). By 1995 a new upgrade had been prepared. The time period studied here starts with the first EU–Mercosur meeting and ends with the signature of EMIFCA. This is not accidental; the EU–Latin America and EU–Mercosur relations were clearly interdependent. Though this was the case during the whole time-frame of the policy, the level of interdependence was more marked at this stage.

By the end of this stage (October 1995), EU relations with Latin America were disconnected from the ones with Asia, as shown in the Commission's final communication: 'The European Union and Latin America: the present situation and prospects for closer partnership' (European Commission 1995a). In that document, the EU finally considered variations *within* Latin

America and, as a consequence, a specific document was prepared for Mercosur. Thus, a distinct Mercosur–EU relationship relatively independent from the official framework of EU–Latin America relations was founded by the end of this stage.

Changes in the guidelines: the Commission or the Council?

The 1990 guidelines (European Commission 1990) were approved by the Council in the Council conclusions of November of the same year. However, the Council asked COREPER to 'continue its discussions in the light of the positions expressed during the meeting in order to be able to adopt a set of guidelines as soon as possible' (European Commission 1995a). By December 1990, the Commission was asking the Council for a decision on financial and technical cooperation for the 1991–1995 period. In April 1991, the Commission presented to the Council a draft for the Council regulation. Having been redrafted after the EP's demands for more detailed information, it was finally adopted by the Council in February, 1992 (EEC 1992a).

In the guidelines for cooperation, the Commission asked for 'multi-annual financial objectives' (European Commission 1990) for those five years; additionally, it wanted to restructure the guidelines according to two main points, 'development aid for the poorest countries and population groups' and 'economic cooperation with countries or regions which have high growth potential, to the mutual benefit of those countries and of the Community' (European Commission 1990). An increase in the amount of aid was requested; as far as economic cooperation was concerned, it was suggested that efforts be directed in particular to the relatively more advanced countries, with a focus on three main areas: (1) the transfer of economic, scientific and technical knowledge; (2) the economic environment; and (3) schemes to help firms (European Commission 1990: 654). Environmental considerations were to be taken into consideration as well. The aid and economic cooperation budget for the 1991–1995 period was 2.570 million ecu, with 65% intended for Asia and 35% for Latin America (Ayuso 1996).

It was the Commission that sent a communication to the Council. The Commission very often addressed proposals promoted by others with the intention of upgrading relations with Latin America. The person behind this proposal was the commissioner responsible for the Latin American region. According to his testimony, the aim was 'to define the philosophy and the general framework of future relations', at a point when the possibility of separate budgets for Asia and Latin America was a real question for the Commission (Agence Europe 7/7/1995). It seems that the Commission was asked by Latin America to do so: 'Latin America is both uniform and diverse; it calls for the Union to vary its approaches tailoring them to national and regional circumstances' (European Commission 1995a). Therefore, it was the Commission that was asking for changes and offering options but, at the same time, Latin America was doing the same. This will be explained in more detail in the following sections. It can be noted here, however, that this was a constant characteristic of Latin American relations with the EU, suggesting upgrading which according to the Commission was a natural development in EU–Mercosur relations. The guidelines will be explored in more detail in the following chapter.

Effects on EU–Mercosur relations

The main result of the new guidelines on EU–Mercosur was a more definite and active EU policy towards Latin America and, therefore, the Mercosur countries. A major consequence was the upgrading of investment facilities between the two regions, from which Mercosur countries benefited. This was the 'European Community–International Investment Partners Financial Facility for Countries of Asia, Latin America and the Mediterranean Region' programme. It was more than a 'policy': it could be understood as a tool for economic purposes, for the mutual benefit of both partners with a focus on developing countries. The budget for this policy, however, was actually smaller than for the previous one. So it is more a complementary tool for the general development of EU policy towards Latin America. It is obvious that Mercosur countries, being the most developed in Latin America, would be among the main beneficiaries of this facility.

The main objective of this programme was the promotion of investment in the form of joint ventures. The investment partners would be private economic actors from the EU and from a particular developing country (European Commission 1991a). This plan was set in motion after a communication from the Commission in 1986; a year later, 'the Council called on the Commission to devise new instruments for cooperation with certain developing countries in Latin America, Asia and the Mediterranean' (European Commission 1991a). As a consequence, the first 'European Community–International Investment Partners' facility started in 1988 for a three-year trial period with a budget of 30 million ecu. In March 1991, in its proposal for council regulation, the Commission asked for a further five years' trial from January 1992 (European Commission 1991a), but received only three years (EEC 1992b). This council regulation was intended to provide regulation in those areas not already covered by the treaties, necessary for this new three-year trial (EEC 1992b). The new regulation had in mind the 1990 guidelines mentioned previously and had a larger budget than the previous trial: 31.4 million ecu for 1992 and 39 million ecu for 1993 and 1994 (European Council 1998).

This stage of EU–Latin America relations was affected by issues other than the guidelines. However, these issues were also in some part a product of the guidelines. The reorganization of EU–Latin American relations is linked to the reformulation of the structure of the GSP (Cepal 1999). The revision was planned for 1991 but was postponed until 1995 due to the delay in the General Agreement on Tariffs and Trade (GATT) (Sanahuja 1999). Arguably this had an effect on the new GSP as the new GSP set tariff rates depending on how suitable the products were for EU producers, as well as how developed the country was (Sanahuja 1999). Because the tariffs were lower for developing countries, Mercosur countries would lose their access to the GSP, since they were among the most developed in Latin America. This might leave Mercosur countries more willing to develop a trade agreement with the EU, but this does not mean that it was a conscious policy of the EU to place Mercosur countries in that position. After the end of the Uruguay Round, due to the concessions made and considering the competitiveness of some countries such as Brazil in the agricultural sector, it seems more likely that such actions were taken by the EU in order to protect its own agricultural sector.

These guidelines can help us measure the level of ambition and commitment. The plans set up in these guidelines, together with the fact that guidelines exist at all, point to a medium level of ambition.

In the case of commitment, there is mixed evidence. The amount of aid assigned to Latin America in the guidelines – especially if there is an increase – and the upgrading of investment facilities are evidence in favour of a high level of commitment. On the other hand, the repercussions of the reorganization of the GSP has a negative impact on commitment.

A wave of EU agreements with Latin American countries and regions including Mercosur

The EU became the most important aid donor to Latin America. The use of the GSP was considered a way of stabilizing democracy in Central America and a way of helping the Andean Community (Caetano et al. 2010). The agreements that were created in the 1990s (the third-generation agreements) included the democratic clause – the signatories had to respect democratic values and be democracies.

The guidelines of 1990 were the basis for the inauguration of third-generation agreements with Latin American countries (Laporte Galli 1995; Ribeiro Hoffmann 2004). By 1993 all South American countries had made such agreements (Laporte Galli 1995): Argentina and Bolivia in 1990, Venezuela and Uruguay in 1991, Chile in 1990, 1996 and 2002, Mexico in 1991 and 1997, and Paraguay and Brazil in 1992. Agreements were also made with sub-regions: the Andean Community (Bolivia, Colombia, Ecuador and Peru, and formerly Venezuela, and sometime member Chile) and CACM in 1993; Mercosur in 1995 (Ribeiro Hoffmann 2004).

These agreements had common characteristics as well as country- and circumstance-specific stipulations. The most innovative aspect was in respect of human rights and the evolutive opt-out, which made it possible to increase new cooperation in new sectors (Aldecoa Luzarraga, 1995; Laporte Galli 1995; Ribeiro Hoffmann 2004).

The EU had cooperation agreements with most developed Latin American countries from the 1970s (Uruguay, Brazil, Argentina and Mexico), excluding Chile , which at that time was under the dictatorship of Pinochet. At the beginning of the 1990s a new wave of cooperation agreements was developed with the same countries, a 'network of new framework cooperation agreements with Latin America countries' (Agence Europe 22/3/1991). These agreements are called 'third generation'. In relation to Latin American countries, this 'impl[ied] an enlargement and development of cooperation and a revision clause and explicit reference to the respect of human rights and democratic principles' (Agence Europe 23/4/1991). Mercosur countries and Chile and Mexico were prioritized over other Latin America countries, being offered privileged association agreements. This might have been due to their economic importance in relative terms to the rest of Latin America or because of their relative political stability in the 1990s. However, given the fact that, until the mid-1980s, the 'prioritized' countries (excluding Mexico) were under dictatorships, it seems more likely that in this case economic development was more influential.

The interest of Spain in the progress of a policy towards Latin America was represented by the Spanish commissioner in charge of this area, Abel Matutes, but it should be noted that, towards the end of this stage, Jacques Delors, the president of the Commission, had started to pay more attention to the issue. It could be argued that thanks to the engagement with Latin America, countries and regions with different economic situations were increasingly 'visible' to the EU. In fact, Delors visited Chile, Mexico and Argentina (although not any other Latin American countries) in his week-long visit to Latin America, since it was 'considered in Brussels [that this region was] likely to play an increasingly important role on the international scene now that they [were] coming out of a period of serious economic difficulties and political instability' (Agence Europe 10/3/1993).

The Commission was going a step further towards Latin America after continued pressure by Spain and Portugal. Delors was progressively developing an interest in Latin America through the work of Matutes. This does not mean that the Commission had gained this new interest just because of the Iberian interest in the region. The reasons behind Delors' sudden interest in those countries are also related to interdependence. Delors, on his visit to those countries, stressed 'the need "better to control world interdependency together" … the planet today having become a village' (Agence Europe 20/3/1993). Coming back to the discussion of engagement, these visits by Delors should be seen as evidence of a high level of commitment, since they symbolize the brand-new interest that was growing within the Commission or at least the attention Mercosur was gaining.

In addition, the EP had economic reasons to give its support: 'The EP invites the Commission to negotiate free trade agreements in the near future with the main supplier of customers from Latin American countries' (Agence Europe 25/4/1994). A few months later, another MEP was asking for the involvement of the economic ministers in EU–Latin America relations (Agence Europe 24/10/1994). Delors considered Mercosur 'an important step towards a Latin American Common Market' (Agence Europe 20/3/1993). It is no surprise, then, that a third-generation agreement had the aim of opening markets first at the sub-regional level (such as Mercosur), as a first step towards the opening of the whole Latin American market.

This support by the EP again adds to the evidence of a medium level of ambition; since the EP has always shows support towards Latin America it cannot be considered a totally new ambition on its side.

Prioritization of Mercosur

The relationship between the EU and Mercosur has been characterized first by great speed and close cooperation, and second by the ambitiousness of the final aims, the development of an FTA that would include both regions. These two characteristics make the EU's policy towards Mercosur distinctive since there are no other cases with this combination of features. When (or if) it is realized, the FTA with Mercosur will create the largest free trade area in the world with a market of over 200 million people. The chances of an inter-regional FTA between the EU and Mercosur being created were higher than between the EU and other Latin American regions (or even with other regional groups in general). Why should EU–Mercosur relations have been so unique?

The countries in the Andean Community benefited from the GSP. Because of the economic situation of the Andean countries, lower tariff levels would be imposed in their trade with the EU. This regional group had been created in the 1960s and, due to historical, political and economic reasons alongside the economic agreements already achieved, would naturally be in a better position to develop an inter-regional relationship with the EU. Mercosur, which was a creation of two countries (Argentina and Brazil) started its integration as late as the mid-1980s; it had no official links to the EU until its creation. Yet it had come the closest to achieving an inter-regional position with the EU. Even the Central American countries, where the links with the EU had for political reasons already been created in the 1980s, had a more distant relationship with the EU. What were the reasons for this prioritization of Mercosur?

As early as 1987, Grabendorff was clear about the implications of South American integration for the EU: 'In the Southern Cone, the Community faces its most intractable sub-regional situation, due not only to the specific tensions which exist between itself and Argentina, but also to the traditional competition which has existed between Argentina and Brazil for regional leadership in the area of foreign commerce' (Grabendorff 1987: 77). He goes on to explain, however, that the success of the integration process between these two countries (beginning in 1986) might bring Uruguay, Paraguay and Chile into the process later. In that case, due to its degree of development and economic potential, it would become the most interesting partner for the EU.

In the literature, there is not much discussion of Mercosur's priority position, or the process by which this priority was established, and little empirical data is presented to support what little discussion there is of these issues. It *is* stated in the literature that Mercosur became a priority (Cienfuegos 2003), but the reasons for it are not clearly explained. For some (Aldecoa Luzarraga 1995; Gillespie et al. 1995; Laporte Galli 1995; Sanchez Bajo 1999; Cienfuegos 2003), Mercosur is a priority because common historical, cultural and social patrimony made important contacts possible. The common interests of the EU and Mercosur are also given as a reason (Cienfuegos 2003). The importance of Mercosur in relative terms compared with other countries in the region is mentioned; the integration of Brazil and Argentina – the most important economies in the region – makes Mercosur especially important for the EU (Smith 1998); Mercosur includes two of the three largest markets in Latin America (Arenas 2002: 2). More explicitly

> Mercosur is a promising partner for the EU, because it represents its main market quota at the commercial and investment level. At the same time Mercosur constitutes an exceptional opportunity for European companies to penetrate the Latin American continent ... the Southern Cone meets one of the EU's sensitive requirements for negotiating international agreements, such as having a democratic system and respecting human rights. In more that one sense the relationship between both blocs constitutes a natural strategic association. (Cienfuegos 2006: 257)

It also appears to some that Mercosur and the EU are 'natural partners' (Kanner 2002), sharing similar values and ideas (Arenas 2002)

The EU–Mercosur agreement will be discussed in detail in the next section. But first it will be useful to look at other agreements between the EU and other countries/regions. This will give an understanding of the peculiarities of agreements with Latin American countries and regions such as Mercosur as well as providing the context in which to analyse the EU's level of commitment to Mercosur.

The EU–Mercosur agreement in comparison to other agreements between the EU and third countries

The legal base of the agreements sets the rules for policy- and decision-making (see Chapter 2). Room for manoeuvre is left for those actors who offer agreements, however, for instance, in terms of what is offered by each side at the outset, and what might be offered after the agreement has been made. The relative level of precision in agreements can therefore be analysed, and reasons given for the differences between agreements in this regard. According to Smith:

> The extent of the network of partners illustrates the influence of law on the EU's external relations: a great deal of what the EU does in international relations is to develop relations that are based on law, that is, on legal agreements. But power is not absent, and the Community can wield its instruments for political purposes. The decision to conclude an agreement with a third country or regional grouping is, in the first place, political. (Smith 2003: 55)

All third-generation agreements with Latin America have in common the 'political conditionality regarding democracy, the environment, and human rights, by means of the so-called democracy clause, and they could be renegotiated with total flexibility, as set out in the so-called 'evolutive clauses' (Ribeiro Hoffmann 2004: 5). Space is left within that framework for issues to be developed further by the evolutive clause.

Ribeiro Hoffmann (2004) makes clear distinctions between formal (empty) and substantial legal commitments. Agreements with the ACP group, the Central and Eastern European countries and former Soviet and Mediterranean countries contained from the beginning 'specific legal commitments concerning topics such as trade, competition, etc' (Ribeiro Hoffmann 2004: 8). That is not the case in agreements with Latin America. Some of these were substantiated later, as is the case of Mercosur, Chile, and Mexico; others, such as the agreement with the Andean Community, remained formal and without substantial commitments (Ribeiro Hoffmann, 2004). These agreements were 'filled' later, either by the conclusion of a new agreement, as in the one with Chile of 2002 and the Mercosur one, or directly in the same agreement, as in the case of Mexico, with the incorporation of Decision 2/2000, which promoted the liberalization of trade in goods, and Decision 2/20001, about the liberalization of trade in services and FDI (Ribeiro Hoffmann 2004). Table 5.1 shows the differences between EU agreements with different Latin America countries/regions quite clearly.

It must be noted that the intention of the EU towards Latin America changed from the early 1990s. By the mid-1990s, the EU was offering more concrete agreements to some of the Latin American countries. Still, none of them managed to garner the level of commitment that the EU had made with countries in other regions. There appears to be a clear list of priorities

Continued

Table 5.1 EU agreements with third countries/regions and their legal commitment

Countries/regions	Type of agreement	Trade	Legal commitments		
			Treatment of foreign firms	Capital movements	Financial protocol
Latin American countries					
Andean Community 1993	Cooperation	No	No	No	No
CACM 1993	Cooperation	No	No	No	No
Argentina 1990	Cooperation	No	No	No	No
Uruguay 1991	Cooperation	No	No	No	No
Brazil 1992	Cooperation	No	No	No	No
Paraguay 1992	Cooperation	No	No	No	No
Mercosur 1995	Cooperation	No	No	No	No
Chile 1991, 1996	Cooperation	No	No	No	No
Chile 2002	Association	FTA goods and services	Yes	Yes	No
Mercosur, under negotiation since 1999	Association	FTA goods and services	Probably yes	Probably yes	Probably no

Table 5.1 EU agreements with third countries/regions and their legal commitment—cont'd

Countries/regions	Type of agreement	Legal commitments			
		Trade	Treatment of foreign firms	Capital movements	Financial protocol
Mexico 1991	Cooperation	No	No	No	No
Mexico 1997	Association	FTA goods and services	Yes	Yes	No
Non Latin American countries/regions					
Central and Eastern European countries	'European'	FTA asymmetrical calendar	National treatment	Yes	Non-quantified, mentions Poland and Hungary: Assistance for Restructuring their Economy (PHARE)
Russia 1994, Ukraine 1994, Belarus 1995	Partnership and cooperation	Most favoured nation	National treatment	Yes	Non-quantified, mentions Technical Aid to the Commonwealth of Independent States (TACIS)
Tunisia 1995, Egypt 2001, Lebanon 2002, etc.	Euro-Med Association	FTA asymmetrical calendar	Confirm GATT obligations	FDI	Non-quantified, does not mention Mediterranean partners
ACP	Lome-Cotonou	Non-reciprocal preferences (WTO waiver)	Non discrimination	No	Quantified from EDF funds

Source: Torrent (1998); Ribeiro Hoffmann (2004).

for the EU when it comes to agreements with third countries/regions. As Smith (2003) claimed, agreements are political decisions. Ribeiro Hoffmann, identifying the relative emptiness of some agreements, reaffirms the political side of them. For her:

> The logic behind the execution of empty agreements is their political meaning. One political reason pointed out as a factor for the execution of such agreements is that they were seen as a strategy by the EU to reinforce its presence worldwide and consolidate the international legal personality of the Community as distinct from its Member States vis-à-vis third parties. Another is that such agreements met the Commission's interests in expanding its competence and the Council's interest in justifying its work since most agreements –whether full or empty- create bilateral institutional arrangements such as joint Committees, Commissions, and Sub-Commissions that meet periodically to manage relations. (Ribeiro Hoffmann 2004: 8–9)

It seems, then, that the wave of agreements with Latin America was not as ambitious as it was presented to be. This could correspond to the priority that the EU placed on becoming a global presence. At the end of this stage, other interests were created that led to some of the regions/countries in Latin America – such as Mercosur – becoming more of a priority for the EU. This could have given the misleading impression that Mercosur was a priority in itself. Mercosur was a priority within Latin America but it was not the EU's only priority in the region because Chile and Mexico also secured association agreements with the EU. Furthermore, it should also be noted that EU–Mercosur relations were definitely not much of a priority within the broader context of EU external relations. In addition to this, the fact that the EU institutionalized relations with Latin America might also have been because the EU was in a position where it 'had' to do something with the region, but had no real interest, or strategy, which explains why the agreements are empty from a legal point of view.

What should be very clear at this point in the discussion is that Latin America was not a top EU priority. According to Smith (2003), the pyramid of privileges ran as follows (from top to bottom): the Central and Eastern European countries, Cyprus, Malta and Turkey; South-East European countries, the Cotonou Convention partners; the Euro-Mediterranean partners; other countries (the former Soviet republics, Latin American countries, ASEAN countries) (Smith 2003). The only significant change from earlier periods was that the ACP group used to be at the top and now were overtaken by the EU's closest neighbours (Smith 2003; Marsh and Mackenstein 2005).

This discussion of the legal content as a way of looking at the EU's behaviour is extremely interesting for the analysis of the level of EU engagement. The lack of concrete content in the agreements shows a very vague ambition towards the region. However, the fact that these agreements seem to be the exception rather than the rule shows not just a vague ambition but a distinct lack of it, and low commitment as well. It is not the intention here to discuss the entire complex of EU external relations, but rather to contextualize where Mercosur stands within the global spectrum of EU relations with other regions; and that is clearly at the bottom. However, when Mercosur is studied within the context of just EU–Latin American relations, it is clear that Mercosur is the priority or at a minimum is the most successful region in getting the attention of the EU, which illustrates that it is not pure indifference that the EU feels about Mercosur. As a consequence of the evidence proffered in this section, the EU engagement appears lower than might be expected after the discussion in the previous section.

This section has demonstrated how, at this stage, the EU developed a series of agreements with Latin American countries which did not, in and of themselves, reveal the EU's real expectations for EU–Latin America relations. The lack of legal commitment compared to other EU agreements is evidence that relations with Latin American countries were not included within, or covered by, a clear strategy. Moreover, this shows the EU's ambiguous stance as regards Latin America. It meant that the desires or demands stated by Latin American countries in these cases were relatively more important than in other EU external relations. In order to develop a semblance of EU–Latin America policy Mercosur is prioritized within the Latin American groups, as are Mexico and Chile, since all have achieved association agreements, but they are not priorities in comparison to other EU external relations

The EU–Rio Group relations: a forum for everything and anything, including EU–Mercosur relations

The Rio Group was introduced in the previous chapter. It is important to note that by 1990 there were eleven members of the Rio Group, including Argentina, Bolivia, Brazil, Chile, Colombia, Ecuador, Paraguay, Peru, Uruguay and Venezuela. It was the most important forum for the discussion of political and economic issues in Latin America. The EU started as an observer of the meetings, and then informal meetings naturally developed between both groups.

It is important to highlight how the institutionalization of the annual meetings was driven from the Latin American side. The Rio Group asked the EU for the institutionalization of the meetings and the EU agreed. In December 1990, the Declaration of Rome institutionalized the relations between the EU and Rio Group. The annual meetings between the groups signified the construction of a forum in which the two sides could develop their relations further. In the Declaration of Rome, the following were included as areas for discussion: commerce, general economic cooperation, science and technology, investment, debt, aid for development, regional cooperation and integration, environment, drugs, terrorism, consultation on global issues, and cooperation projects.

The Declaration of Rome was not a surprise; the conference in Rome had been called in order to institutionalize this forum (Ayuso 1996). It could be argued little improvement in the relations resulted, apart from discussions and promises to cooperate, which tended to remain unrealized. The role of the EU–Rio Group relations is better understood from the point of view of the EU's interests in the region. Given the low level of EU interest in Latin America, the mere possibility of having regular contacts was at that point important as a means to closer, future cooperation (Ayuso 1996).

This forum gave some access in particular to the EU perspective on areas of mutual interest, as well as to perspectives of all other participating actors more generally. The Spanish foreign minister, Fernandez Ordonez, agreed to the idea of including the topic of financing from the EIB in Latin America during the Luxembourg declaration. This issue was pursued again in the following meeting in 1992. The issue was closely linked to that of opening the economies of Latin America, a notion accepted by Latin American countries themselves. At the same time, however, Latin America was asking for the opening of the EU market – that is, a liberalization of trade in the region. This took on special importance with the launching of the European Common Market and concomitant developments in Central and Eastern Europe. These latter moves apparently spooked the Latin American countries since they threatened the expected increases in trade between the regions.

The ministerial meetings of the EU–Rio Group proved to be multi-purpose and multi-functional affairs, where Latin American countries demanded, above all, more accessible trade with the EU. In October 1992, a meeting took place between representatives of the Rio Group and the Commission. A variety of issues related to trade were discussed, including the Uruguay Round, the European Single Market and the impact of the reform of the CAP and the future of the GSP (Agence Europe 30/10/1992).

The main actor within the EU was the commissioner in charge of this area. Until 1992, the office was held by the Spanish commissioner Abel Matutes; the following year, another Spaniard, Manuel Marin, took over the role. Following the Latin American countries, Matutes used the forum to announce changes in the EU towards Latin America. Matutes highlighted the importance of these meetings and confirmed the intention of the EU to help Bolivia and Peru – the poorest countries in Latin America – through the provision of aid (Agence Europe 23/4/1991). In these meetings, Matutes stated the intention of the Commission to open a delegation in Lima that would deal with both Peru and Bolivia, and another one in Buenos Aires (Agence Europe 26/4/1991). In the main, however, it was the Latin American countries that requested changes from the EU (as in the case of the EIB or the GSP). The EU had to react to these petitions, which it did in a more or less positive way. Marin (as will be seen in the next section) also used this forum to communicate with Mercosur countries, but only to some extent, since EU–Mercosur relations were then relatively independent of wider EU–Latin American or EU–Rio Group discussions.

In terms of EU engagement, this section presents evidence which questions the level of EU ambition because the Latin American side was the one asking for the institutionalization of the annual meetings. The changes requested on the Latin American side related to the GSP and the EIB and do not support the claim of a good level of ambition, especially since both the GSP and EIB are EU instruments whose use is decided unilaterally by the EU. Therefore, in a way, the EU was being told what to do, which does not suggest a high level of ambition. On the other side, the fact that the EU agreed to some of the suggestions is evidence of a sort of commitment on the EU side, although it was directed by Latin America. These requests from the Latin American side do not demonstrate very strategic behaviour by the EU.

The fact that again the main EU actors were Spaniards – the Spanish foreign minister, Fernandez Ordonez, and the Spanish commissioners, Matute and Marin – show the continuity of the path started in the previous stage with the Iberian membership.

Effect on EU–Mercosur

These annual meetings helped in the development of the EU's relations with Mercosur in its initial stages, giving each of the parties the opportunity to contact the other, and even to negotiate informal agreements. It was a good base from which the EU could develop its relations with Latin America, and vice versa (Hoste 1999). Latin America took the opportunity in these meetings to demand concessions since, until 1999 when the first summit of heads of state of Latin America and the EU was celebrated, these were the only official meetings between the parties. EU–Mercosur relations developed unofficially within the EU-Rio Group forum before becoming autonomous (Hoste 1999).

An important ministerial meeting with the Rio Group, bringing the Mercosur countries to Europe, took place in Luxembourg on 26–27 April 1991. Two days later they visited the European Commission in Brussels, meeting President Delors, Vice-Presidents Bangerman and Pandolfi and Commissioner Matutes. 'The aim of the visit was mainly to present to the Commission the objectives and cooperation of the Mercosur common market. It is significant that the first 'international action' by Mercosur countries was to present their achievement to the EU, especially since the treaty that created Mercosur was signed only a month before their trip to Europe. It indicates Mercosur's 'willingness to develop relations with the

Community in particular' (Agence Europe 23/4/1991). The importance for Latin America of these meetings – as a forum in which to discuss important issues with the EU as well as detailing for the EU their own position – is obvious. It helped Mercosur to understand the EU position on many issues as well as to develop, informally, meetings in relation to their own interests and projects. Mercosur introduced itself to the world in this first visit to Europe. This meeting produced a desirable outcome for Mercosur only a year later: in a subsequent EU–Rio Group ministerial meeting, the EU and Mercosur signed an administrative cooperation agreement (Agence Europe 29/5/1992).

Moreover, as the 'Communication from the Commission to the Council and the European Parliament, the European Community and Mercosur: an enhanced policy' of 1994 explains clearly:

> a Union strategy aimed at strengthening relations with Mercosur, Mexico and other Latin American regions cannot be seen as an alternative to the dialogue with the Rio Group. It should instead be considered a means of deepening and extending that dialogue, within which the Community's interests demand that it recognize and take account of regional specificities. This means that the Community's proposed new strategy towards Mercosur must not be developed in isolation, but as part of a broader Community strategy towards all the Latin American countries, and in particular the Rio Group. (European Commission 1994a: 3)

It can be said then, that Mercosur was one part of the general EU strategy towards Latin America. The Rio Group and Mercosur were not in competition, but were meant to complement one another. This supports the notion that EU relations towards Mercosur were an inseparable part of EU policy towards Latin America.

In relation to the analysis of EU engagement, once again the EU seems to be the one taking on initiatives from the outside more than developing its own. The fact that Mercosur was the one coming to Brussels, seeking to start some sort of relations with the EU, does not evidence much ambition on the part of the EU. Since the EU and Mercosur signed their first agreement a year after their first official meeting, this does show a good level of EU commitment. The fact that the EU is the one receiving offers from Mercosur and developing the relationship based on these offers does not help the image of the EU as a strategic actor.

EU–Mercosur relations

This section discusses EU–Mercosur relations at this stage, focusing on agreements that were made and any evident problems associated with them. It explains the causes of the agreements, showing the extent to which they were part of an EU strategy and/or responses to Mercosur's demands.

EU–Mercosur agreements: the productive side of the relations
The development of agreements between the EU and Mercosur was the most productive part of the policy at this stage. This could also be considered the most productive stage of the policy studied here. The agreement made in 1992 was minor, without far-reaching intent or consequences; in 1995, another agreement upgrading EU–Mercosur relations with the aim of creating an association agreement was signed, but the negotiations have not finished yet, as will be explained in detail in the following chapter.

The EU's first contact with Mercosur was in April 1991, a month after it had signed the treaty that created the Common Market of the South. The foreign ministers of the four member states of Mercosur – Guido di Tella (Argentina, acting secretary), José Francisco Rezek (Brazil), Alexis Frutos (Paraguay) and Hector Gros (Uruguay) – visited the Commission on 29 April for talks with commissioners Delors, Matutes and MacSharry.

This visit had several aims. The first aim was to introduce the new regional group to the EU. It was welcomed by Delors and his colleagues and the importance of integration for political stability and the economic development of the countries involved was highlighted. Secondly, the possibility of cooperation between the EU and Mercosur was discussed. There also were talks regarding a cooperation agreement (Cienfuegos 2006), to be made on the basis of Article 228 of the Treaty of Rome, once Mercosur institutions were developed. Similar discussions were entered in the areas of trade. The foreign ministers of the Mercosur countries held a meeting with representatives of the Commission in Brussels on 21 April 1991 in order to present the new regional group and to request a cooperation agreement: 'On the question of the terms of trade between the Community and the Mercosur countries, the Commission representatives said that the Commission could, at the opportune moment, propose measures to take account, in the application of its own commercial policy instruments, of the progress made by Mercosur in establishing its customs union and common external trade policy' (European Commission 1991b). Soon after this meeting, Matutes had a working meeting with the Council and it was decided that, once the Treaty of Asunción was ratified, an inter-institutional agreement between the Commission and Mercosur would be signed (Agence Europe 5/5/1992).

The presidency of the EU was held by Portugal at this time. On 2 May 1992, an informal meeting took place in Guimaraes (Portugal) between the European Union foreign ministers and their Mercosur counterparts, where a potential agreement was discussed. After this meeting, the ministers asked the Commission to work on a paper in which different ways of improving relations with Mercosur would be discussed (Agence Europe 5/5/1992). At the Guimaraes meeting, it seems that the ministers of Mercosur countries criticized the EU's agricultural protectionism (Agence Europe 5/5/1992). It is not clear what the EU wanted to do with Mercosur, but it was clear that the agriculture sector would be a point of contention in EU–Mercosur relations. In Chile, on 29 May 1992, the first Inter-institutional Cooperation Agreement between the Commission of the European Communities and the Mercosur Council was signed.

The EU's level of engagement seems to start to confront the most important obstacle, the agricultural sector. This issue, as will be shown in the next chapter, will become the centre of the discussion due to its negative effect on EU engagement towards Mercosur. Again, the work of Matutes as commissioner and the Portuguese presidency worked to the benefit of EU–Mercosur relations, once more demonstrating the path dependence created by the Iberian membership. In terms of strategic behaviour, again the EU does not seem to have a clear plan since Mercosur is the one asking for changes, and updates.

The Spanish commissioner Manuel Marin took over Matutes' portfolio in 1993. He visited Uruguay in early 1993; in March of the same year Delors paid visits to Chile, Argentina and Mexico in order to 'take the pulse' of the continent and of those countries specifically, since they were considered by Brussels potentially important players on the international scene (Agence Europe 10/3/1993). At this point, the Commission seemed to be considering different approaches to Mercosur. In April 1993, an informal meeting took place in Copenhagen within the EU–Rio Group framework (Bizzozero 1995). The contacts between the groups were constant; the idea of upgrading the relationship seemed to be in the air at this point. From that moment, the speed of events was frenetic. The annual EU–Rio Group meeting of April 1994, which discussed the options for an upgrading of EU–Mercosur relations in earnest, was crucial. After April 1994 a series of diplomatic gestures were made on both side of the Atlantic. First, in June 1994, the General Affairs Council meeting in Luxembourg discussed the evaluation of the Commission with regard to relations with Mercosur. After Commissioner Van den Broek's (external relations commissioner at that time) thoughts on the EU's relations with Mercosur were heard, the Council affirmed its desire to 'strengthen relations between the European Union and that important Latin American regional grouping'; the Council also took note of the communication by the Commission to be submitted in the near future, linked to these relations (European Commission 1994b). The presidency's conclusions at Corfu a few days later reaffirmed the intention of the EU to strengthen its relations with Mercosur. Mercosur countries responded to these gestures positively, welcoming them and, crucially, reaffirming on their part a wish to intensify the economic and trade issues and 'to contribute to the liberalisation of world trade' (Agence Europe 16/8/1994). Finally, on 19 October 1994, the Commission proposed an 'enhanced policy' towards Mercosur (European Commission 1994a). This was presented to the press by Manuel Marin on 19 October.

In this policy, the Commission was offering two potential scenarios for the years up to 2000:

• Scenario 1: No change in current trends.
• Scenario 2: Liberalization of trade between the EU and Mercosur. This scenario assumed the establishment of a free trade area with Mercosur (European Commission 1994a).

The EU's institutional machinery put in motion traditional procedures; it was decided a few days later in the General Affairs Council meeting to send the communication to COREPER for its perusal, with a request that the subsequent report to the Council be delivered within one month. This would give time for the preparation of the Essen European Council (European Commission 1994c). As Box 5.1 shows, the Commission had suggested different options for the development of EU–Mercosur relations.

The Commission favoured the third option, thereby demonstrating a certain interest in developing an agreement with Mercosur. However, before the Essen Council was able to convene, the four Mercosur ministers of foreign affairs met Delors, Marin and Van den Broek in Brussels (European Commission 1994d). This was not a coincidence: Mercosur wanted a chance to discuss the Commission communication before the Essen Council's decision on the Commission's proposal of an inter-regional EU–Mercosur association was made (European Commission 1994d). Mercosur had already been incredibly active and present in the upgrading of its policy, putting continuous pressure on the Commission.

The conclusions of the Essen Council presidency gave yet another push to the relations: 'It urges the Council and the Commission, working on the basis of the Council report, to create as quickly as possible the conditions for an early opening of negotiations with the Mercosur countries on an inter-regional framework agreement, including a Memorandum of Understanding' (European Council 1994). On 22 December 1994, the Solemn Joint Declaration between the Council of the EU/European Commission and the Member States of the Mercosur was signed (European Commission 1994e).

The objectives of the inter-regional association in the official documents were a mix of economic and value-based interests, coming from the EU side:

• To foster inter-regional flows to the advantage of both partners and within the bounds of the Uruguay Round Final Act.
• To promote strategic investment by firms.
• To strengthen political cooperation at international level, in particular by seeking to reach joint positions in international forums on issues of mutual interest, including world peace and security.

Box 5.1 Options for EU–Mercosur relations

Option 1: A trade cooperation agreement

This option would give priority to the trade cooperation aspect. While continuing the work begun under the existing inter-institutional cooperation agreement, priority would be given to measures that would help strengthen Mercosur's structural capacity to manage effectively the trade-related aspects of its integration and the trade element of its cooperation with the EU in preparation for the liberalization of trade. This option reflects the need to deepen trade links, with the political and structural side of relations taking second place.

Option 2: An inter-regional framework agreement on trade and economic cooperation

Compared with the previous option, this one offered the advantage of being a more active response to Mercosur, demonstrating the EU's express desire to contribute to Mercosur's consolidation process. This approach is genuinely political, and not simply economic.

Option 3: An inter-regional association agreement

Set against the other options, this one pre-empts Mercosur's consolidation by proposing the immediate negotiation of an inter-regional association between the EU and Mercosur. This agreement would include the provisions needed to bring about, according to a fixed timetable, a free trade area of the type outlined above.

Cooperation under such an agreement would cover the same areas as the preceding option, but would be reinforced by the introduction of joint financial instruments through the raising of substantial funds by both parties. Compared with the other options, this would be a proactive approach on the part of the EU aimed at accelerating the regional integration process by acting upstream even of initiatives by Mercosur and its members.

Source: European Commission (1994a).

- To improve the efficiency of the EU's external activities by establishing a new framework for relations with partners of a similar nature. (European Commission 1994a)

The Commission was already considering the presentation of draft negotiating directives to the Council in early 1995 (European Commission 1994d).

In April 1995, in the General Affairs Council meeting, communication from the Commission to the Council regarding the negotiating mandate for the inter-regional framework with Mercosur was welcomed. As usual it was passed to COREPER for analysis (European Commission 1995b). Later in June, the General Affairs Council adopted the directives of negotiations (European Commission 1995c). On the other side of the Atlantic, Mercosur countries were preparing for their meeting with the EU in Brussels on 14 September 1995.

In Montevideo the Commission and Mercosur negotiators initialled the agreement (European Commission 1995b), and on 15 December 1995 in Madrid, the EMIFCA was signed.

The level of engagement shown by this agreement seems higher than previously thought because the agreement proposed (and the association agreement) involves more than the general cooperation or only trade agreements. Association agreements are offered to countries or regions to upgrade the relationship; this shows an increase in the levels of both ambition and commitment, which as a consequence involves an increase in the level of engagement.

Who supported this policy and who did not?
There were some obstacles to the agreement within the EU because of the agricultural question. 'The majority of the ministers of industry, economic and foreign affairs from the EU member states appeared to support the negotiations with Mercosur. But the French, Irish and Dutch ministers of agriculture and fisheries, under pressure from their domestic lobbies, were opposed to this mandate' (IRELA 1999, quoted in Santander 2005: 296). The UK did not want to start negotiations until the end of the WTO Round. Even within the Commission there was disagreement: the commissioner of agriculture, Franz Fischler, his colleagues from France, commissioners de Silguy and Cresson, and from Ireland, Flynn, also opposed the project (Santander 2005). In the end it was voted on by the Commission and a decision was taken to go ahead with the association agreement with Mercosur (Interviewee 9).

At the same time there were other obstacles within the EU against developing an economic agreement. These obstacles were based on the argument in Article 24 of the GATT (*El País* 6/4/1995). On the other side, Manuel Marin argued that Article 24 of the GATT would allow 'the progressive liberalization of all sectors establishing exceptions and transitory periods for the most sensitive products if it does not pass the 20% of the total. The other obstacle is the norm of the WTO that expects the creation of the free trade area in 10 years maximum' (*El País* 6/4/1995). Apparently, Marin was able to convince them, since the negotiation mandate was eventually conceded. When asked, he argued that the exchange of agricultural products was only 14% of the trade between the regions. However, Mercosur was an exporter of cereals, meat and dairy products, all of them super-sensitive products for the EU (*El País* 16/12/1995). In the case of free trade between the two regions, it would be interesting to know to what extent the EU would increase its imports from Mercosur without the constraints of the CAP.

The EU–Mercosur agreements: the most productive side of the relationship

The EU was involved in controversy over its CAP before it signed any agreements with Mercosur. This began as early as 1986, when the agricultural issue was included in the Uruguay Round after pressure from the US and the Cairns Group (Meunier 2000). The Cairns Group is a coalition of developing countries that export agricultural products and was formed in 1986 to give its members an international voice. Crucially, the four members of Mercosur were members of the Cairns Group. The agricultural importance of Argentina and Brazil at the international level was clear. The agriculture issue was a problem for the EU at all levels and with many regions. In relation to Mercosur, many problems could be foreseen at the outset as the parties' positions varied on the matter. However, there was scope for optimism after the so-called Blair House Agreement was reached, leading to the EU's 1992 CAP reforms.

There had been talks beforehand about not including agricultural sector trade in the EU–Mercosur agreement of 1995 (Agence Europe 12/10/1994). Of all the commissioners, René Steichen, the commissioner of agriculture, was the most recalcitrant in his rejection of the agreement. In Brasilia, just days before the commission led by Marin presented a report on a possible EU–Mercosur agreement, Steichen stated his opinions on the matter quite openly: both sides would be in direct competition on several products and procedures but the EU would protect the most sensitive sectors (Agence Europe 12/10/1994). A day later, during the same visit, the president of Argentina, Carlos Menem, and the ministers of agriculture, foreign affairs and trade were treated to similar outbursts from Steichen. He indicated that Argentina was one of the principal beneficiaries of the Uruguay Round and also profited from the impact on world trade of the reform of the CAP (Agence Europe 12/10/1994). He claimed that the reforms of the latter and the Uruguay Round meant that the EU would be producing less, exporting less, and importing more, leaving little to offer Argentina in this area so far as the liberalization of the EU market for Argentinean products was concerned (Agence Europe 12/10/1994). 'Mr Steichen used the same argument with Brazil and the WTO: Brazil was one of the countries that would benefit from the Uruguay Round and the Blair House agreement, therefore Brazilian taxation on European whiskeys differently from Brazilian whiskeys should be modified' (Agence Europe 13/10/1994). As mentioned above, these talks took place days before the Commission proposed a 'pioneering agreement' with Mercosur (Agence Europe 19/10/1994). Marin, as the 'father' of this proposal and of most of the EU's advances towards Latin America, was very optimistic. He emphasized the singular characteristics of the 'first inter-regional agreement' (Agence Europe 19/10/1994).

However, this announcement did not smooth over the issue of agriculture. Days later an exchange of views on it took place. This agreement would not cover agriculture automatically; Argentina and Brazil responded clearly: the Argentinean minister for the economy, Domingo Cavallo, declared that 'negotiations in which the first item was not agricultural trade would have no significance' and that 'negotiations limited to industry and services would be worthless' (Agence Europe 9/11/1994). The Brazilian president Fernando Henrique Cardoso said it would be 'very difficult' to conclude an agreement with the EU because 'an agreement that did not include a chapter on agriculture would not make sense' (Agence Europe 9/11/1994).

EU engagement in Mercosur

In order to assess the level of ambition at the different stages, it is necessary to contrast with the status quo the presence of offers of negotiation mandates or agreements, EU official policy pronouncements, promises to Mercosur and plans for a potential relationship. The different levels of ambition are shown in Figure 5.1.

This chapter has explained that in the area of ambition the new guidelines indicate that there was a good level, as well as the support of the EP towards a development on the EU side. Also evidence of ambitions is the fact that the EU agreed to an association agreement with Mercosur, considered a preferential type of agreement.

However, the fact that the EIB requests came from the Latin American side, as did the requests for the institutionalization of the Rio Group and the requests for the development of agreements, balances the level of

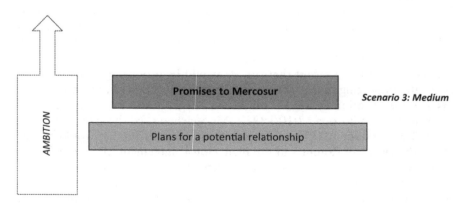

Figure 5.1 Level of ambition: second stage

ambition. Also on the negative side is that the EU agreements had no legal content and the initial negative reaction in some parts of the EU to the inclusion of the agricultural sector in any of those agreements. Therefore the final level of ambition is medium, higher than in the previous stage.

The link between commitment and engagement is that you need the first one to have the second one. This is the case especially in an area such as South America which has been ignored for decades. The more concise and less abstract the commitments are, the more verifiable this criterion is. If there is no commitment, involvement will come as a reaction to the other players, or as an unintentional action. It is important to note whether strategy existed or not.

In order to assess the level of commitment it is necessary to pay attention to certain indicators: prioritization of negotiations over other agreements/ negotiations, substantial content of agreements and of offers during the negotiations, aid, funding or technical help provided by the EU, meetings either official or unofficial at any level. Figure 5.2 shows the assessed level of commitment.

The amount of aid assigned in the guidelines can be seen as evidence confirming commitment, as can the upgrading of investment facilities. Also boosting the level of commitment are the visits by Delors to the region, and the acceptance of requests for the inclusion of Latin America in EIB loans, and the institutionalization of the annual meetings. Finally in favour of commitment is the fact that the EU signed two different agreements in a very short period of time.

However, the reorganization of the GSP is a negative indicator of the EU commitment towards Mercosur countries as well as the legal emptiness of the EU agreements with Mercosur. Also pushing down the level of commitment is the indecision about the inclusion of the agricultural sector in the

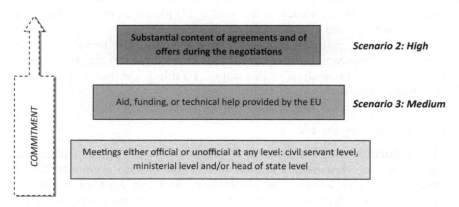

Figure 5.2 Level of commitment: second stage

Table 5.2 Measurement of the dependent variable, engagement: second stage

		Top	High	Medium	Low	None
				Ambition		
	Top					
Commitment	High			Second stage: med/high		
	Medium					
	Low				First stage: low/low	
	None					

agreements. All of the evidence together points to a high level of commitment, the highest of the three stages.

The level of engagement is somewhere between high and medium, as shown in Table 5.2. This is a large change from the previous stage, where EU involvement was qualified as low. The component of engagement which improved the most was commitment, since during this stage of the policy two official agreements were signed between the EU and Mercosur in a short period of time. Also in general terms, as this chapter has shown, these years were the most productive of EU–Mercosur relations. Ambition has been assessed as medium, since although Mercosur is the EU's priority within Latin America, it does not mean that the EU has enormous ambition in this region compared with other EU foreign policies such as the policies towards Eastern European countries. EU ambition towards Mercosur is high within Latin America, but low within EU global ambitions, therefore it is fair to be placed at medium level.

Once the dependent variable has been assessed, the focus is on the competing arguments. On this occasion, three of the six explanations meet the outcome of the analysis of this stage, as Table 5.3 shows and as evaluated further below.

Counterbalancing the US

The explanation for EU actions as a counterbalancing strategy against the US at this stage has been discussed in Chapter 2. This argument would expect the EU to increase its involvement in Latin America if the US increases its involvement. In relation to the US's involvement, the idea behind this explanation is the possibility of the FTAA. This plan was

Table 5.3 Competing arguments and the independent variables: second stage

Independent variable	Expectation	Independent variable value	Expectation value	Met/confronted
Counterbalancing the US	If the US increases its involvement in LA, the EU should increase its involvement. ↑US = ↑EU in LA	High	High	Yes
Global aspirations	If the EU increases its presence in international affairs, the EU's involvement in LA should also increase. ↑EU in the world = ↑EU in LA	High	High	Yes
External federator	If LA becomes more integrated, the EU will increase its relations with LA. ↑LA integration = ↑EU in LA	High	High	Yes
Affinity	An increase of shared values between the regions should develop EU policy. ↑LA shared values = ↑EU in LA	Top	Top	No
Interdependence	If trade and investment between the EU and LA increase, EU policy should also increase. ↑LA trade = ↑EU in LA	Low	Low	No
Iberia	If the influence of Spain and Portugal increase within the EU, then the EU's involvement in LA should increase. ↑SP + PT influence = ↑EU in LA	Medium	Medium	No

Notes: LA = Latin America; PT = Portugal; SP = Spain.

launched during the Summit of the Americas in Miami in December 1994 which brought together the heads of state of thirty-four American states. The process had been started in 1993 by the US Clinton administration, headed by Vice-President Al Gore. At the Miami Summit, the heads of state signed a declaration with the aim of creating an FTA in America by 2005 (Devlin et al. 2003). In December 1994, the European Council asked the Commission to work on the agreement with Mercosur and Chile and Mexico; this is compelling evidence in support of the 'US influence' argument at this stage in EU–Mercosur relations.

Although there is certainly some kind of competition between the EU and the US for influence/control of the Latin American market, this should be considered to be a natural element of the international economic system where the globalization of markets means that economic competition now takes places at a global level rather than just an inter-regional level. However, as discussed in the previous section, the amount of trade between the EU and Mercosur countries highlights just how little economically Mercosur means to the EU. It has been noted that the EU could not compete with the US in Latin America due to the advantage that the latter already had there (*El País* 17/6/1994; Interviewee 7). Nevertheless, the evidence suggests that the Commission was already planning an upgrading of the EU–Mercosur relations in 1993 after Mercosur demands.

Global aspirations

The basis of this argument – that the EU was expected to increase its involvement in Latin America as a consequence of the EU's increased involvement in the world – seems to have been realized, since these relations did indeed intensify with the end of Cold War. The new globalized world brought new opportunities for the EU. The agreement with Mercosur could be seen as one way of developing the EU's economic influence in the different regions rather than being a result of the end of the Cold War. According to the Argentinean government, in a globalized world Europe clearly had an interest in achieving influence in the new economic regions (*El País* 9/12/1995). When the EU upgraded its policies towards Latin America with the new strategy for 1996 to 2000, Manuel Marin explained the upgrading in these terms: 'The EU must be equally present in the emerging zones at world level such as Latin America' (*El País* 27/10/1995).

This argument has been mentioned several times in this chapter. The question remains, however; whether the EU actually had the political will to achieve the requisite degree of involvement with Latin America to fulfil its global strategy. The EU's agreements appear more as compensatory attempts to fill the gaps in the common foreign and security policy (Petiteville 2004, cited in Santander 2005: 303). If that is indeed the case, then the political emphasis of those agreements is clear.

For some, it has been important to stress that the EU's role in Latin America – even if it is part of the broader strategy to increase the EU's political and economical role at global level – is still less prominent even than the EU's role in Asia (Dinan 1999). For Freres (2000) this is not explained by a lack of power, but rather by a lack of common will. It has been explained in this chapter that, relative to other external agreements, those with Latin American countries (including Mercosur) were treated differently by the EU, initially in terms of the legal commitments offered when signing the agreements. It has also been mentioned that the EU's pyramid of preference has never given Latin America priority; it has, in fact, always been (and now remains) at the bottom of the heap, as it were.

Promotion of regional integration

The promotion of regional integration has been one of the arguments given in the literature. For this stage, emphasis on the promotion of regionalism has special significance, probably because of the speed of the development of Mercosur institutions and the involvement of the EU in the process. The expectations related to this argument would be realized if the EU increased its involvement in Latin America in response to an intensification in Mercosur's integration. This seems to have been the case. The agreement of 1992 allowed the transfer of knowledge (know-how) and funding from the EU to Mercosur. On 26 and 27 July 1992, the Lisbon European Council 'emphasized the importance of supporting moves towards regional integration in Latin America such as that represented by Mercosur' (European Council 1992). The first meeting of the Joint Advisory Committee was in July 1992, and it was asked to focus initially on the topics of customs, technical standards and agriculture (EC–Mercosur 1993).

Mercosur secured a considerable amount of funding from the EU for the development of the institutions in a relatively short period of time, as presented in Table 5.4. Moreover, in 1993, the Training Centre for Regional Integration was created in Uruguay by the EU in order to provide know-how in the area of regional integration. The European Institute of Public Administration in Maastricht administered the development of the programme (Bizzozero 1995).

The involvement of the EU in the development of Mercosur institutions was intense and it is clear that the Mercosur institutions are modelled on the EU institutions outlined in Chapter 1. Much literature in this area has been dedicated to comparing the similarities and difference between the institutions in the two regional groups. According to Marin, this type of agreement was pioneering and became a possibility for other parts of the world where there was both integration and emergent economies (IRELA 1994). In other words, the EU model could be considered to be an example for other regions to follow.

Table 5.4 EU cooperation with Mercosur, 1992–2000

Area	Projects under the 1992 inter-institutional cooperation agreement and the EMIFCA	EU contribution (€)
Institutions		
Customs cooperation	Macro-economic policy-coordination	2,500,000
Statistics	Statistics	4,135,000
Technical standards	Standards	3,950.000
Mercosur's bodies	Administrative Secretariat of Mercosur (I)	900,000
	Administrative Secretariat of Mercosur (I)	900,000
	Joint parliamentary commission	917,175
Support to single market and macro-economic coordination	Customs	700,000
	Customs	5,300,000
	Support to the single market	4,600,000
Civil society		
Social dimension of Mercosur	Labour and social dimension	950,000
Others		
	Mercosur Agriculture	11,200,000

Source: European Commission (2002c).

The 'external federator' tag for the EU's behaviour towards Latin America in general and Mercosur in particular is justified by this evidence. Even an official from the European Commission, working at the Mercosur desk, confirmed that the promotion of regional integration was the clearest way of explaining EU–Mercosur relations: 'if one adopts a perspective of supporting and furthering regional integration, then the European Union–Mercosur relationship and its future possibilities ... suddenly becomes much clearer' (Klom 2000). Jean Grugel (2004) believes an adequate explanation of EU policy towards Mercosur might potentially draw on many factors, including perhaps trade and investment, but considers Mercosur's replication of the EU example a very important reason. Grugel develops her argument further based on the idea of the 'partnership' that was offered to Mercosur (and other regions) by the EU. She argues that the EU is 'using new regionalism as a way to lay down an identity marker of what it perceives as a more humane governance model for Latin America than that of the USA' (Grugel 2004: 1). The problem is that she believes that, since the intention is to compete with the US, the EU is treating Mercosur and the other regions in Latin America similarly. This is clearly not the case. Like many authors, Grugel considers many explanatory models, but vacillates rather than chooses one particular explanation.

It was Latin America and Mercosur that took the initiative in dealings with the EU, particularly in respect of the possible upgrade of agreements and the institutionalization of relations or meetings. Therefore, the idea of the EU using these agreements as an incentive to achieve regional integration is not a sustainable argument. Nevertheless, this does not mean that the EU does not want regional integration. Two officials from the European Commission admitted that the EU is in favour of regional integration, but that it could not force Mercosur to integrate (Interviewees 7 and 8). Certainly, the EU cannot force Mercosur, but it *can* do more than make suggestions. The EU is still not using all its tools to achieve regional integration in Mercosur, and at the same time it is offering individual agreements to Mercosur countries. The term 'external federator' seems too big for the EU in this case. Looking at the evidence, we can discount the argument of promotion of regionalism.

Affinity

This argument explains that the involvement of the EU in Latin America is due to an increase in the sharing of values between the regions. Therefore, if Latin America and the EU shared a higher degree of common values at this stage, the EU would increase its involvement in the region. This was not the case, however: political, economic and cultural values did not change in any of the regions at this stage.

Interdependence

The interdependence argument makes reference to the level of trade and FDI between the two regions in its explanation of EU–Mercosur relations. The argument expects an increase in the EU's involvement in Latin America if there is an increase in the level of trade and FDI between the regions. Table 5.5 presents the levels of trade between the EU and Mercosur in this period in both relative and absolute terms, showing that there was a low

Table 5.5 EU exports and imports with Mercosur countries, 1991–1995 (values in US$ million)

	1991	1992	1993	1994	1995[1]
EU imp from Mercosur	14,500	15,500	14,000	17,500	18,000
EU imp from world	1,578,945	1,654,045	1,487,610	1,690,635	2,050,935
EU imp from Mercosur as % of total	0.91%	0.93%	0.94%	1.03%	0.87%
EU exp to Mercosur	7,000	9,000	12,000	17,000	21,500
EU exp to world	1,492,780	1,584,275	1,488,885	1,702,895	2,083,745
EU exp to Mercosur as % of total	0.46%	0.56%	0.80%	0.99%	1.03%

Sources: The author's own elaboration with the data from IRELA (1995, 1999), WTO Statistics Database and Eurostat Database.
Note: [1]Austria, Finland and Sweden joined the EU.

level of trade as a percentage of the total EU trade. The highest level is barely 1% of the total imports and exports, evidence enough of its relative insignificance. This table also shows that there had been a considerable increase in the area of EU exports, so much so that EU exports increased threefold. However, this is still only 1% of the total. It is difficult to sustain the argument that Mercosur was of particular economic importance for the EU at this stage.

The idea of interdependence is difficult to defend at this stage. Also, Latin America has never been the EU's priority from an economic point of view. The agreements with Mercosur were driven by political factors, not economic ones (Interviewee 7).

Spanish and Portuguese influence in the EU

Spain and Portugal have been key actors in the development of EU–Mercosur relations, but they are not the only reason for the development of EU's policy towards Mercosur. The argument for the Iberian influence in the EU expected that the EU's involvement in Latin America would increase if Spanish and Portuguese influence increased in the EU. At the end of this stage, the EU increased its membership from twelve to fifteen states, decreasing the power of Iberian countries within the EU. Therefore, the argument's expectations are not met at this stage. This does not mean that

Spain and Portugal did not have influence in the EU: their influence was necessary, but not sufficient to produce the actual outcomes found at this stage.

Spain did play a crucial role. The commissioners involved and directors of portfolio in the Commission were Spanish. Marin himself admits that he did everything possible for the development of EU–Latin America relations (Marin 1995). There has also been major progress in EU relations with Latin America during the Spanish presidencies; the Spanish presidency of 1995 secured signatures on the EMIFCA. However, Spain was not as entirely pro-regional integration in relation to economic interest as Marin was. Spain opposed Latin American products such as bananas being imported into the EU. Marin went further and warned of the possibility of treating regions of the Mercosur as individual states. The EU agreement with Mercosur was also welcomed by a Brazilian ambassador who thanked Spain and Portugal for the 'obvious and proven' role that they played, particularly because their membership of the EU sensitized the EU towards issues relating to Latin America, whereas before the Iberian membership there was not much in the way of contact between the two regions (*El País* 20/11/1994).

Compared with other EU members, Germany, Spain, France, Italy and the UK are the EU countries that invested the most in Latin America (IRELA 1995). In the case of Brazil, Germany and Italy were the biggest investors. Spain also had a strategy of increasing its investments in the area if there was a process of privatization in Brazil similar to the ones that took place in Argentina and Chile (*El País* 16/9/1995). In general, in 1992 most of the investments in Latin America were destined for the privatization of former public companies in Mercosur countries. In the case of Argentina, 80% of the $10,000 million came from Europe (IRELA 1995). These figures can be problematic and looking at the amount of money invested in general terms by each country does not give a true picture; rather one should look at the proportion of its GDP because Spain was at that time one of the poorest nations in the EU, whilst Germany could afford to invest more in absolute terms.

In the area of aid, again Spain and Germany were the main actors:

> Over the period 1991–1997, only two countries, Germany and Spain, can be considered major region wide donors. Both provided a cumulative total of more than two billion dollars. Germany was the top European donor throughout the 1990s; in 1996 its aid for Latin America was twice that of the United States. In that year, Spain's ODA [official development aid] for the region was only slightly lower than that of the United States. (Freres 2000: 42)

Again in relative terms, Spain prioritized the region, giving more than half of its aid to Latin America. If Spain had not increased the amount of aid that it gave to Latin America in the early 1990s, Latin America would have received less funding from the EU than in previous periods (Freres 2000). This confirms the lack of, or at least decline in, interest shown by the EU in Latin America. It also demonstrates just how important Spain was to the region. Spain's prioritization of Latin America is cited by many member states as an obstacle to the coordination of aid plans at the national level (Youngs 2000). The EU's priority tended to be the poorest countries in the world and Latin America in general and Mercosur in particular were not in this category. At the supranational level, due to Spanish pressure, the Commission did increase the level of funding to Latin America and, more specifically, the Spanish government acquiesced on the enlargement of the EU in terms of the Eastern European countries after securing an increase of funding for Latin America (Youngs 2000). However, it seems that this Spanish pressure backfired. One of the reasons that the EU member states did not give more aid to Latin America was that they assumed that Spain would take care of Europe's responsibilities in this area (Youngs 2000).

This chapter has also shown that the Commission, the EU institution in charge of the development of the policy towards Latin America, and Commissioner Matutes first and later more specifically Commissioner Marin were key to the development of EU relations towards Mercosur. They confronted the commissioners of agriculture, and the French and Irish commissioners, and managed to develop some kind of agreement with the region. Iberian countries persistently tried to increase their influence in the EU and certainly without their effort it would not have not been possible to develop the policy towards Mercosur. However, it must be noted that this would also not have been possible without the assistance of other countries, such as Germany, who also contributed. The initiative and demands of Mercosur were also a necessary feature that made the development of the EU policy possible.

The path dependence created by the membership of Spain and Portugal is as applicable as in the previous stage. Moreover, this stage helps to show the consequences of the path dependence created in the first stage, which have effects in the third stage because the consequences do not tend to be immediate. The path dependency created in 1986 keeps being followed with the evolution of the cooperation policies towards Latin America in general and Mercosur countries in this case. Moreover, the EU finally managed to develop independent guidelines towards Latin America, separate from the ones for Asia. At the end of this stage the development of some knowledge on Latin America was shown with the division of policies towards the different regions in Latin America instead of being directed at the whole region.

With regard to the process of Europeanization, there had been more changes in the way the EU dealt with Latin America, and Iberian countries had not changed the way they dealt with their former colonies. However, it should be stated and highlighted how Spain in particular had been trying to behave as a bridge between the EU and Mercosur, placing Spain in a powerful position as an intermediary. Also, like any other EU country, Spain and Portugal tried to have some influence in the EU when holding the presidencies. Iberian countries tried to pursue their interest in Mercosur at the EU level, but again it cannot be described as Europeanization since there was not a massive change in the EU towards Mercosur. In other words, Spain and Portugal did try to provoke a sort of Europeanization process which would initiate the uploading of their national foreign policies by the EU.

As explained before, the central argument in this monograph is related to the degree of Europeanization which comes from the influence of Spain and Portugal within the EU when dealing with Mercosur. This was not sufficient, however, and the proactive role of Mercosur countries was necessary. It seems that the path dependence created was not strong enough on its own to create a policy towards Mercosur that could overcome the obstacles.

Conclusion

This chapter has shown how this period was the most productive period of EU–Mercosur relations. The first agreement between Mercosur and the EU took just a year to be reached. It was given the green light at the first meeting between the two regions. Almost immediately, Mercosur took the initiative and made efforts to have the policy upgraded (which the EU could not concede until Mercosur became a customs union because the policy involved inter-regional trade). The development of EU–Mercosur relations had also been influenced by the productive EU–Latin America relations at this stage, which led to the creation of new cooperation guidelines between the regions, new agreements with the individual countries and the consolidation of the institutionalization of the EU–Rio Group meetings. Once again it should be noted that this political forum was institutionalized at the request of the Rio Group.

In terms of the analysis of the EU's engagement with the region, this chapter's evidence has helped the assessment of the EU's ambition and commitment, with an outcome of 'medium' and 'high' respectively; as a consequence, the level of EU engagement has an outcome of 'high'. In relation to ambition, the new guidelines and the support of the EP together with the EU compromise helped to develop an association agreement. However, the fact that it was the Latin American side that requested the EIB, the institutionalization of the annual meetings and different agreements does not lend support to a high level of ambition. In fact, the lack of legal content in the EU agreements offered to Mercosur and Latin American countries suggests an undefined, unclear and uncertain level of ambition on the EU side. That there were already voices against the inclusion of the agricultural sector does not help the level of ambition.

In relation to commitment, the outcome is more positive, with a final assessment of 'high'. There are several pieces of evidence in support of that, such as the increase in aid assigned in the new guidelines, and the upgrading of the investment facilities, together with the visits of the president of the Commission, Delors, to the region and the inclusion of the countries of Latin America as candidates for EIB loans. Moreover, the institutionalization of the annual meetings with the Rio Group and the fact that two agreements between the EU and Mercosur were signed in a period of five years do help this assessment. Against the measure of commitment are the fact that the reorganization of the GSP left Mercosur countries out of the scheme, and the lack of legal content in the EU agreements offered to Latin American countries and regions.

This chapter has also looked at the different arguments that can be found in the existing literature which try to explain these events. In particular, the discussion above has examined to what extent these explanations can or cannot explain the development of EU policy towards Mercosur. Here it was argued that the contradiction in the EU's actions leaves gaps in most of the explanations. The EU claims to promote regional integration but at the same time has offered agreements to individual countries. The EU also claims to have economic interest in the region, but trade figures and the lack of priority shown towards the region when compared to other regions contradicts that. The 'counterbalancing the US' argument is not credible since the EU and Mercosur had been discussing the upgrading of relations years before the US started to become more involved in the region. Spain and Portugal clearly supported further development of EU–Mercosur relations. However, the evidence presented above suggests that the Iberian countries were not powerful enough to bring this region to the same status as the former colonies of other EU member states.

This chapter has also demonstrated that there was a link between Mercosur petitions and Spanish – and, to a lesser extent, Portuguese – support for those petitions. This comes from the path dependence created with the Iberian membership which had an effect at this stage and also in the following stage. Consequently, there had been an upgrading of the cooperation policies achieved at this stage; there were now guidelines towards Latin America that were independent from the ones on Asia. Moreover, the new guidelines towards Latin America finally acknowledged an obvious fact: Latin America is so diverse that it could not be treated as one entity, therefore different policies were planned for the different regions and countries.

Finally, Spanish and Portuguese support was essential for the development of EU–Mercosur relations but not sufficient to develop these relations more significantly. Therefore, continuing with the central argument of this monograph, the EU has been *responsive* to Mercosur petitions and EU–Mercosur relations were developed as a result of Spanish and Portuguese interest in the region. Mercosur is not a priority for the EU compared to other regions such as the ACP, although EU–Mercosur relations were more of a priority for the EU compared to other Latin American groups and countries.

6

The first attempt to negotiate the association agreement

Introduction

This chapter aims to explain the phase in EU–Mercosur relations which saw the negotiation of the association agreement without reaching a successful ending. Both parties developed those negotiations under the EMIFCA. It was agreed that this agreement would be carried out in two phases. The first phase related to the preparation of the ground for future negotiations by comparing standards, statistical systems and trade procedures, whilst the second phase centred on trade liberalization. The second phase of this agreement was also focused on the actual negotiations. In the end, the parties were unable to reach an agreement and the negotiations were halted in October 2004.

By looking at how these two parts of the policy were developed, and how far both sides went in both their statements and actions, it will be possible to discuss the level of engagement on the EU side towards Mercosur. It seems that within the EU there were actors willing to increase and decrease the level of ambition and commitment. Mercosur countries helped to overcome some of the obstacles and this should be considered in order not to attribute the whole outcome solely to EU behaviour. The EU developed the association agreement towards Mercosur at this stage because of the efforts of the commissioner in charge of the policy until 1999. This was also the result of the clear pressure and demands made by Mercosur countries and Spanish ministers in the European Council and Spanish MEPs. The business associations, where again there was a strong Spanish presence, were also in favour of this agreement. However, despite having various sources of support, these forces were not powerful enough within the EU. The mandate given to the Commission was linked to the WTO negotiations. This proved to be an obstacle which led to the cessation of the negotiations without a successful conclusion until the WTO finished its negotiations. In addition to the pressure exerted by the agricultural lobby groups at the European level, French commissioners and Council members were opposed to the agreement. Argentina also decided to stop the negotiations until the results of the Doha Round of the WTO was over. Five years later, the negotiations were restarted. These initial renegotiations were ambitious in that they were designed to be concluded during the Spanish presidency of the EU in 2010. This did not happen, but the work of the Spaniards before their occupation of the presidency was key to relaunching the negotiations. As in the previous stages, the effect of the path dependence created with the Iberian membership is clear.

The period between 1995 and 2004 is important because it is the point where the actors that were against the agreement clearly voiced their dissent. During the period leading up to the end of the policy, new actors either started to participate or became more prominent in EU–Mercosur relations. This period highlights the differences of opinions and views among commissioners and among EU member states. It will be demonstrated that this lack of agreement could not sustain EU–Mercosur relations nor could it lead to the development of a clear and coherent EU strategy, and this affected the overall level of engagement. Exploring these issues between 1995 and 2004 is fundamental to examine the validity of the six different arguments which have been developed to explain EU–Mercosur relations. In fact, as has been discussed already in previous chapters, the interest of Spain and Portugal, combined with a strong desire on the part of Mercosur actors, made possible the development of relations between the two regions to some extent, although those relations did end somewhat unsuccessfully.

This stage is also the period when there were more contacts and more discussions between the two regions. The discussion below will also demonstrate that the EU continued to adopt the role of a reactive actor, responding to the demands and initiatives emanating from Latin America. However, it must be acknowledged that the EU was not simply the voice of Latin America in Europe. Below it will be demonstrated that even though it was always Mercosur that tried to further develop relations and policies between the regions, and EU the one reacting to its demands; the EU did not agree to all Mercosur's demands. In other words, Mercosur was always the one fighting (being proactive) to develop relations further and the EU, to a certain extent, repeatedly played the role of the responsive/reactive actor, with Manuel Marin once again being the channel and defender of Mercosur requests within the EU.

At the end of the first part of the policy the negotiation mandate was accepted 'in extremis' due to the pressure of Spain, Marin and Mercosur on the French embassies in their countries. This was also the result of the pressure mounted with the first summit of the heads of state of the EU and Latin America. Prior to this, the EU had been attempting to delay any policy decision for several years. When the negotiations started with Romano Prodi in charge of the Commission, Mercosur was once again very keen but the EU proved to be less interested in the region than ever.

Again we examine the six explanations for EU–Mercosur that can be found in the existing literature. In relation to the argument which suggests that the EU would seek to counterbalance the influence of the US, the EU should have been at its most aggressive at this point. In other words, the EU should have been very generous towards Mercosur because the FTAA was being negotiated at the same time as the association agreement with the EU. As far as the global aspirations expectation is concerned, again the EU should have been more active in order to achieve the first inter-regional agreement in history and not leave Latin America lagging behind on the EU's overall external relations agenda. The idea that the EU would act as an external federator suggests that the EU's priority would be to promote regional integration in other parts of the world, and the next argument – which points towards the long-standing political, economic and cultural ties between the Iberian countries and Latin America – would also suggest that these ties should have made the agreement possible. The interdependence argument also predicts that business issues should have been prioritized too, particularly in the agricultural sector, during the attempts to seek an agreement which would bring more interdependence between the regions by increasing FDI. Finally it is suggested in the existing literature that Iberian influence in the EU should have been able to demand a more generous offer for Mercosur countries which would have made negotiation of the agreement less complicated.

This chapter is divided into three main sections. The first section will examine the first part of EMIFCA at the level of the EU directives. The focus will then move to the EU–Mercosur negotiations. This is followed by an analysis of both the role and interests of the various key actors involved in this process.

EMIFCA's negotiations at the internal level: EU directives

EU policy-making towards Mercosur took on a new dimension after the signature of the EMIFCA in Madrid on 15 December 1995. It is important to acknowledge that this agreement was signed whilst Spain was holding the presidency of the EU; which shows again the interest of Iberian countries channelled through the path dependence. At the time of the signature in 1995, it was agreed that this agreement would be developed in two phases. The first phase was designed to prepare the ground for future negotiations by comparing standards, statistical systems and trade procedure. The second phase was designed to focus on trade liberalization (Agence Europe 9/4/1997). As already explained in the introduction, the EU promised to start the process of trade liberalization at the beginning of the twenty-first century. In order to start the liberalization, which would require further negotiations between the two sides, the Council had to pass directives to the Commission. The second phase is the heart of the discussion in the next section.

This section examines the internal negotiations and debates within the EU in relation to the granting or not of the directives to start the negotiations of EMIFCA. This discussion will highlight the degree of interest shown towards these directives by the Council, since the different positions of the members of the Council are the basis of the outcome. The Council is the main actor to consider in this part of the policy and indeed in this chapter. This section will analyse to what extent there was any ambition and commitment within the EU, revealed through the negotiations of the directives that would give the Commission power to start negotiations for an association agreement with Mercosur.

During the first phase of the agreement, actors involved in the policy showed either their support or opposition very clearly through the debate related to the directives that the Council had to give to the Commission. These directives were necessary if negotiations of an association agreement with Mercosur were to begin. In fact, it was during this period that it became much clearer who exactly was in favour and who was opposed to the creation of an association agreement. It could be argued that this was a result of there being a substantial leap from the previous stage where discussions had been held in relation to small issues such as technical cooperation. During this stage, the EU was about to develop an inter-regional agreement with a region that was not geographically close to it, a region which until then had never truly been of any great interest to the EU because there was not any significant security risk to the EU, nor did Latin America provide any real economic competition to the EU in sectors such as agriculture. It seems that this was the first time that both supporters and the opposition believed there was a chance of opening up trade relations with Mercosur. During this time the EU was deciding whether or not to approve the directives. Furthermore, a series of meetings were held between the EU and Mercosur in order to resolve a number of technical issues. Some of these meetings happened within the framework of the EU–Rio Group annual meetings. At one of these annual meetings it was decided that a summit for the heads of state of the EU and Latin America would be held in 1999. This decision would prove to be an important moment in the development of EU–Mercosur relations.

This section will now explain, firstly, what happened during the negotiations of the directives, before going on to discuss the actors who were either in favour or opposed to the association agreement. This will shed some light in relation to the following questions: Why did it take so many years to approve the directives? Who was involved? Was it difficult to reach a consensus within Mercosur? During this period of the policy, how involved was Spain and Spanish officials in Brussels, especially Manuel Marin before he left the Commission? To what extent did the EU perception of Mercosur change during this period? And finally, was this agreement really Mercosur's top priority, and if so, why?

How to delay a decision until the last minute

As mentioned above, the creation of the directives took several years to be approved. Meanwhile, representatives of both the EU and Mercosur held meetings, during which time they resolved many of the technical issues related to future negotiations. In addition to this, these meetings helped to maintain the momentum that had been created and avoided a watering-down of the promises behind the EMIFCA. The derailing of the whole process was a possibility, given how comments coming from both sides relating to the agricultural sector had created tensions in EU–Mercosur relations at certain moments.

As a consequence of the signing of EMIFCA in 1995, a Joint Committee with representatives from both the EU and Mercosur was created. The Joint Committee held its first meeting in mid-June 1996. Its task was 'preparing the ground for future trade liberalisation, approve the protocol for customs cooperation currently on the table, examine the rules for the functioning of consultation intended to settle trade problems, and examine the main avenues of trade cooperation' (Agence Europe 17/4/1996). The first sign of just how problematic the agriculture issue had become was clear after the inaugural meeting of the EU–Mercosur, when farmers' representatives met in Brussels in mid-June 1996. On the one side, Mercosur's position 'allowed for agricultural trade issues to be tackled in a realistic fashion and less ideologically' (Agence Europe 18/6/1996). On the other side, the European farmers, grouped under the Committee of European Agricultural Organization (COPA), were more reserved, stating, 'We are in favour of more liberalized trade but under harmonized social and environmental conditions' (Agence Europe 18/6/1996). With this, COPA tried to put in place some obstacles to developing inter-regional trade by highlighting EU regulations that did not exist in Mercosur countries in relation to social and environmental issues.

Mercosur went further and asked to hold meetings twice a year, a proposal that was rejected by the Europeans, who claimed that these discussions should take place within the International Federation of Agricultural Producers, as well as claiming that Mercosur farmers were too divided to be able to develop a common position (Agence Europe 18/6/1996). In any case, in December 1996 the EU and Mercosur signed a cooperation agreement (Agence Europe 16/4/1998), a sign of the enduring desire and persistent efforts aimed at further developing EU–Mercosur relations. The creation of the Joint Committee was a good indicator of the level of ambition shown by the EU. The content of the meetings held by that committee and the actions developed in the framework will show the level of commitment on the EU's side. It is clear that COPA opposed from the very beginning any agreement with Mercosur that included the agricultural sector. However, when discussing EU engagement, we are looking at the EU and its members, not to third parties that tried to influence the EU (sometimes successfully) and therefore the EU engagement.

The commissioner in charge of Latin America, Manuel Marin, was working on the evolution of EMIFCA and announced that by the end of 1997 both sides would assess the first phase of the agreement. Marin also requested that 'political arbitration' be given to the Council in 1998 in order to provide a brief for moving into the negotiation on trade liberalization (Agence Europe 9/4/1997). The calendar prepared by Marin was welcomed by Mercosur countries apart from Uruguay. Whilst three Mercosur countries had already ratified the agreement, only three EU member states had done so (Agence Europe 9/4/1997). As a result, an entire section of the agreement which is under shared responsibility had not been enforced and the Joint Committee had not been able to meet formally to discuss the liberalization of services and intellectual property since it was fully under the states' competence (Agence Europe 9/4/1997). As has been explained, if there is no ratification of an agreement, the negotiations cannot start. The lack of progress in the ratification of the agreement had a clear impact on the activities of the Joint Committee, Therefore, it could be said that the commitment shown by the EU did not match the expectations of either the Joint Committee or Mercosur since both were interested in starting the negotiations.

By November 1997, the Trade Subcommittee of the Joint Committee met in Uruguay to analyse trade flows since 1990 in the 'area of goods and services, and practices related to trade standards and disciplines' (Agence Europe 19/12/1997). This analysis would be used by the Commission for its proposal for a negotiating brief. 'In accordance with the agreed calendar, the technical working groups finalised their work in April 1998. The assessment served as a background document for the negotiation of the interregional association agreement between the European Community and Mercosur' (Adiwasito et al. 2006: 8). By early 1998, it was becoming more difficult for the EU representatives to justify to Mercosur countries the lack of agreement. The EU created things such as a 'photograph' or snapshot of trade relations. The snapshot was simply a mechanism to save face (Interviewee 1). Once the snapshot was completed, it was expected that a political decision would be taken (Agence Europe 14/5/1998). In a way, the EU was trying to create some extra time to reach a decision, whilst Mercosur was putting more and more pressure on the EU to reach a decision more quickly. Again the Joint Committee tried its best to keep alive the 'intention' set up with the 1995 signature of EMIFCA but so far the commitment shown did not match the expectations.

On top of the problems relating to ratification by the member states, some commissioners to the Council voiced their opposition to the proposal in relation to the negotiation mandate led by Mr Marin. The resistance came from the two French commissioners, Edith Cresson and Yves-Thibault de Silguy, and the German commissioner of agricultural, Franz Fischler. Their opposition stemmed from the sensitive nature of agricultural issues for their particular countries (*El País* 9/7/1998). In fact, Fischler asked for an extension of a week to analyse the impact of the liberalization of the EU agricultural market (*El País* 9/7/1998).

The situation became even more difficult when France and Germany took the issue to the Council of Ministers. According to a spokesperson for the French government, it was argued that the liberalization of trade between the regions posed a 'great real and potential risk for the Union agriculture model' (*El País* 21/7/1998). On a more positive note, the UK, Denmark and Sweden supported Mr Marin's project (*El País* 21/7/1998). Another problem for Brussels was that the rules established at international level would also influence the nature of their trade agreements. The WTO explicitly said in its Article XXIV that FTAs between its members must substantially cover all trade. It has been accepted in the literature that this means that the FTA must cover around 90% (Griffith 2006) or between 80% and 90% (Hilpold 2003) of the total trade, and that no individual sectors should be left out of the agreement, and that agreements should be implemented 'within a reasonable length of time' (agreed interpretation is ten years except in exceptional circumstances) (Griffith 2006). It appeared that Brussels wanted to exclude 13.9% of the trade negotiations, but due to the WTO rules it had to cover 90% of trade negotiations (*El País* 21/7/1998). Leaving aside the matter of percentage of trade to be covered, it was by now clear that the EU wanted to omit agriculture from the negotiations, whilst Mercosur, especially Brazil, was particularly insistent that agricultural issues were included.

On 22 July 1998 a decision was finally taken. The Commission passed a recommendation to the Council asking for a negotiating brief for Mercosur even though four commissioners, Fischler, de Silguy, Cresson and Flynn, voted against it (*El País* 23/7/1998, Agence Europe 24/7/1998; Interviewees 10 and 15). After this the Council was the one that had to decide this issue. Yves Doutriaux, spokesman for the French foreign minister, could not have been clearer when he stated:

> France will, at Council level, point out its stance on the inappropriateness of this Commission proposal as conceived. While fundamentally in favour of deepening relations between Europe, Mercosur and Chile, in the framework of the agreements signed in 95 and 96, France considers that the Commission's proposal does not take account of the major hurdles facing the Union, especially Agenda 2000 and the preparation of negotiations within the World Trade Organizations. The establishment of a free trade area proposed by the

Commission, moreover, poses a problem of compatibility with the Union's common policies, and foremost the common agricultural policy and the European model of agriculture, reaffirmed by last December's European Council. It could considerably further burden the Union's budget, in the order of several tens of billions of francs a year. The Council of Agriculture Ministers already expressed its concerns on this issue on 20 July. (Agence Europe 24/7/1998)

This statement explains why the French were looking to develop a different kind of relationship with Mercosur. It also shows that the French would object to the proposal as it stood at that particular time. French complaints were repeated but this time by the president of France, Jacques Chirac. At the same time, in 1997 it was agreed to arrange a summit of the heads of state of the EU and Latin America. This suggestion, put forward by Spain and France after the annual meeting with the Rio Group, was accepted and was to be held before 1999. Being the first summit of that kind, it put extra pressure on the EU. During the first six months of 1999, the presidency of the EU was held by Germany. Up until this point, Germany had tried to get the directives approved in the General Affairs Council on 31 May 1999 in order to avoid going to the Rio Summit with nothing to offer to Mercosur (Agence Europe 27/5/1999). The summit was to be held in Rio de Janeiro on 28–29 June 1999. Two weeks before the General Affairs Council, France and the UK were attempting to halt any progress in relation to the directive (*El País* 12/5/1999).

Wording issues also became important. France, Ireland and the UK refused the term 'free trade area' and suggested the 'possibility of a free trade area' (Agence Europe 27/5/1999). In contrast, Spain and Portugal explicitly wanted the words 'free trade area' in order to maintain the political impact of the agreement, whilst the German presidency proposed the phrase 'tend towards free trade' which was also supported by the Benelux and Scandinavian countries (Agence Europe 27/5/1999). The French explanation for this language issue, according to Yves Doutriau was:

We have framework agreements with Mercosur and Chile that need to be followed up with more specific agreements. In these framework-agreements, it was agreed that there would be a gradual and reciprocal liberalisation of trade. These framework agreements did not provide for the establishment of a free-trade agreement. There is now a Commission proposal that does not comply with what was agreed, what was the subject of an agreement between the European Union and the countries of Mercosur. Reciprocal and gradual liberalisation does not mean a free-trade area. We have never said anything else. (Agence Europe 24/7/1998)

On 31 May, as a result of France's position on this matter, the General Affairs Council failed to reach an agreement (Agence Europe 31/5/1999). The next attempt to approve the text before the summit in Rio took place at the Cologne Summit on 3–4 June. At this point it was clear that France, Ireland and the UK were against the agreement. These three countries felt that the negotiations should not start before they knew the results of the agriculture negotiations at the WTO (Agence Europe 1/6/1999). Apart from the 'free trade' words, another issue was impeding the approval: the creation of a timetable to start the negotiations. The German presidency proposed to start negotiations on non-tariff issues in the second half of 1999 and negotiations on tariff reductions and services before 1 December 2000 (Agence Europe 1/6/1999). A group of countries supported the German proposal on timetables, but Spain, Portugal and Sweden wanted to start negotiations on tariff issues as soon as possible, in addition to accepting the German proposal as long as the objective of a free trade area was clearly indicated in the directive (Agence Europe 1/6/1999). Italy also supported the proposal, which confirmed that there was a balance between the different member states in relation to the extreme positions in favour of or against the agreement. However, France rejected the idea of starting negotiations on tariff issues by 1 December 2000, proposing instead that negotiations be started on 1 July 2003, the date by which they predicted the WTO negotiations would have concluded (Agence Europe 1/6/1999). The UK also wanted to wait until the end of the WTO negotiations, whilst Paris insisted that negotiations on the FTA objective be eliminated from the negotiating brief (Agence Europe 1/6/1999).

The Cologne Summit did not resolve these issues and Chirac vetoed the German proposal of splitting the dates for starting negotiations (*El País* 6/6/1999). Chirac explained that until the end of the WTO negotiations, which he expected to be concluded by 2003, he did not want to discuss anything because doing so would jeopardize a million tonnes of French sugar (*El País* 6/6/1999). Nevertheless, it was verbally agreed that this issue would be discussed again during the Council meeting on 21 June 1999 (*El País* 6/6/1999), although hopes were not high that these issues would be resolved at this meeting, which would take place just four days before the summit with the heads of state of Latin America in Rio. In addition to this situation in Europe, in Latin America there was pressure for an agreement. In fact, at this point, Jorio Dauster, a former Brazilian ambassador to Brussels, stated very clearly, 'Mercosur must make no concessions to the EU as long as this economic bloc maintains its protectionist position in relation to Latin American exports' (Agence Europe 10/6/1999). In relation to France, Dauster claimed that 'Its attitude is surprising after all this diplomatic work ... Globalization discourse is increasingly false and hypocritical. The rich countries are not globalizing because they are not opening their markets, especially agriculture' (Agence Europe 10/6/1999).

Finally, when it seemed that all hope was lost, the unexpected happened. On 21 June 1999 an agreement was reached. In the preceding days, Spain had further pressed France for a possible agreement (Agence Europe

21/6/1999). It seems that the pressure put on the French embassies in Latin America had some influence in addition to the pressure being mounted by the Commission and Spain (*El País* 22/6/1999). In the end, it was agreed that the negotiation on tariff reductions and services would begin on 1 July 2001 (Agence Europe 21/6/1999). The pressure exerted on France appears to have had an impact because France eventually accepted an offer that was worse than the one offered to them during the Cologne Summit, when the Germans had proposed negotiations started on 1 July 2002, after the French elections (*El País* 22/6/1999). However, France was able to secure one of its objectives – that the negotiations could not be concluded before the WTO round (Agence Europe 24/6/1999). At the diplomatic level, France continued to pursue this issue. Firstly, during the Rio Summit, Chirac argued that: 'Against what I have read lately, I reiterate that France supports without reservation the beginning of these negotiations, because they correspond to our strategic view in the long term' (*El País* 29/6/1999).

However, during the Rio Summit the EU asked that the Council of Ministers' mandate that was passed to the EU Commission be included word for word in the joint communication of EU–Mercosur. This request was refused by Mercosur because it was considered an internal EU document (Agence Europe 29/6/1999) and therefore had nothing to do with Mercosur. The directives were approved officially by the General Affairs Council in September 1999 (Agence Europe 15/9/1999).

This section has shown how, in terms of ambition, the EU was divided, with Spain and Portugal and the Spanish commissioner having great ambition, Germany, the Benelux and Scandinavian countries having medium ambition and Ireland, France and their commissioners having very low ambition. As a consequence, the EU had a medium level of ambition overall, since most of the countries were somewhere in between the two positions. In relation to commitment, there is a similar picture, giving a medium level of commitment.

Again, success in this part of the policy was due to the pressure that Mercosur countries exerted on the French embassies in their countries, together with the pressure created with the first summit of the heads of state between Latin America and the EU. The suggestion for another summit came from Latin America, and Mercosur was very keen on promoting this summit, as they showed in the Joint Committees. This undermines the level of ambition attributed to the EU in its policy towards Mercosur.

The path dependence is once again clear if we look at the behaviour of Marin – the Spanish commissioner called the 'father' of the agreement – and the drive of Spain and Portugal towards a positive agreement with Mercosur. The impact of the Iberian membership of the EU at this stage is underestimated in the literature. As this monograph has explained, the impact was more long-lasting than any other study has yet considered – it influenced both the second and third stage of the policy.

EMIFCA's external negotiations: the negotiations with Mercosur for the association agreement

The negotiations between Mercosur and the EU towards an association agreement were the most problematic of the whole EU policy covered in this monograph. This was mainly due to the lack of interest the EU showed in Mercosur's agricultural sector. The fact that the teams of negotiators did not have complementary goals and were trying to get the best deal without sacrificing their own market competitiveness only complicated matters. In fact, playing around with their options led to the negotiations being characterized as a 'poker game' (see Russau 2005). At this stage, the EU was trying to protect its agricultural sector from the extreme competitiveness of Brazilian and Argentinean agricultural products. Similarly, Mercosur countries were trying to protect other sectors of their own national and regional economies. Furthermore, EU–Mercosur negotiations were not helped by the Doha Round of the WTO negotiations. This part of the policy lowers tremendously the level of EU commitment because the EU was not willing to overcome the obstacle of agricultural negotiations. Also, the EU's level of ambition was not very high since it linked the EU–Mercosur negotiations to the WTO negotiations in a way that set the limits of the outcome of the EU–Mercosur agreement before the negotiations started. The level of engagement in this part of the policy lowers the previous levels.

EU–Mercosur negotiation meetings

As has already been discussed, Mercosur refused to include the Council's negotiating mandate on a word-for-word basis. During the ministerial meeting of February 2000, before the first EU–Mercosur Biregional Negotiations Committee meeting, Mercosur countries insisted that they were not bound by that mandate and that they wanted the negotiations to address all issues (Agence Europe 24/2/2000). In the area of political dialogue, it was argued that:

> Political co-operation between the Parties should cover the aspects of mutual interest and any other international issue the Parties should consider appropriate to discuss in their Political Dialogue: Particularly, on the grounds of peace and stability, prevention of conflicts, confidence and security building measures, promotion and protection of Human Rights, democracy and the Rule of law, sustainable development taking into account economic, social and environmental dimensions, common action against drug trafficking and related felonies, arms trafficking, organized crime and international terrorism. (EU–Mercosur 2000a)

This statement makes it clear that Mercosur felt that the negotiations 'should consider [it] appropriate to discuss' a full range of topics, but the objectives in this area are not clear. In the area of cooperation, there was more organization and a number of groups were created in order to ensure the 'smooth functioning of negotiations' (EU–Mercosur 2000a). Furthermore, in the area of cooperation the structure of the discussion is clearer than in the area of political dialogue, implying that in this area both sides had a clear set of aims. The following subgroups were created at this meeting:

1 In relation to the Subgroup on Economic Co-operation: industrial co-operation, co-operation on technical regulations and conformity assessment, co-operation in the field of services, investment promotion, macro-economic dialogue, scientific and technological co-operation, energy co-operation, transports, telecommunications, information technology and information society, co-operation on agricultural and rural sector fisheries, customs co-operation, statistic co-operation, environmental co-operation, consumer protection and data protection;
2 In relation to the Subgroup on Social and Cultural Co-operation: social co-operation, education and training, social dialogue, drugs and related organised crime, cultural co-operation;
3 In relation to the Subgroup on Financial and Technical Co-operation: public administration modernisation, inter-institutional co-operation, co-operation on regional integration. (EU–Mercosur 2000a)

Finally, in the area of trade, the most important area in this agreement, it was considered essential that this agreement had proper organization and that these negotiations were planned in greater depth than the negotiations relating to cooperation. In order to achieve this, the following technical groups were created:

1 Technical Group 1: trade in goods, covering both tariffs and non-tariff measures, including inter alia sanitary and phytosanitary measures, standards, technical regulations and conformity assessment procedures; antidumping and counter-vailing duties and safeguards, rules of origin, and customs procedures and mutual assistance in customs matters;
2 Technical Group 2: trade in services, intellectual property rights and measures to encourage an open and non-discriminatory investment climate;
3 Technical Group 3: government procurement, competition and dispute settlement. (EU–Mercosur 2000a)

It is clear that these trade discussions were far more wide-reaching and based on objectives that were both clear and straightforward. For example, these trade discussions aimed to develop the: 'Exchange of information in all areas of negotiations; Discussion on specific objectives and modalities on non-tariff measures; Ways of addressing non-tariff obstacles to trade;

and exchange of working texts' (EU–Mercosur 2000a). Furthermore, the unofficial discussion of non-tariff trade in the first meeting, although it could not start officially until July 2001, proves the interest in developing trade. Table 6.1 gives a timeline of the meetings and discussions, in parallel with the development of the WTO

The Mercosur–EU Business Forum (MEBF) mentioned in the seventh meeting was established in 1999 to provide an informal forum for business people to identify what they regarded as the key issues in the trade and industrial relationship between the two regions. This forum was also created to develop recommendations to the public authorities of both regions, on steps that could be taken to improve market access, facilitate business dealings and encourage investment (European Commission 1999). The twelfth meeting, which took place prior to the third summit of heads of state from the EU and Latin America in Guadalajara, was working towards the deadline of October 2004. The Guadalajara Summit included a discussion on the offers exchanged prior to the summit. On 21 May 2004, the EU had prepared an improved offer on agriculture which would allow

Table 6.1 Timeline of EU–Mercosur meetings and the evolution of the WTO

EU–Mercosur meeting	WTO	*Content of meeting*
First meeting, Buenos Aires, April 2000	Seattle, 1999	Political dialogue: very broad and ambiguous during the discussions.
Second meeting, Brussels, June 2000		Political dialogue: agreement reached for an exchange of texts in relation to the third meeting. Cooperation: meetings of the different groups and discussions but nothing specific was agreed. Trade: exchange of information and the setting of some deadlines: • By 30 June: both sides to exchange a list of names of experts in order to facilitate information exchange; • By 31 July: information requests identified at the second round to be submitted; • By 31 July: analysis of information submitted so far and submission of follow-up questions; • By 30 September: both sides to submit new information requested in the follow-up questions, and the EU to submit a proposal regarding specific objectives.

Table 6.1 Timeline of EU–Mercosur meetings and the evolution of the WTO—cont'd

EU–Mercosur meeting	WTO	*Content of meeting*
Third meeting, Brussels, June 2000		Political dialogue: exchange of negotiating texts which was the basis for a draft of a joint text. Cooperation: less positive than in the political dialogue. Trade: more progress with the three technical groups working on specific issues and agreeing to send draft documents a month before the next meeting.
Fourth meeting, Brussels, March 2001	Doha Round, 2001	Political dialogue: discussion on the draft Mercosur had presented at the previous meeting and the draft that the EU sent in advance of the meeting. Cooperation: some joint texts were produced in the field of social and cultural cooperation to be discussed in the following meeting. Trade: this group worked intensively and focused on the proposals put forward by both delegations. Also they agreed that experts from both sides would work together continuously and send proposals a month in advance of the following meeting.
Fifth meeting, Montevideo, July 2001		Political dialogue: discussed draft joint texts. Cooperation: the subgroup on economic cooperation agreed on joint drafts in the area of customs cooperation, competition cooperation, statistics cooperation and scientific and technological cooperation. The subgroup on social and cultural cooperation also agreed on texts in the field of cooperation in combating drugs and related organized crime. Trade: The EU presented its offer on tariffs and negotiating texts for good, services and procurement, including a progressive and reciprocal liberalization without excluding any sector during a period of 10 years.
Sixth meeting, Brussels, October 2001		Political dialogue: more talks were held. Economic cooperation: more joint texts on the economic cooperation group were produced but nothing specific was agreed. Trade: An offer from Mercosur was presented in response to the offer presented by the EU during the previous meeting.

Continued

Table 6.1 Timeline of EU–Mercosur meetings and the evolution of the WTO—cont'd

EU–Mercosur meeting	*WTO*	*Content of meeting*
Seventh meeting, Buenos Aires, April 2002		Political dialogue: agreed to improve the political and cooperation area of the negotiations as well as measures for business facilitation. Cooperation: the analysis was focused on the draft on the principles, objectives, nature and scope of the association, political dialogue and institutional framework. Parties examined the incorporation of the principle of 'good governance' and the regularity and content of meetings of heads of state and government. Trade: progress in the area of business facilitation where they analysed 'trade facilitation measures with a view to their adoption in Madrid, taking into consideration the recommendations of the Mercosur–EU Business Forum. These included customs, standards, regulations and conformity assessment, sanitary and phytosanitary measures, and electronic commerce' (EU–Mercosur 2002a).
Eighth meeting, Brasilia, November 2002		Tariffs: there was discussion relating to the methodology for market access and the EU made some offers, reminding Mercosur of the target date of 28 February 2003 agreed by both sides; Customs procedures: there was discussion of the EU proposal as well as a discussion on the negotiations of the regulation of the rules of origin. Services: there was a broad discussion on the objectives in this area and in relation to intellectual property rights. Both sides presented their proposals, which were circulated before the meeting, first by Mercosur in March and then by the EU in October. Competition: the discussion was focused on a proposal made by the EU, leading to a consolidation paper being produced. Dispute settlement: both parties followed Mercosur's text prepared on 9 October, but this time the EU offered to prepare a proposal for the next meeting instead of agreeing completely on the one produced by Mercosur. Business facilitation: indepth discussion of the proposal presented by Mercosur on the implementation of the measures agreed in Madrid.

Table 6.1 Timeline of EU–Mercosur meetings and the evolution of the WTO—cont'd

EU–Mercosur meeting	WTO	Content of meeting
Ninth meeting, Brussels, March 2003		Tariff offers: completed. There was a discussion relating to the Action Plan on Business Facilitation, cooperation for development, sustainable development and EU enlargement.
Tenth meeting, Asunción, June 2003	Cancún Round, September 2003	Tariff offers: some requests to improve the tariff offers on government procurement. The EU could not discuss anything without a Mercosur offer, but Mercosur was ready to discuss the methodology in the absence of offers.
Eleventh meeting, Brussels, December 2003		More discussion on the progress of different working groups.
Twelfth meeting, Buenos Aires, March 2004		'Commitment' to improve offers a month after that meeting.
Thirteenth meeting, Brussels, May 2004	Annex A of 2004, July package	Hervé Juoanjean, the deputy director general of the Commission, highlighted the extreme importance for Brussels of this meeting to exchange improved offers on services, investment, government procurement and goods, including agriculture.
	Hong Kong, 2005	

Sources: EU–Mercosur (2000a, 2000b, 2000c, 2001a, 2001b, 2001c, 2002a, 2002b, 2003a, 2003b, 2004a, 2004b).

duty-free and preferential treatment that would cover more than 99% of current imports of agricultural products to the EU from Mercosur (European Commission 2004). It was possible to complete the agreement in October 2004 because of the extra effort expended in the final few months by both the EU and Mercosur.

The foundations for negotiations were 'on the table', according to Commissioner Franz Fischler before the Guadalajara Summit (Agence Europe 27/5/2004). In June, Commissioner Pascal Lamy did not rule out the idea of asking the Council to eliminate the link between the EU–Mercosur discussion and the WTO negotiations if there was enough progress since its discussions with Chile were already completed in that vein (Agence Europe 28/5/2004). At this point, France was once again showing its opposition to the agreement by claiming that the situation was far from being concluded, at what was a very sensitive moment in the negotiations and just days before a deadlock was created (Agence Europe 1/6/2004). Other actors present at the Biregional Negotiations Committee meetings were expecting there to be a successful ending to these discussions. However, the deadlock was created at the next meeting, in June 2004. This did not seem to worry Karl Falkenberg (the director general of trade) too much because he confirmed that there was no reason to think that there would not be a successful conclusion by October 2004 (Agence Europe 29/6/2004). The deadlock remained following the meeting held in July. In August, both sides started to blame each other for the continuing stalemate. Mercosur complained that the EU was not offering enough in terms of agricultural negotiations, whilst the Commission claimed that Mercosur's offer on public tendering and services did not match EU expectations (Agence Europe 10/8/2004). At the end of September 2004, Mercosur put forward a new offer which was studied carefully by the Commission and individual EU member states in the Article 133 Committee (Agence Europe 28/9/2004). A few days later, the EU improved its offer at the last minute, leaving almost no time for further negotiation, which suggests that the EU probably expected its offer to be accepted by Mercosur. It might be argued that the EU could have been more flexible during the negotiations. The fact that there was a possibility of breaking the link between these negotiations and the WTO negotiations but it was not pursued, shows a low level of commitment.

When October arrived, Portugal was the holder of the EU presidency. Despite this, there was no last-minute agreement this time, as had happened 1999 with the negotiation mandate. On this occasion, the blame was directed at Argentina because it decided, at the last minute, to wait to see what would happen in the WTO, much to the dismay of Pascal Lamy, who wanted to reach an agreement before his departure from the EU Commission (Interviewees 7 and 8). Therefore, it seems that both Falkenberg and Lamy had high expectations that there would be a successful ending to the negotiations. It could also be argued that both Falkenberg and Lamy offered as much as they thought it would take to get Mercosur to accept the offer, even though neither made any further last-minute offers in order to secure an agreement. This might be seen as a typical behaviour when negotiating trade agreements, but it reduces the level of ambition to reach an agreement since it seems that they could have done much more.

The negotiations and the WTO

In the discussion above it was suggested that the negotiations were intentionally linked to the outcome of the WTO negotiations in terms of the mandate that the EU Council gave to the Commission. However, the Commission did consider asking the Council to take that link out of the directives during the negotiations. There were many offers, and there is not room here to discuss the technicalities of the negotiations, but Table 6.2 provides an outline of the offer made by the EU in September 2004. This was the most significant offer because it is the last offer to be made by the EU and is clearly linked to the WTO negotiations.

Table 6.2 EU tariff-rate quotas offer, September 2004

Product	Duty	Quantity (tons)	
		1st step EU–Mercosur agreement	2nd step WTO negotiation
Bovine meat	10%	60,000	40,000
Pork meat	€125/tonne net (5%–10% AVE)	6,000	5,000
Poultry meat	€49.7/tonne net (1%–5% AVE)	45,000	30,000
Milk and cream powder	€640/tonne net (30%–66% AVE)	6,500	6,500
Butter	€434/tonne net (19%–21% AVE)	2,000	2,000
Cheese	€401.4/ tonne net (7%–17% AVE)	10,000	10,000
Garlic	4.8%	6,000	4,000
Bananas	€37.5/tonne net (12% AVE)	30,000	0
Low quality wheat	€6/tonne (5% AVE)	120,000	80,000
Maize	€24.5/tonne (4%–8% AVE)	400,000	300,000
Rice	€29/tonne (7%–17% AVE)	26,000	14,000
Ethanol	$5.1–9.7/hl (9%–23% AVE)	600,000	400,000

Source: Kutas (2006).
Note: AVE: ad valorem equivalent (a tariff that is not a percentage (e.g. €/tonne) can be estimated as a percentage of the price using the ad valorem equivalent.

During the first step (see Table 6.2),

> [The tariff-rate quotas] will be carried out through equal instalments over a
> period of 10 years, starting from the entry into force of the agreement ... As
> regards the second quantity, the volume granted to Mercosur is linked to the
> WTO negotiations in the Doha Round because the EU does not want to 'pay
> twice'. As a consequence, the second quantity that Mercosur will effectively
> obtain will be inversely linked to the increase in the current volume of the
> EU WTO TRQs [tariff-rate quotas] that will be negotiated at the WTO. For
> every percentage point of increase in the EU bound WTO TRQs, the second
> quantity devoted to Mercosur shall be reduced by a corresponding five per-
> centage points. Therefore, if no increase of EU bound TRQs is negotiated at
> the Doha Round, Mercosur shall be granted the full second quantity men-
> tioned ... Conversely, if the Doha Round results in an increase equal or
> superior to 20%, no second quantity shall be given to Mercosur. Finally, if
> an increase of 10% of the bound TRQs is negotiated at the WTO, Mercosur
> shall be granted half of the second quantity. (Kutas 2006: 37)

As pointed out by Kutas (2006), an increase in imports in the WTO
negotiations does not necessarily mean that Mercosur would be the one
obtaining the increase since it will compete with the other WTO members.
In other words, an agreement within the WTO includes other actors,
therefore, the amount of imports that the EU will allow to enter the
European market in certain conditions is offered to all the WTO members.
However, the EU–Mercosur negotiations only allow Mercosur countries to
have access to the European market under the conditions agreed.

Lack of interest: lack of commitment and ambition?

In terms of interest shown by the EU towards Mercosur, EU Commissioner
Chris Patten explained what could be considered to be the official line since
the same speech was given by a member of the Council Secretariat (Interviewee 4) and a permanent representative of a country (Interviewee 9).
Patten claimed that

> Mercosur is today an area of peace, progress and growing prosperity. It may
> still have many challenges to overcome (economic development, social justice,
> and environmental degradation). But its efforts during the past decade to
> restore democracy, and the respect of human rights, and to restructure and
> open up its economies are to be applauded. Some say that the European Union
> does not sufficiently recognise this reality. They say we do not assign sufficient
> priority to its relationship with the Mercosur countries delegating them to a
> second division when it comes to the attention we pay them. I would like to
> answer those critics honestly. I say to you: there is inevitably some truth in
> that Mercosur takes up less of the European Union's time than other parts of
> the world. And we – and the countries of Mercosur – should be grateful for
> that. Because Mercosur does not need to be a priority like the gruesome war

in Kosovo. Or the bloody slaughter in Chechnya. Or the killing fields in Rwanda. Or the human misery following Hurricane Mitch. (EU–Mercosur 2000c)

Despite acknowledging that the EU had not given Mercosur the same attention as other regions, the speech outlined an argument for why the EU had not done so. Patten failed to mention why other countries that were former colonies of the UK and France, such as ACP countries or the Mediterranean countries, or even ASEAN countries, had a larger share of the EU's attention than other regions such as Mercosur.

Within the EP, the view was different from the one put forward by Patten. For example, José Ignacio Salafranca, a Spanish MEP, argued that 'discrimination towards this [Latin America] continent in EU external relations is not justified' (Agence Europe 1/3/2001). In relation to discrimination, a Brazilian ambassador pointed out that 'it is a well-known fact that the Member States are less enthusiastic about these negotiations than the Commission' (Agence Europe 7/11/2002). During the negotiations, Spanish MEPs Marset Campos and Salafranca also directed their comments directly at Commissioner Patten. The MEPs provided a report with suggestions for changing the negotiating mandate. This report requested a specification of the legal basis of the agreement and the elimination of the link to the WTO (Agence Europe 8/2/2001). As has already been noted, the negotiation mandate did not change, and in 2001 Patten was not ready even to contemplate the type of change that Lamy considered in 2004. In addition to this, the link between the agreement negotiations and the WTO negotiations still remained intact. In relation to the legal basis, Patten explained that it was not going to be just a mere trade agreement, but an association agreement (European Commission 2001a; Agence Europe 1/3/2001). Furthermore, he also stated that the exact articles for the legal basis could only be determined at the end of the negotiations, as had been done during similar negotiations (European Commission 2001a; Agence Europe 1/3/2001). The EP also asked for the discussions to be based on Article 310 (ex Article 238) (Agence Europe 1/3/2001).

In the previous chapter there was an analysis of the legal base for the agreements compared to other EU agreements. It was clear from Patten's comments (on the negotiations with the WTO) that it would continue to be ambiguous and imprecise. When an agreement is so ambiguous and open to interpretation as this one was, the personal commitment and diplomatic skills of the individuals involved can carry enormous weight. But having in mind the lack of interest in Mercosur, in this case it has to be assumed that there was a lack of ambition, characterized by the ambiguous nature of the agreement.

This shows that the EU may not have had a clear strategy because once again it appears that if Mercosur wanted to develop a broader relationship with the EU then Mercosur would have to be the one demanding such a relationship and would also have to be the flexible side during the negotiations. It could also be argued that this was yet another occasion where the EU assumed the role of the reactive actor that simply responded to the demands of Mercosur in a way that appeared to depend upon who was in charge of the EU's negotiation team. Furthermore, it seems that the success of these negotiations may have depended upon the EU negotiator rather than the EU having a clear and coherent policy agenda. This argument is supported by the fact there was so much disagreement between EU member states. This lack of strategy does not help to support a good level of ambition.

This section has shown again the importance given by the Spanish and Portuguese in the Commission or the EP to these negotiations. It is clear that the efforts of the Iberian countries in the different EU institutions helped to advance EU–Mercosur negotiations. Again this reflects the path dependence created with the Iberian membership of the EU.

After the failure to reach an agreement in October 2004, the next important stage in EU–Latin American relations and policy development was the political partnership that the EU offered to Brazil in 2008. This was part of the EU's strategy which aimed to establish new political partnerships with the leaders in other regions such as Brazil, Russia, India and China. Although this was the official line, one interviewee (Interviewee 9) claimed that this was a direct decision taken by the president of the Commission, José Manuel Barroso. It seems that Argentina asked for a similar agreement but it was not accepted.

The role of other actors

This section will examine the role played by the other actors during this stage of EU–Mercosur relations and policy development. It begins by considering the role of the EU Commission and various commissioners and moves on to discuss the role played by civil society.

The Commission and commissioners

The reasons for each commissioner's support or opposition for the agreement had different roots. The Spanish commissioner, Marin, was the most involved in the agreement and his support was not matched by the others. Marin left his post in 1999 when the whole Commission resigned under allegations of corruption; it has been proved since then that he was not involved in the corruption case at all. The negotiations restarted, but there was more trouble ahead for EU–Mercosur relations. Arguably, with Marin still in charge of the portfolio, the agreement could have been reached. Marin played an important role until two of the most difficult aspects of the agreements were successfully resolved. He proved to be very persistent during the negotiations leading to the signature of EMIFCA, as well as being very determined at the beginning of the negotiations in 1999. The predisposition of the Spanish commissioner during the negotiations was very different to that of other commissioners, particularly in relation to trade issues (Interviewee 2). Spanish commissioners were said to be more willing to give better offers, as well as being prepared to tell Mercosur actors that other commissioners would not be willing to do the same (Interviewees 1 and 2). Furthermore, the attitude and skills of individual negotiators is a variable that tends to be underestimated when analysing the success or failure of these cases (Interviewee 2).

Chris Patten argued that 'What is at stake in the negotiations between the EU and Mercosur is the possibility for a strategic, political and economic alliance between the only two real common markets in the world' (EU–Mercosur 2000c). Using phrases and terms such as 'alliance' and 'the only two real markets in the world', Patten's statement appears to suggest that the actions of the EU were very much part of a clear strategy. It sounds as if EU relations with Mercosur were based on the EU's interests and the EU's position in the world. However, Patten later went on to adopt a more normative position when claiming that

> The prospective association agreement will not only provide for short-term financial gains and closer political ties. It will create a free trade area covering nearly 600 million people. By doing this, it will generate democratic development, growing prosperity and respect of human rights. Where prosperity reigns, democracy and human rights can take firm root. (EU–Mercosur 2000c)

These claims appear to focus more on the idea of promoting human rights, democracy based on the economic development of a region, which is normal. Patten then went on to claim: 'A fair distribution of wealth and the elimination of extreme poverty make sense not only politically, but also economically: with increases in consumption capacity comes new investment possibilities' (EU–Mercosur 2000c).

Nowhere in this speech does Patten appear to provide a clear reason for an association agreement in terms of political or trade interests. It could be argued that this ambiguity was due to the lack of a real EU strategy prior to this agreement and the fact that the EU had adopted the role of being reactive to Mercosur requests. The requests that the Mercosur put forward to the EU were channelled through Marin, who was extremely committed to improving EU–Mercosur relations. In fact, in Latin America some diplomats complained that Patten was less sensitive to the problems of the region than Manuel Marin (*El País* 17/11/2002). When Marin had to leave after the problematic Santer Commission, cooperation and aid to the region decreased tremendously (*El País* 15/7/2000). Under Prodi, the number of staff in the Latin America section of the Commission was less than half of previous levels (*El País* 15/7/2000).

In contrast to Patten, Pascal Lamy, the trade commissioner, considered EU–Mercosur policy to be of great strategic importance to the EU. In 2000, Argentina complained about the absence of high-level European representatives during the EU–Mercosur meetings held on the fringes of the UN Assembly. When the MEBF scheduled for September 2000 was cancelled, Lamy responded by saying that 'increasing the pressure is part of the tactics' of negotiation – as if the cancellation was nothing more than a game. He continued, 'The negotiations will take time. The Mercosur is very complicated: compared to it, the European Union seems to be a monster of simplicity. We have a mandate from the Council that we are following' (Agence Europe 20/9/2000).

It would also seem that Lamy's trip to Brazil was of strategic importance. For example, he claimed that, 'As a central pillar of both Mercosur and the WTO, Brazil is a unique and essential partner for the EU. During my visit I look forward to further cementing our trading relationship in both the regional and multilateral contexts' (European Commission 2001b).

Therefore, it could be argued that the EU's interest in establishing strong links with Brazil was evident as early as 2000. Furthermore, Lamy also explained:

> It follows that this negotiation must not detract our attention from the pursuit of the Doha Development Agenda. I am glad that this is a view firmly shared by Mercosur countries. Why does the EU care about Mercosur? Because above and beyond providing a market to our exports and stability to the region, Mercosur reinforces the multi-polar nature of the international system. (European Commission 2002a)

This would suggest that, for Lamy at least, developing EU–Mercosur relations, particularly in the area of trade relations, was, to a certain extent, part of the EU's wider inter-regional agenda.

Civil society

The EU's Economic and Social Committee has always supported relations with Mercosur. However, it does not seem to have been particularly influential. As early as 1997, the Economic and Social Committee (ESC) from the EU met with Mercosur's Foro Consultativo Economico y Social (FCES). To mark the first official meeting in Montevideo on 16 December 1997, both parties signed a 'Memorandum of understanding for institutional cooperation between the Economic and Social Consultative Forum of Mercosur (FCES) and the Economic and Social Committee of the European Communities (ESC-EC)' (European Commission 1998a). This memorandum of understanding provided for: 'a regular exchange of information and experience, possible joint projects and studies, technical assistance and familiarization visits. It was agreed that a working meeting should be held once a year when the joint work programme would be drawn up' (European Commission 1998b). It was also agreed that this alliance would: 'Pursue the establishment of an ESC–FCES Joint Consultative Committee within the framework of the inter-regional political and economic association agreement, in order to institutionalize their discussions' (European Commission 1998b).

The business sector was arguably the most active body to lobby the EU in terms of developing EU–Mercosur trade initiatives, prioritizing an agreement between the EU and Mercosur as soon as possible. As explained earlier in this chapter, the MEBF was created to provide an:

> informal forum for business people to identify what they regard as the key issues in the trade and industrial relationship between the two regions and to come up with recommendations to the public authorities of both sides on steps that could be taken to improve market access, facilitate doing business and encourage investment. (European Commission 1999)

The MEBF was also very much are aware of its own influence. For example, it was claimed that:

> Many of our recommendations, including the ones made during the last MEBF Plenary Conference held in Brasilia in October 2003, have been adopted by officials of the European Commission and the Mercosur Governments and are now at the core of their current negotiation agenda, while some others are subject to deep discussion. (MEBF 2004: 3)

Pascal Lamy also supported this initiative because he supported the idea of liberalizing inter-regional trade (European Commission 2001b). In fact, the meetings that were held during the negotiations helped both sides in the area of business facilitation to the point that it created an EU–Mercosur Action Plan on Business Facilitation agreement; Commissioner Liikanen from enterprise and society and Lamy and Patten thanked the forum for its proposals (European Commission 2002a). In fact, Liikanen said, 'I am very pleased with the positive results of this week's meeting. Our dialogue with the Mercosur–EU Businesses Forum is part of the strengthening of our dialogue with civil society in both regions' (European Commission 2002b).

However, despite praising the efforts of the MEBF, Liikanen did not discuss the role played by other parts of civil society that were not represented in these negotiations, such as the efforts by the Economic and Social Forum. Therefore, it could be argued that those groups in civil society, such as the MEBF and the agriculture groups, were the groups that the EU either listened to or were influenced by. However, agriculture groups, particularly European ones, had a different view of the EU–Mercosur agreement. For example, the largest associations, COPA and the General Committee for Agricultural Cooperation in the European Union, complained about the agreement from the very beginning. Nevertheless, it seems that these groups influenced EU policy towards Mercosur because agricultural issues were an important factor for why such an agreement was not reached. And finally, the evidence presented in this section also suggests that the EU did not have a coherent policy agenda towards Mercosur beyond the development of trade relations.

EU engagement in Mercosur

There are several pieces of evidence that suggest a top level of ambition. Priority was given to the development of an association agreement, the first trade agreement between two regions in history. The Joint Committee that was created supports a good level of ambition. The level of ambition within the EU has varied, and that has had an impact on the overall ambition. Spain and Portugal have been the most pro-Mercosur, and on the opposite side, Ireland and France were critical of Mercosur due to the importance of the agricultural sector in their countries. It should be noted that agriculture is still very much an important sector in Spain and Portugal but their links to Latin America were more important, generally speaking. As in the previous chapters, the level of ambition should not be overestimated since the ambition on the part of Mercosur helped increase ambition on the EU side. Once the negotiations had been started, the level of ambition increased again, as they were working towards the achievement of an association agreement, which was considered a privileged agreement.

On the negative side, the ambition shown so far deflated due to the fact that the EU did not do everything it could have done to achieve an agreement with Mercosur, as shown by the linking of the negotiations with the WTO, and the fact that the EU did not try to improve its offer in order to secure the agreement (Figure 6.1).

The change of actors within the Commission played a big part in the lack of full ambition. Once Marin left, commissioners Lamy and Patten did not ever intend to pursue the same level of ambition.

In order to assess the level of commitment it is necessary to pay attention to different indicators. Here the picture is less positive, since the EU's actions did not match its level of ambition. For example, in relation to the Joint Committee, the lack of progress for several years was due to the lack of commitment shown by some actors in the EU, including the French and Irish commissioners and the commissioner of agriculture. The lack of final agreement is the best example of how the EU did not do its best to achieve a successful outcome; it has been shown that there were other unpursued options that could have improved the negotiations. The insistence on the linking of the negotiations to the WTO and the lack of agreement in the agricultural sector do not show a high level of commitment (Figure 6.2).

If there is more ambition than commitment, the EU's behaviour could be described as having more strategy than interest, or pretending to be more

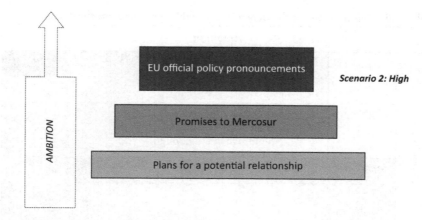

Figure 6.1 Level of ambition: third stage

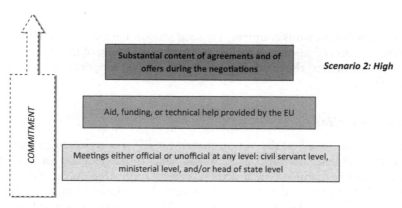

Figure 6.2 Level of commitment: third stage

interested than it really is. In the case that there is more commitment than ambition, there would be more interest than strategy. In that case it would seem that the EU was not very organized. Altogether, ambition and commitment show the real engagement of the EU.

As a consequence of all of this, the assessment of the level of engagement is high, is the highest level of the whole policy. Table 6.3 shows the assessment of the dependent variable in the three stages. Once the dependent variable has been assessed and compared with the values given at this stage of the policy to the independent variables of the six competing arguments, the conclusion is that none of the six independent variables reached the level of of the dependent variable (see Table 6.4).

Table 6.3 Measurement of the dependent variable, engagement: third stage

		Top	High	Medium	Low	None
				Ambition		
Commitment	Top					
	High		Third stage: high/high	Second stage: med/high		
	Medium					
	Low				First stage: low/low	
	None					

As with the previous chapters, the final section here will consider the six different expectations that were laid out at the beginning of this monograph, to assess whether the evidence presented above supports any of these arguments.

Counterbalancing the US

The argument based on the notion that, if the EU was trying to counterbalance the influence of the US, it would lead to an increase in the EU's involvement in Latin America does not seem applicable during the period 1996–2004. Not only did the commissioners have different views, many of the EU member states were opposed to the agreement. It should also be clear by now that there was not a clear strategy towards the region. On top of that, the aforementioned FTAA that had threatened the EU–Mercosur agreement was dead before the EU–Mercosur deadlock of October 2004 (*El País* 9/7/2004), yet the negotiations between the EU and Mercosur continued. It is also quite clear that the EU did not want and was not capable of competing with the US (Interviewee 4). Pascal Lamy, who was in charge of trade, was extremely clear about how much the actions of the US were an influence upon him: 'I am not going to lose any sleep about Bob Zoellick pursuing an FTA with Morocco ... any more than he is worried about me doing one with Mexico' (Agence Europe 5/11/2003). The EU would not have been able to compete with the US in Latin America, even if it had wanted to. Certainly, there were declarations made by some EU members about the intention to compete with the US, such as those made by Chirac (*El País* 11/3/1997), but once again it is clear that France

Table 6.4 Competing arguments and the independent variables: third stage

Independent variable	Expectation	Independent variable value	Expectation value	Met/confronted
Counterbalancing the US	If the US increases its involvement in LA, the EU should increase its involvement. $\uparrow$US = $\uparrow$EU in LA	Low	Low	No
Global aspirations	If the EU increases its presence in international affairs, the EU's involvement in LA should also increase. $\uparrow$EU in the world = $\uparrow$EU in LA	Top	Top	No
External federator	If LA becomes more integrated, the EU will increase its relations with LA. $\uparrow$LA integration = $\uparrow$EU in LA	Top	Top	No
Affinity	An increase of shared values between the regions should develop EU policy. $\uparrow$LA shared values = $\uparrow$EU in LA	Top	Top	No
Interdependence	If trade and investment between the EU and LA increase, EU policy should also increase. $\uparrow$LA trade = $\uparrow$EU in LA	Low	Low	No
Iberia	If the influence of Spain and Portugal increase within the EU, then the EU's involvement in LA should increase. $\uparrow$SP + PT influence = $\uparrow$EU in LA	Low	Low	No

Notes: LA = Latin America; PT = Portugal; SP = Spain.

was never entirely serious about doing so because it was opposed to the agreement all the way through. Furthermore, Patten himself commented on how:

> Some wish that the EU compete in LA with the US. It is not our intention, the US has a geopolitical and strategic relation that no other region can have. There is a geographic continuity, a great economic interdependence and common problems of security and an exchange of population that cannot be compared with the one existing in Latin America and the EU. (*El País* 17/11/2002)

Global aspirations

The global aspirations argument expects that an increase in the EU's involvement in Latin America would be an important part of the developing agenda of the EU in which the EU would play a greater role in the international arena. It is difficult to support this argument at this point because there were some questions about the usefulness of FTAs and of the ill-thought-out promises the EU made towards third world countries. Furthermore, the Commission was seen as incompetent when developing a global agenda: 'The criticisms are addressed first and foremost to the European Commission, which does not seem to have developed a comprehensive debate on this problem and appears to have launched its free trade plans without due consideration' (Agence Europe 14/2/1996). To be more accurate:

> If Vice-President Marin was given the responsibility of relations with the Mediterranean and South African countries, what could be more normal than for him to take initiatives to build closer relations? ... It is the other Commissioner who must point out the repercussions of free trade areas on the sectors under their responsibility. The President must impose comprehensive reflection on the effects of free trade areas. (Agence Europe 14/2/1996)

It seems clear that there has been a lack of coordination within the Commission, let alone the Council, when developing FTAs. It also seems apparent that the main actors developing the agreements are the commissioners in charge of geographical portfolios. For example, a few months later it was also clear that the Agriculture Council shared the Italian president of the EU's position in relation to the increase in the number of proposed areas of free trade conceived in Brussels and that an increase in goods imported from Latin America would have a detrimental effect on the agricultural sector in the EU (Agence Europe 7/5/1996). Again there is a mix of interests in the EU related to FTAs with third world countries that makes it difficult to support the argument that the EU's relationship with Latin America was a constituent feature of a strategy designed to strengthen the EU's presence in the global arena, because no such strategy actually existed.

With the Prodi Commission, Patten relaunched the debate on EU policy towards third countries with a paper in which he questioned the whole organization. Among other things, Patten claimed: 'certain Member States' invitations to the Commission are more like Mafia offers that cannot be refused' (Agence Europe 8/6/2000); instead, regarding external relations, he supported 'the necessity of establishing a rigorous hierarchy of priorities, and the requirement of making available financial means corresponding to objectives' (Agence Europe 8/6/2000).

If the commissioner in charge of EU external relations questions the organization of the Commission, it seems that the EU had failed to develop a clear strategy towards Mercosur. Therefore, it is hardly possible to talk about EU global strategy. Instead, it seems that the EU Commission was a place where different national interests were pursued rather than the EU Commission pursuing a unified strategy agenda. On top of this, Pascal Lamy, the commissioner in charge of trade, questioned the usefulness of FTAs with third countries, claiming that

> I personally believe this kind of traditional free trade area of the 20th century, based on total market liberalisation, to be a formula that is today a little outdated despite its political symbolism. If we want the trade and investment relationships to reach their full potential, then we should tackle the regulatory obstacles, and, for the time being, put our 'ambitions' aside with regards to market access, leaving that to the multilateral arena where it belongs. Frankly speaking, the difficulty that Europe experiences with the idea of a free trade area is that it is not absolutely clear that this is what our trade relations really need. (Agence Europe 14/1/2003)

Here, the person in charge of the portfolio of trade is against the very idea of creating FTAs between countries. In fact, Lamy's comments suggest that there was an obvious lack of agreement, plan or strategy towards third countries within the EU. If this was the case at this stage in policy development towards Mercosur (1996–2004), then it is difficult to accept the existence of a global strategy in the previous stages of the EU–Mercosur policy.

External federator

In the area of regional promotion, the EU continued to provide funding and the transfer of know-how. This is something the EU had done from the very first moment and reinforced it with the agreement based on region-to-region negotiations. This means that the EU was demanding that Mercosur comply with a common external and internal tariff in order to be able to negotiate trade issues between the regions. Therefore, when the Commission voiced its frustration at the lack of integration as one of the reasons for the lack of an agreement, it seems possible that the main force for the EU policy towards Mercosur was the development of a regional group that was modelled on the institutional framework of the EU. To copy the EU's structural framework would be extremely flattering as well as giving the EU further influence in Latin America. However, the Commission was not going to force regional integration on Latin America. In fact, interviewees suggested that there was only so much that the Commission could do if the countries in Latin America did not want to integrate (Interviewees 7 and 8). The problem was that, when the EU was promoting regional integration on the one hand and on the other hand was offering a political partnership to Brazil in 2008, it was sending a message which undermined any suggestion that the EU was committed to regional integration and establishing inter-regional relations with Latin America as a whole. In other words, by showing preferential treatment to a particular member of Mercosur, the EU was not demonstrating a solid commitment to regional integration in Latin America in terms of a coherent policy agenda (Interviewee 9).

Affinity

The argument that the EU's involvement in Latin America would increase because of the historical ties and shared values between the regions is difficult to sustain during the third stage of EU–Mercosur relations. This is evident in the fact that most EU member states showed a serious lack of interest in the region. The discussion throughout this chapter has shown that individual commissioners have also shown either opposition or a distinct lack of interest in developing relations with Latin America. More specifically, the discussion above has shown that the EU did not express a desire to develop EU–Mercosur policy as a consequence of long-standing political, economic or cultural ties and values.

Interdependence

The argument which suggested that an increase in the EU' s involvement in Latin America would develop as a consequence of increasing trade and FDI in Mercosur cannot be supported at this stage. The influence of business associations such as MEBF was higher in Latin America than in the EU because the Mercosur was producing more information on business-related issues. In terms of trade, it has been shown that Latin America was of minimal importance to the EU, hence there had been a lack of agreements between the two regions. Furthermore, if the EU did have any real interest in Latin America, then the development of any relations/policies would have been restricted to agricultural issues rather than more substantial levels of inter-regional interdepence.

Spanish and Portuguese influence in the EU

The argument which suggested that there would be an increase in the EU's interest in Latin America as a result of the influence of Iberian countries in the EU is also not sustainable when looking at EU–Mercosur relations between 1996 and 2004 because the preparations for the 2004 enlargement had an impact on the influence of Spain and Portugal, which after 2004 was completely diluted when ten new countries joined the EU. Nevertheless, the Iberian countries continued to support Mercosur and did try to influence the policy towards Mercosur. Despite this, the Iberian countries were unable to develop any substantial policy developments. To some extent, Spain and Portugal had undoubtedly been the biggest supporters of EU–Mercosur policy within the EU. During this stage of EU–Mercosur relations, Spanish officials in the Commission (Marin), in the EP (Spanish MEPs such as Salafranca) and in the Council (Aznar or Zapatero) persistently showed their commitment to developing EU–Mercosur relations. However, it seems that they were not able to achieve the type of progress and policies that they would have wanted and, in the end, the lack of an agreement proves just how little power they had within the EU. This is most evident in relation to the Prodi Commission, when Marin was no longer a commissioner. More specifically, during this time the Latin American section in the Commission was downgraded, levels of interest decreased, as did the levels of cooperation and aid given to Latin America, which show just how little the Iberian countries were able to achieve. Finally, this stage of the policy demonstrates how Spain and Portugal were not strong enough to further develop a degree of Europeanization that would have made possible the agreement between the two regions.

Conclusion

This chapter has discussed the third phase of the EU policy towards Mercosur. The first section outlined the difficulties encountered until the negotiating directive was approved in 1999. Here it was argued that the difficulties were mainly due to the opposition shown by France. It was also explained that it was the influence of Spain and the Latin American countries that finally led to the first summit of the heads of state of Latin America and the EU. In the second part of the chapter, the discussion focused on the negotiations and how EU interest in Latin America declined during this period. The discussions were intimately connected to the importance of the WTO negotiations. It was suggested that agricultural issues were the main obstacle to an agreement being reached and as a result policy negotiations were unsuccessfully concluded in October 2004, just before the change of Commission. It was also suggested that the EU showed a change in direction in terms of its approach to relation with Mercosur. More specifically, the EU regional policy towards Latin America was undermined by the decision to offer a political partnership to Brazil, the largest and least integrated member of Mercosur. The final section of this chapter focused on the main actors involved in shaping EU policy towards Mercosur by paying attention to the individuals' position during this phase of EU–Mercosur relations. Looking at the arguments laid out in the introduction to this book, none of the expectations has any real purchase in terms of explaining policy development between the two regions. In fact, it could be argued that this is the case because of the EU's general lack of interest in the region.

Considering the evidence offered above, the EU engagement has been assessed as high. More specifically, in relation to ambition, the Joint Committee shows evidence of ambition in both the EU and Mercosur in achieving an association agreement. The development of an association agreement which includes the first inter-regional FTA is quite exceptional. But, as in the previous stages of the policy, caution should be taken when analysing the level of ambition, since the pressure from Mercosur countries to achieve progress has been key for the development of the policy, which undermines the level of EU ambition. An example of this was the pressure put on the French embassies to achieve the signing of the negotiating mandate. The fact that the EU did not offer enough concessions to achieve the association agreement since it was linked to the WTO negotiations also undermines the apparent ambition. With the departure of Marin, the Commission had lower ambition, as the pronouncements of commissioners Lamy and Patten showed.

In relation to commitment, the outcome is similar for ambition because, even though the negotiations were launched, the commitment was slow. This is shown in the lack of progress in the Joint Committee, to the point where it was embarrassing for the EU representatives, who had to come up with snapshots and other exercises to gain time. Moreover, the EU did not achieve a successful end of the negotiations. As a consequence, the assessment given to commitment is high. And, since ambition achieved the same assessment, the final outcome is high.

Finally, this chapter has shown that the EU did not have a clear and coherent strategy towards Mercosur. Instead, the EU tended to follow both the initiatives and interests put forward by the Iberian countries, and the EU once again undertook the role of the responsive actor that simply reacted to the demands of Mercosur countries.

7

The second attempt to negotiate the association agreement

Introduction

From the moment the EU and Mercosur stopped negotiations there was no progress or a real intention to restart the negotiations until 2010. Officially the EU and Mercosur continued negotiating the association agreement, but it is fair to say that after such a failure at the last minute in October 2004, both sides had become cautious in their hopes for a successful agreement. Considering that the negotiations had failed publicly, it is understandable that some years of 'healing' were needed before a new attempt could be broached.

One more time, the right momentum was necessary to facilitate the relaunch of the negotiations. The economic environment was completely different from 2004. At this moment Europe was recovering from a financial crisis and from a weak eurozone, while the international crisis had not had that much of an effect in Latin America. However, in 2004 Brazil and Argentina were recovering from the economic crisis of the late 1990s and early 2000s. The negotiations between the EU and other Latin American regional groups and individual countries had been successful. At the same time, a third major investor and trader became an important piece of the puzzle – China. To some extent this could be seen as a more promising context for reaching a successful agreement between the EU and Mercosur. The facilitator of the relaunching of the negotiations was once again the Spanish presidency of 2010. Since then, several meetings have taken place between the EU and Mercosur, the last one in Brussels in mid-June 2015. Throughout 2015, a new kind of scenario became possible – a two-speed type of negotiation: one with Brazil and other countries such as Uruguay and Paraguay, and another one with Argentina. Venezuela did not participate in the negotiations because its protectionist approach made it particularly difficult for the country to take part. Venezuela's restricted participation was further complicated by the fact that it became a member of Mercosur after the negotiations had already started. Considering both the views of

Evo Morales and the economic development of this Andean country, Bolivia's potential membership of Mercosur would also further slow down the negotiations.

The overall argument is again supported through these negotiations. The EU's policy towards Mercosur is a reaction to the agenda being put forward by other actors. Mercosur in general and Brazil in particular are very keen to develop an agreement after the failure of the Doha Round. The facilitation of the negotiations had been made possible by the continued interest of the Iberian countries, especially Spain. The fact that Mercosur countries are willing to negotiate individually with the EU indicates how keen and proactive they are to develop this agreement. The diplomatic efforts of Spain were necessary in order to: (1) facilitate dialogue between the two regions; (2) bring Mercosur's views to the EU table; and (3) pursue a favourable EU reaction to Mercosur's suggestions.

The relaunch of the negotiations and the actors involved

The relaunching of the negotiations, as has been mentioned, was during the 2010 summit in Madrid. Although the negotiations had stopped in 2004, it did not mean a complete breakdown of the relationship. In fact, at the 2008 EU–Mercosur summit in Lima an agreement was signed to expand relations to three new areas: science and technology, infrastructure and renewable energy.

Leaders emphasized the close cultural, economic and political values which bonded the two regions together. They underlined that, with a combined population of more than 700 million people, high combined GDP and biregional trade close to €100 billion annually, cooperation between the two blocs generates reciprocal advantages and positive spillovers at the global level. 'The leaders are aware that substantial efforts will have to be made, and underlined their full commitment to engage in these negotiations' (EU–Mercosur). Both sides stressed their commitment to strive for a conclusion of the negotiations without delay' (EU–Mercosur Summit Joint Communiqué Madrid, 17 May 2010). In the meantime the EU continued to support the development of the Mercosur project.

The Regional Indicative Programme attached to the 2007–2013 EU–Mercosur Regional Strategy Paper outlined provisions for a total budget of €50 million, focusing on three key areas: institutional support, preparation for a future EU–Mercosur association agreement and support for civil society. After a mid-term revision, a decision was made to focus on two key issues: €2 million of support for the development of bio-technologies in Mercosur (replacing the previously anticipated support to strengthen Mercosur institutions) and €15 million towards further developing the Mercosur project, including the implementation of the future association agreement (European Commission 2015).

How did it happen?

Just before the beginning of the Spanish presidency, there were talks about the relaunching of the negotiations between the EU and Mercosur. European foreign affairs ministers placed these negotiations within EU–Latin America relations, which also includes association agreements with the Andean Community and Central America (Agence Europe 10/12/2009).

It is important to understand that there were some substantial changes in context between the 1995 and 1999 agreements and the relaunch of negotiations in 2010 (Caetano et al. 2010). In the previous negotiations there was progress in the areas of cooperation and political dialogue, however there was little progress in terms of trade. Furthermore, there was a lack of progress in relation to dealing with the lack of social cohesion and the uneven distribution of economic and political power in Mercosur (Caetano 2010).

There are several reasons to believe that the EU considers the negotiations with Latin America relevant (Caetano et al. 2010). Caetano et al. point to reasons provided by Celestino del Arenal (2009), the most important of which are: a change in the international arena focusing more on the Asia-Pacific region; the international economic crisis and changes in US foreign policy; the enlargement of the EU and the shift towards right-wing governments across the EU; and the weakness of the Latin American lobbies.

It is of extreme importance to remember the asymmetries between the two blocs to understand the weight that each side carries in the negotiations. Table 7.1 shows the disparities that exist between the EU and Mercosur in terms economic resources. We also need to identify the EU and Mercosur's main trading partners before the relaunch of the negotiations in order to identify both the actors and the different interests which kick-started the relaunch of negotiations. Table 7.2 helps us to understand the priorities of different actors.

With the economic crisis having a profound impact and the lack of a successful outcome during the Doha Round of negotiations in 2010, Spanish and Argentinean presidencies of their respective was yet another for the relaunch of the negotiations. On the Mercosur side the possibility was discussed during the last summit in Montevideo in 2009. The official documents described the positive view:

Table 7.1 GDP of the EU and Mercosur, 2007

Region	GDP (millions)	GDP per capita
Mercosur	$1,630,558	$6,753
EU-27	€12,303,961 (around $9,000,000 – 450% more than Mercosur	€24,800

Source: Caetano et al. (2010).

Table 7.2 Main trading partners of Mercosur countries and the EU-27, 2012

Main trade partners of Brazil	Main trade partners of Argentina	Main trade partners of Paraguay	Main trade partners of Uruguay	Main trade partners of EU-27
EU-27: 22.4%	Brazil: 26.8%	Brazil: 24.5%	Brazil: 17.8%	US: 15.2%
US: 14.9%	**EU-27: 18.7%**	Argentina: 17.0%	**EU-27: 17.1%**	China: 11.4%
China: 9.7%	China: 11.5%	US: 15.2%	Argentina: 12.3%	Russia: 9.7%
Argentina: 6.2%	US: 10.9%	**EU-27: 9.4%**	China: 10.8%	Switzerland: 6.2%
Japan: 4.7%	Chile: 4.3%	China: 7.3%	US: 7.5%	Norway: 4.7%
Nigeria: 4.1%	Mexico: 2.5%	Mexico: 2.5%	Paraguay: 4.6%	
Chile: 3.5%	Paraguay: 1.6%	Paraguay: 1.6%	Mexico: 3.0%	
South Korea: 2.3%	Russia: 1.6%	Uruguay: 1.5%	Nigeria: 3.0%	
Mexico: 2.2%	Uruguay: 1.5%	Japan: 1.3%	Russia: 2.5%	**Brazil: 2.2%**
Russia: 2.1%	Japan: 1.3%		South Africa: 2.3%	

Note: Figures are percentage of total foreign trade.
Source: http://europa.eu/.

[the Presidents] celebrated the Meeting between Mercosur and the European Commission in Lisbon on November 4 to 6, 2009, and expressed their support to furthering the relations, inclusively before the end of 2009, between the future Pro Tempore President of Mercosur (Argentina) and the European Commission as well as advancing work in order to reach the greatest possible progress in the negotiations in view of the presidential meeting scheduled within the LAC–EU Summit for May 2010 under Spain's EU Presidency. (Pena 2009)

At the same time, the pressure on Mercosur also came from other actors that had been present during the previous negotiations – the business associations. The presidents of the MEBF, Inaki Urdangarin on the European side and Carlos Mariani Bittencourt on the Mercosur side, provided a declaration to the four Mercosur countries explaining the need to end the negotiations successfully (Pena 2009). It is interesting to see that even at the time of the relaunch of the negotiations there was an attempt to create a two-speed process that would facilitate flexible negotiations (Pena 2009). In doing so, it seems that different degrees of commitment were expected by certain Mercosur countries. This issue will be explored further at the end of this chapter.

The EU decided to relaunch the negotiations with Mercosur as there were clear economic benefits for both the EU and Mercosur (European Commission 2010). According to the European Commissioner for Trade, Karel De Gucht:

> negotiations such as these are challenging but the moment is right to take a fresh look at the state of discussions so far. Any agreement must be ambitious bringing increased access for a range of EU businesses, including agriculture, into the Mercosur region. It is critical that certain key EU demands are met if these negotiations are to be fruitful at the end of the day. (European Commission 2010)

The biggest obstacle to the agreement was the negotiations in the agriculture sector. The EU wanted better access to the industrial sector, while Mercosur asked for lowers obstacles to their agricultural exports to Europe.

Once again Spain and Portugal were key actors in terms of facilitating EU–Mercosur relations. After the actions of the Iberian countries have been discussed, the remainder of this chapter will focus on the actions of other EU countries. The relative importance of these negotiations in EU external issues does not generally provoke discussion and opinions in the twenty-eight countries, and therefore the analyses will focus on the countries that have a strong opinion on this policy – France, Ireland and Greece – since they are the ones acting in a distinct way. After focusing on the EU member states, the discussion will turn to focus on the role of EU institutions, particularly the actions of the European Commission and the EP, which have had opposing views on this policy. Finally we will examine how the position of Mercosur countries has been underestimated by showing that they did have considerable influence in the relaunch, as they had done the first time around in the 1990s.

The European Union

Spain and Portugal

The Iberian countries traditionally give more importance to EU relations with Latin America than other European countries do. The Iberian support for the relaunch of the EU–Mercosur negotiations has been shown on several occasions. In November 2009 – almost a month before the start of the Spanish presidency, there was a meeting in Madrid where the role of Spain was specifically discussed by Juan Pablo de Laiglesia, the Spanish secretary of state for Iberoamerica (*El País* 25/11/2009). Here it was decided that they would push for the negotiations at the following Iberoamerica summit a month later (*El País* 25/11/2009).

The importance of the Spanish presidency of the EU in advancing the negotiations with Mercosur was highlighted by the director of the European Commission on Latin America (*El País* 25/11/2009). On the other side of the Atlantic, this was also observed when an MEP claimed: 'if with the Spanish presidency there is not progress with Latin America, forget about it' (*Clarin* 2/1/2010). The sub-secretariat of economic integration in Mercosur, Eduardo Sigal, admitted that the Spanish presidency and the role of Spain was one of the key factors in terms of improving this relationship (*Clarin* 7/3/2010). Moreover, the Spanish vice-president at that time went to Buenos Aires to discuss the issue with the president of Argentina and was straightforward: 'This is a very important occasion, it is not going to be repeated in a long time, Spain will preside over the EU, and Argentina over Mercosur, and we both can influence the priorities and the agendas of the organizations' (*El País* 9/11/2010) Spain knew that the next presidencies of the EU would ignore Latin America and therefore pressed forward any agreement talks with this region (Agence Europe 20/5/2010).

Spain planned and tried to conclude negotiations with Mercosur during the six months of its presidency, but it was obvious that there were some doubts about what could be achieved. According to the Spanish minister of foreign affairs, Moratinos: 'We will continue the ambitious negotiations but will it be possible to conclude talks by May? It is difficult to say but we will do all we can to achieve this in Madrid' (Agence Europe 5/2/2010). Statements such as this reveal just how different the political rhetoric was from the reality of the negotiations. The conclusion of the negotiations in May 2010 was entirely unfeasible.

Other EU countries

Although there was complaints from France during the first EU–Mercosur association negotiations, the number of countries complaining increased considerably during the second round of negotiations. Crucially, during the negotiations that ended in 2004, there was only fifteen EU member states. By the time of the second round of negotiations the EU had expanded to twenty-eight member states. Moreover, most of the new members considered the agricultural sector to be important to their national economies. In 2010 the economic situation was not the same as it had been in 2004, especially for countries such as Ireland and Greece.

These complaints increased in intensity in the weeks before the summit of the heads of state of the EU and Latin America which was held in May 2010 in Madrid, during the Spanish presidency of the EU. The French minister Bruno Le Maire declared that the EU could not go ahead with the negotiations due to the negative influence that they would have on the

French and European agricultural sector (*Clarin* 6/5/2010; *El País* 7/5/2010). In fact, the main farmers' trade union in France asked French President Nicolas Sarkozy to veto the negotiations altogether (*El País* 7/5/2010). Bruno le Maire argued that the EU had already made concessions that would benefit the Brazilian agricultural sector during the Doha Round negotiations in July 2008 (*Clarin* 6/5/2010). On the other side, the Argentinean newspaper, *Clarin*, criticized that fact that France received more than 20% of the aid budget that provided for the agricultural sector, which disadvantaged Mercosur agricultural products (*Clarin* 6/5/2010). This debate echoes the situation in the late 1990s before the first Rio Summit, as has been explained in Chapter 4.

Initially, seven countries expressed their dissatisfaction when the European Commission announced on 4 May 2010 that the negotiations would be resumed: Austria, Finland, France, Greece, Hungary, Ireland and Poland (Agence Europe 15/5/2010). A few days later, the ministers of agriculture of several EU countries complained again about the official relaunch of the negotiations on 17 May 2010 during the summit: Austria, Belgium, Cyprus, France, Greece, Hungary, Ireland, Italy, Lithuania, Luxembourg, Poland, Portugal, Romania, Slovenia and Slovakia (Agence Europe 18/5/2010). The argument used was again related to the concessions granted in July 2008 and the fact that the countries felt that they would pay for the concessions twice, leading them to ask the Commission to conduct further research into the effects of this agreement.

The level of dissatisfaction continued, this centring on the discussions relating to, among other things, the standard of Brazilian products, with the French minister Bruno Le Maire arguing that: 'agriculture is not an exchange currency. We will not go further on the negotiations with the WTO. Europe is not an outlet for agricultural products from South American countries' (Agence Europe 16/9/2010). The Irish MEP Marian Harkin also complained that 'the Russians and the Americans will not permit the importation of Brazilian beef and have good reasons for those decisions. The EU has been far less demanding in regard to standards and traceability of food products. Commissioner De Gucht's suggestion that a trade agreement would benefit EU exporters and investors has to be viewed with suspicion' (Agence Europe 16/9/2010). The answer from European Trade Commissioner De Gucht was clear: 'The Commission does the negotiating, and it has to be respected. The French position is well-known – it's the same as it always says' (Agence Europe 18/9/2010). A few months later the Irish Farmers' Association claimed that De Gucht had failed to represent European interest, while also accusing the trade commissioner of double standards when dealing with EU and non-EU agricultural products (Agence Europe 23/2/2011). It is clear by now that both France and Ireland were the countries that most vehemently rejected the negotiations. However, Mercosur had a supporter of some weight within the EU. The German

Chancellor, Angela Merkel supported the agreement and considered it beneficial for Europe (*Clarin* 18/10/2011).

European Union

The EU decided to relaunch the negotiations in 2010 but it is crucial to remember that, only a couple of years before, there had been no intention on either side to relaunch them until the Doha Round was completed (Agence Europe 20/5/2008). This supports the overall argument of presented throughout this monograph: that there was a lack of a clear EU strategy towards Mercosur. In fact, the EU followed the momentum created every so often by the Spanish and Portuguese presidencies of the EU to improve EU–Mercosur relations. More often than not, any momentum in this direction was not initiated by the EU, even though Commissioner Ferrero-Walder tried to give a different impression during the EU–Latin American Summit of 2008: 'We are confident that, if we continue with the same will, we will be able to conclude the agreements before the end of 2009' (Agence Europe 7/5/2008). At the same time, Ferrero-Walder hoped that the summit would give 'renewed momentum' to the WTO. This, again, suggests that there was clear discrepancy between the rhetoric and reality when it comes to the progress of these negotiations.

In 2010, the Spanish presidency of the EU and the Argentinean presidency of Mercosur lead the European Commission to believe that there was now right the momentum required time to relaunch negotiations (*El País* 25/11/2009). As the Spanish Minister of External Affairs pointed out, the Doha negotiations was going nowhere at this point (*El País* 25/11/2009). It was in this moment that the Director of the Latin American Area for the European Commission admitted that in the context of the financial crisis both regions needed new markets to help improve their respective economic situations (*El País* 25/11/2009). However, it seemed that in contrast to France and Germany, some countries within the EU, such as Spain, were willing to be more generous towards Mercosur (*El País* 25/11/2009).

During the negotiations, the EU clearly accused Mercosur in general and Argentina in particular of being responsible for stopping the progress between the regions. In fact, Commissioner De Gucht directly accused Argentina's protectionist stance of causing problems to the point where he threatened the Mercosur country with an official complaint to the WTO (*Clarin* 15/4/2011). Here De Gucht was alluding to the barriers faced by European exporters to Argentina – a matter that had also been raised by several EU countries. Argentina responded immediately, claiming that the De Gucht was trying to create divisions amongst Mercosur countries (*Clarin* 15/4/2011). However, in contrast to Argentina, it seems that Paraguay and Brazil were showing greater more flexibility in their efforts to reach an agreement, although Argentina would claim that Brazil was simply just better at disguising its real strategy (*Clarin* 5/5/2011). Support for the agreement also came from other EU actors such as Catherine Aston; the EU high representative for foreign affairs stated that 'negotiations with Mercosur must be resumed' (Agence Europe 22/4/2010).

Mercosur

The discussion of the negotiations should cover the views of all the actors, especially since Mercosur has been very active in EU–Latin American relations. Mercosur countries wanted this agreement in the first place, and it was felt that the second opportunity which the Spanish presidency of 2010 presented was not to be ignored. Argentina and Brazil tried to put aside their problems and drive the agreement (*El País* 18/5/2010). At this point, there were several reasons why Mercosur wanted to reach an agreement. While Uruguay had always supported the agreement, the reasons for reaching an agreement included improving Argentina's image on the international stage through an agreement with the EU, and broader concerns within Mercosur that Brazil would make its individual agreements with the EU (*El País* 18/5/2010).

Argentina had always been the Mercosur country with deeper reservations regarding any agreement with the EU (*El País* 18/4/2010), and on this occasion, Argentina again presented further some obstacles in terms of blocking imports from the EU. Countries affected by this issue, such as Greece, complained directly at the European level since it violated international norms of commerce, and the EU as a consequence asked Argentina to halt these actions (*Clarin* 28/6/2010). It also seems that Greek exports, valued at $2,400 million, had also been cancelled or suspended (*Clarin* 28/6/2010). When Greece asked Argentina for an explanation, the latter refused to give one. As a result Greece threatened to block negotiations between the EU and Mercosur (*Clarin* 28/6/2010). Argentina justified the blocking of exports as being occasional rather policy and they claimed in a meeting of the WTO that the European accusations were politically motivated (*Clarin* 5/7/2010).

Brazil tried to keep the negotiations going. This included President Lula organizing meeting in Brasilia with the president of the European Commission, José Manuel Barroso, and the president of the European Council, Herman Van Rompuy (*El País* 15/7/2010a). Brazil had been in a similar position with Argentina, with Brazilian products being blocked at the Argentinean border. However, on this occasion Lula was trying to progress the required preparatory work for reaching an agreement before he left the Brazilian presidency (*El País* 15/7/2010a). When discussing his role as president of Mercosur, Lula clearly stated that: 'I have assumed the presidency of Mercosur and I have the task of trying to persuade the EU to sign an agreement' (Agence Europe 17/7/2010). Lula also referred to the French president's view on the agreement, noting that: 'As the comrade who has done most ... is my great friend Nicolas Sarkozy, it will be my responsibility to try to convince [him], to win the hearts of the French to get this agreement before the end of my presidential term of office' (Agence Europe 17/7/2010).

At the same time, Argentina needed both the EU and Spain to be more diplomatic if it was to be persuaded to change its stance towards Europe. This led to the Argentinean president holding discussions with the president of the European Commission, José Manual Barroso in 2008 during the EU–Latin America summit, as well as further talks with the Spanish vice-president during her visit to Buenos Aires in 2009 with a view to improving political relations (*El País* 18/4/2010).

Another reason for Argentina to improve relations with the EU and Spain was to improve the image of Mercosur (*El País* 18/4/2010). The accusations of lack of progress in the Mercosur integration project came from all sides, including Latin American countries. At this stage, Uruguay considered that the end of 2010 pivotal for the integration project in Mercosur, primarily because of the lack of political economic coordination in Mercosur and the growing strength of other regional projects such as the Union of South American Nations (UNASUR) (*El País* 10/12/2010). Even Spanish politicians such as Carlos Solchaga, the former Minister of Finance, commented on the fragility of the Mercosur project (*El País* 15/7/2010b). However, the most worrying issue for Argentina was the fact that some sectors in Brazil wanted to develop individual agreements with the EU, believing that Brazil could further advance its own interest independently of the other Mercosur countries (*El País* 17/7/2010).

Mercosur: a happy family of five?

As well as the lack of regional integration, Mercosur had to deal with two difficult issues that were, to some extent, interlinked: the suspension of Paraguay's membership of Mercosur and Venezuela becoming a Mercosur member state. To be more specific, a political crisis in Paraguay provoked the suspension of its membership of Mercosur, which was used as an opportunity to let Venezuela officially join the regional group.

In June 2012 the president of Paraguay was removed from office, allegedly in response to the way that he had handled domestic issues such as the massacre at Curuguaty, and his choice of the security minister without consulting the government's coalition partners (MercoPress 18/4/2013). President Lugo had three days to respond, after which the Senate voted against him, the Senate with 120 out of 125, to remove him from office. Lugo was later replaced by Federico Franco, who at the time was the country's vice-president (MercoPress 18/4/2013). Mercosur and UNASUR claimed that this was a coup and suspended Paraguay's membership of Mercosur was suspended until after the next general election in Paraguay. In fact, Paraguay was also suspended from other groups and summits which included the Iberoamerican summit, the meeting of Latin American and Arab countries and the Community of Latin American and Caribbean States (CELAC) (MercoPress 26/1/2013). However, with the support of the US and Canada, Paraguay managed to remain a part of the Organization of American States, even though Argentina, Uruguay, Brazil, Venezuela, Bolivia, Peru, Ecuador, Cuba and Nicaragua did not agree (MercoPress 26/1/2013). According to the head of the Paraguayan delegation to the Parliament of Mercosur, the suspension from so many forums was orchestrated, with Argentina, Brazil and Venezuela masterminding the plot to limit Paraguay's influence in the international arena.

In January 2013 Paraguay decided not to attend the EU–CELAC summit after Mercosur and UNASUR countries had argued that Paraguay should not be invited (MercoPress 26/1/2013). In fact, the Paraguayan president, Federico Franco stated that 'Paraguay had not been invited' (MercoPress 26/1/2013). This was a critical moment in diplomatic relations given that Paraguay had not encountered any problems with CELAC.

By April 2013 Paraguay was still dealing with this diplomatic problem. However, attention had shifted to the upcoming Paraguayan national elections. In order to ensure that the elections were democratic, the elections were observed by, among others, three Nobel Prize-winners, the EU and the Organization of American States (MercoPress 18/4/2013). Occupying an increasingly peripheral position in the international arena meant that Paraguay could not object to such an imposition.

The suspension of Paraguay was used by the other Mercosur countries as a chance to incorporate Venezuela in the regional group; because of its long-standing political dislike of Venezuelan president Hugo Chavez, Paraguay had for years refused to allow Venezuela to become a member of Mercosur. This created even more friction between Paraguay and Venezuela, particularly between Chavez and Paraguay. Even after Nicolas Maduro became president after Chavez's death, relations did not improve, primarily because Maduro appeared to support the President Lugo following the aforementioned calls from the Paraguayan Congress that he be removed from office. In fact, Maduro called for the Paraguayan people to take to the streets to protest against Lugo's removal (MercoPress 18/4/2013). For Paraguay, however, what really mattered was that the EU acknowledged that Paraguayan was part of Mercosur and that Paraguay could rejoin Mercosur's negotiations with the EU (MercoPress 18/4/2013). Brazil played a key role as a regional leader in forcing Paraguay to accept Venezuela as a member of Mercosur. In principle the suspension was until the elections were held, but after the elections Brazil set the condition that Paraguay could only return to Mercosur if it gave its approval to the Venezuelan membership (MercoPress (23/4/2013).What this issue again reveals is that there were clear asymmetries of power within Mercosur.

At this point, Paraguay demanded respect for 'the country's dignity and rule of the law' (MercoPress 27/5/2013). It was felt that Venezuela's membership of Mercosur had been imposed on Paraguay because the latter's Congress had not ratified the former's membership. By June 2013 Paraguay stated its intention to become a member of the Alliance of the Pacific (MercoPress 16/6/2013). This should be seen as a move towards Mercosur's 'rival' regional group in Latin America, which not only expressed a more liberal agenda, but also enjoyed better relations with the US. Paraguay also had other options apart from Mercosur. The balance of power had certainly changed in Latin America since the creation of Mercosur, and this would have an impact on the need to develop agreements with other regions and countries, particularly in relation to the EU. If the non-Mercosur countries achieved individual better agreements with the EU and the US, this would negatively affect Brazil, Argentina, Paraguay and Uruguay because their exports were not that different from other Latin American countries in terms competitive agricultural and farming products. This helps us to see the economic reality for countries and regional groups such as the Alliance of the Pacific and Mercosur. However, there was also the political agenda at play. Mercosur had not embraced neoliberal economic policies in the same way that the Alliance of the Pacific had done. Changes in the regional power dynamics were also evident: Mercosur, with the weight of Brazil and Argentina, could be seen as the main regional leader, until Mexico and Chile came together with other Latin American countries to form create the Alliance of the Pacific.

Matters were not helped in the first half of 2014 when it was the turn of Paraguay to hold the presidency of Mercosur, which instead was passed to Venezuela. From a diplomatic point of view, Mercosur in general and Brazil in particular behaved in a high-handed way. Paraguay tried to use the weight of the EU to support its case. According to a representative of Paraguay: 'There's no need to rush, Mercosur has a low rating in international politics. Mercosur has violated the law. The European Union will not negotiate with an entity that violates the law and, as comments from acknowledged personalities from Argentina and Brazil have stated, Mercosur is disintegrating politically and juridically' (MercoPress 16/6/2013).

At the same time, Venezuela tried to become an accepted by the other countries as member of Mercosur. For example, it supported the negotiations with the EU but did not demand that it participated in them. Also, Maduro promised to the left-wing president of Uruguay, José Mujica, a 'permanent' supply of petroleum, as well as the signing of a strategic alliance in the energy sector (MercoPress 8/5/2013).

Brazil attempted to mediate in Venezuelan domestic politics, asking Maduro to develop a political dialogue with his political opponents, including Henrique Capriles (MercoPress 14/5/2013). At the same time, Brazil was prepared to supply emergency shipments of food, up to 700,000 tonnes, to help the Maduro administration (MercoPress 14/5/2013).

Other problems that had to be dealt with in Mercosur involved the lack of economic and political consensus between Brazil and Argentina, a situation in which other Mercosur countries were reluctant to intervene. The level of economic and political disagreement between these two countries was not the same level as that which existed between Venezuela and Paraguay. The presidents of the two countries, Fernandez and Rousseff, had different views on both investment and trade – an issue which had the potential to affect the very foundations of Mercosur (MercoPress 20/5/2013). In addition to this, Argentina had started to develop strong links with Russia as a response to the nation's severe economic problems and more specifically because of its high levels external debt. Since Argentina's economic problems would, sooner or later, have an impact on the Brazilian economy, it was widely felt that Brazil should be the one helping Argentina as one of its main trading partners (*El País* 1/8/2014).

The 2015 Brussels Summit: the end of biregional negotiations?

The summits that took place in 1999 between the EU, Latin American and Caribbean countries are indicative of the way that cooperation developed between these regions. However, over time, these summits became an increasingly difficult forum within which to develop bilateral discussions due to expanding number of participants taking part in the discussions (Maihold 2009).

The impetus for the first EU–Latin America summit (Rio de Janeiro, 1999) came from Iberia. It was Spain who would put forward the idea during the Iberoamerican summit of November 1996. This was considered to be the exact moment to try and further advance biregional relations into the twenty first century. The role of Spain in pushing for this particular, and also subsequent, summits was key (Maihold 2009). The second summit (Madrid, 2002) was key feature of the Spanish presidency of the EU and was used to boost the cooperation and negotiations between the EU with regional groups such as Mercosur. The 2010 summit in Madrid further demonstrated Spanish interest in relaunching EU–Mercosur negotiations and the signing of the EU–CACM agreement. Although these summits put pressure on both sides to reach agreements, the declarations emerged from the meetings were, despite good intentions, considered to be rather vague. However, these summits did help to create an EU–Latin American agenda that was subsequently used to reach common positions in relation to issues discussed at other international forums such as the United Nations (Maihold 2009). Furthermore, these summits were also occasionally used by various national presidents to enhance their own personal image and to project their personalities as playing a key role in the outcome of the summit (Maihold 2009). The politicization of the summits – as was the case of the 2010 and 2013 summits – can also negatively affect the development of agreements, especially if a country's president feels the need to react to the fact that other countries have tried to sabotage their attendance at a summit in response to internal national political issues, as happened with Honduras in 2010 and Paraguay in 2013.

In 2014 there were also several announcements that there would be a renegotiation of tariffs, but this did not happen. According to the president of Brazil, Dilma Rousseff, the South Americans created barriers to the proposals while the EU was more proactive. The negotiations have taken so long and the reasons for this were deemed to be quite evident and so difficult to overcome that the option of negotiating individual national agreements with the EU, as opposed to a broader regional group agreement, was considered to be a more feasible solution for some of the Mercosur countries. The former president of Uruguay, José Alberto 'Pepe' Mujica, claimed that the Mercosur project had stalled and risked becoming obsolete if it did not have needed trade agreements with third parties. According to Mujica, Mercosur had become a 'poor customs union' (MercoPress 2/3/2013): 'We can't and should not cheat ourselves: in recent years Mercosur is stalled and with growing difficulties to trade among its partners ... although there is the manifest bilateral determination which we believe will continue to advance with Brazil ... The truth is that in the whole bloc we have pachyderm size difficulties to advance or to try to advance' (MercoPress 2/3/2013). Mujica also issued a warning about the state of negotiations between the EU and the US: 'How do you penetrate such a huge free trade space? We must lift our heads and look around to what is happening in the world. Imagine the growing difficulties for those left out in the cold to have access to those agreements' (MercoPress 2/3/2013).

According to a representative of Brazil, it was EU Commissioner De Gucht who suggested that they cancel the following meeting where both blocs were meant to exchange proposals for the agreement. The EU insisted that they had not given up and that they were waiting to hear positive news from Mercosur in order to speed up the negotiations (*Clarin* 13/12/2013).

For the EU, the main problem was Argentina since the other three countries had offered the expected outcome which stated that 90% of products would not be subjected to custom tariffs, while Argentinean president, Cristina Fernandez would offer no more than 80% (*Clarin* 13/12/2013). Mercosur adopted a two-speed approach so that Argentina could move more slowly, even though it was felt that the EU would rather see Argentina on the outside of the agreement (*Clarin* 13/12/2013). Just before the summit in Brussels in June 2015, the president of Brazil warned Argentina of the risk of being left behind (*Clarin* 11/6/15). In Brussels, Brazil announced that Mercosur was ready to present an offer, while at the same time appearing to put pressure on Argentina, who were opposed the agreement (*Clarin* 11/6/15). This was similar to what had happened in 2004, when again it was Argentina that had refused to sign the agreement at the last minute. In 2015, Argentinean representatives also disagreed with the timetable that Brazil had offered to Europe (*Clarin* 11/6/15). It is also crucial to point out that the president of Argentina, Cristina Fernandez had decided not to attend the summit.

Given that Brazil needed to improve the competitiveness of its exports, they therefore felt that negotiations had to begin as soon as possible. However, the renegotiation of tariffs had to be done by both sides at the same time, meaning that the EU would also have to agree to the renegotiate tariffs (*Clarin* 11/6/15). In contrast to Brazil, the respective interests of the other Mercosur countries were equal, if not even higher. For example, Uruguay had signed a cooperation agreement with the EU and other developing countries. Uruguay explained how important this agreement with the EU was and that it would reach agreement one way or another (*Clarin* 11/6/15).

The fact that Mercosur needed to negotiate as a group is something that was brought to the discussion because it seems that many South American countries wanted to change this rule so that they could develop their own intendent national-level agreements with the EU. In fact, two weeks before the summit in Brussels, both Uruguay and Brazil discussed the excluding Argentina from the discussions with the EU (*Clarin* 4/6/2015). Both countries also appeared to be worried about being displaced by the US when it comes to food exports (*Clarin* 4/6/2015).

Uruguay also admitted that it had tried to advance talks with the EU on its own during the Brussels Summit, while Brazil waited for the outcome of the elections in Argentina to initiate a change in negotiation with the EU (*Clarin* 9/6/2015). In a manner similar to Uruguay, Paraguay had also discussed the negotiation of an individual trade agreement with the EU (*La Nacion* 11/5/2015).

Brazilian agricultural groups also pointed out that it was extremely important to sign the Mercosur regional agreement with the EU and that if Argentina did not want to participate, Mercosur should push on with the negotiations (*El País* 25/2/2014). At the same time, they were also concerned about negotiations between the EU and the US which could have had a catastrophic impact on the Brazilian agricultural sector (*El País* 25/2/2014).

According to European Commissioner Cecilia Malmstrom, there was a need for more technical meetings before renegotiation of tariffs could take place (MercoPress 12/6/2015). Malmstrom also explained that attempts were being made to progress further discussions, claiming that the negotiations are 'in a dead-end street ... we are seeing if we can find an exit ... there is willingness' (Iprofesional 20/4/2015). Malmstrom also suggested that there are problems with the level of ambition being expressed: 'it needs to be seen if the ambitions are the same, if we want the same, there are discussions [sic] meetings to see if it is the case' (Iprofesional 20/4/2015). Spain also seemed to be suggest that a pragmatic agreement between the EU and Mercosur which would also sanction individual agreements between Mercosur countries and the EU (EUBrasil 27/4/2015), while it also appears that the EU was considering the same issue.

Christian Leffler, head of the EU Desk for the Americas, did not discount the possibility of advancing separate national-level agreements with Mercosur as long as this became 'an official, formal communication'. In fact, Leffler admitted during a video conference with Latin American journalists: 'At that point we would have to consider the situation and find a solution', but the fact was that the EU 'wants to reach an agreement with all Mercosur members ... The objective, our main goal is an association agreement between the EU and Mercosur, and we are convinced that this would be the best option both for Mercosur countries and for the EU' (MercoPress 30/5/2015). In effect, this statement suggested that the decision to push on with the negotiations without Argentina had to come from Mercosur, for it seems that the EU did not want to be seen as responsible making this decision.

After the summit in Brussels, it seemed that the EU would now accept a two-speed agreement with both Mercosur and individual Mercosur member states, with the Vice-president of Uruguay stating that 'I think the most positive side of the meeting in Brussels was the fact that German Chancellor Angela Merkel insisted on the need to formalize as soon as possible an EU/ Mercosur agreement, and if necessary a "two-speed" approach was acceptable' (MercoPress 18/6/2015).

EU engagement with Mercosur

In order to assess the level of ambition shown at the different stages of the negotiation process, it is necessary to contrast the presence of: (1) offers of negotiation mandates or agreements; (2) EU official policy pronouncements; (3) EU promises to Mercosur; and (4) plans for a potential relationship (see Figure 7.1). Furthermore, the negotiations discussed above demonstrate a high level of ambition due to the presence of the following:

- EU official policy pronouncements
- Promises to Mercosur
- Plans for a potential relationship.

In addition to ambition, these negotiations also demonstrate a high level of commitment based on the following factors (Figure 7.2):

- Substantial content of agreements and of offers (including clear tariff arrangements) during the negotiations

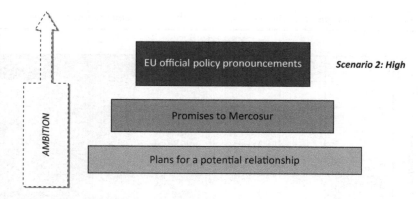

Figure 7.1 Level of ambition: fourth stage

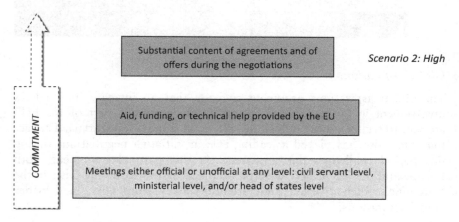

Figure 7.2 Level of commitment: fourth stage

- Aid, funding or technical help provided by the EU
- Meetings, either official or unofficial, at any level: civil servant level, ministerial level, and/or heads of state level.

Engagement is thus measured as high (Table 7.3). In light of the evidence presented above, the final section here will consider the six different arguments that were laid out in Chapter 2 (Table 7.4).

Counterbalancing the US

The argument that the EU was trying to counterbalance the influence of the US does not appear to be applicable during this period, particularly when we consider the fact that the EU and US were also negotiating the Transatlantic Trade and Investment Partnership (TTIP) agreement.

Table 7.3 Measurement of the dependent variable, engagement: fourth stage

		Top	High	Medium	Low	None
				Ambition		
		Top	High	Medium	Low	None
Commitment	Top					
	High		Third and fourth stage: high/high	Second stage: med/high		
	Medium					
	Low				First stage: low/low	
	None					

Global aspirations

The global aspirations argument suggests that an increase in the EU's involvement in Latin America would be an important part of the EU's attempt to secure a more influential role in the international arena. The fact that Mercosur has played a leading role in initiating negotiations during this period challenges this argument. At this particular moment, both Europe and the EU project were preoccupied by the economic crisis in the 'eurozone' which diverted their attention away from pursuing broader global aspirations.

External federator

In regard to promoting regional trade agreements, the EU continued to provide both funding and technical expertise. This is a role that the EU has played from the very outset. The EU continued to play this role by providing funding for the regional integration project in South America. However, the EU's strategic partnership with Brazil in 2007 and the cooperation agreement with Uruguay in 2015, alongside the fact that the EU also seemed to accept bilateral negotiations with Mercosur countries, challenges the 'external federator' argument.

Long-standing political, economic and cultural ties

The suggestion that the EU's involvement in Latin America would increase as a result of the historical ties and shared values between the two regions

Table 7.4 Competing arguments and the independent variables: fourth stage

Independent variable	Expectation	Independent variable value	Expectation value	Met/confronted
Counterbalancing the US	If the US increases its involvement in LA, the EU should increase its involvement. ↑US = ↑EU in LA	Low	Low	No
Global aspirations	If the EU increases its presence in international affairs, the EU's involvement in LA should also increase. ↑EU in the world = ↑EU in LA	Top	Top	No
External federator	If LA becomes more integrated, the EU will increase its relations with LA. ↑LA integration = ↑EU in LA	Top	Top	No
Affinity	An increase of shared values between the regions should develop EU policy. ↑LA shared values = ↑EU in LA	Top	Top	No
Interdependence	If trade and investment between the EU and LA increase, EU policy should also increase. ↑LA trade = ↑EU in LA	Low	Low	No
Iberia	If the influence of Spain and Portugal increase within the EU, then the EU's involvement in LA should increase. ↑SP + PT influence = ↑EU in LA	Low	Low	No

Notes: LA = Latin America; PT = Portugal; SP = Spain.

does seem applicable to the third stage of EU–Mercosur relations. This is evidenced by the fact most EU member states showed a serious lack of interest in the region. Moreover, the fact that the EU was developing additional trade agreements with Asian and African countries – which could be seen as less similar to Europe – further counters this argument.

Interdependence

This argument suggests that an increase in the EU's involvement in Latin America will in response to increasing trade and FDI in Mercosur. The evidence presented above does not support this argument during this particular stage of the negotiations. The influence of business associations, such as the MEBF, played a more proactive role in Latin America than in the EU. Again, it is important to note that trade agreements with South America was not a key priority for all EU member states (see Tables 6.1 and 6.2).

Spanish and Portuguese influence in the EU

This argument suggests that the increase in the EU's interest in Latin America as a result of the influence of Iberian countries in the EU cannot be sustained. While the EU's Iberian member states created forums that would facilitate the negotiations, this momentum was primarily instigated by Mercosur countries. In other words, these negotiations could not be sustained by Iberian interest alone.

In summary, this section has assessed the dependent variable as well as linking it to the values of the independent variables at the third stage of policy negotiations. It has shown how, during this particular stage, none of the aforementioned arguments is sufficient terms of explaining how events unfolded. It has also shown that the degree of Europeanization declined. This supports the core argument this put forward here. The development of the EU policy towards Mercosur very much required the influence its Iberian members. However, this alone was not sufficient by itself. The realization of the EU's policy towards Mercosur was also dependent upon the proactive role played by Mercosur member states.

Conclusion

This chapter has examined the relaunching of the negotiations of an association agreement between the EU and Mercosur since 2010. It has explained how the different possible explanations for the first round of EU–Mercosur negotiations are not fully applicable to this second stage of agreement negotiations. This is due to the fact that these explanations have underestimated the importance of political 'momentum' when it comes to developing

EU–Mercosur trade negotiations, especially the role of Mercosur. They have also underestimated the role played by Spain and Portugal inside the EU, both in relation to Latin America in general and Mercosur in particular.

This chapter has also described how the expansion of EU, which included the integration of twelve new member states who placed strong emphasis on the agricultural sphere of their national economies, also made negotiations more difficult. However, the fact that an agreement was not reached during the Doha Round appears to have helped the Mercosur and the EU to come closer together. We must also acknowledge that was that Mercosur had to improve its reputation as a regional group after variety of concerns expressed on this issue was also an important factor. More importantly, the interest shown by both Spain and Portugal, demonstrated through the Spanish presidency and the efforts of Barroso in his role as president of the European Commission, were also crucial to the relaunch of the negotiations.

Overall, this second round of negotiations encountered additional obstacles, primarily in response to the impact of the 2007 economic crisis, the reluctance shown by both existing and new EU member states towards develop a regional trade agreement with Mercosur and, in particular, Argentina. However, these two regional groups do not relaunch such negotiations if there is no realistic chance of achieving a successful agreement, as was the case with the CACM.

8

Lessons to be learned from the EU policy towards Mercosur

Introduction

> Russia and China, as well as partners in Latin-America, deserve a clear
> European strategy. Africa has, unfortunately, been absent from the EU's
> strategic agenda for years and needs to be reengaged ... The Union can be a
> global actor considering we possess the objectives, principles and instruments.
> Unfortunately the political will is often lacking and the question is whether
> the EU Member States will take action to change this. (Moratinos 2010)

The views of Miguel Angel Moratinos, Spanish minister of foreign affairs
and cooperation, in a speech of 20 January 2010, during the Spanish presidency of the EU, recognize a series of gaps in the strategic behaviour, the
existence of partiality in the strategic agenda, and a lack of will in EU
external relations. This quote suggests that if this was the situation in 2010,
then EU policies during the 1980s and 1990s towards a Latin American
region such as Mercosur were not the most structured nor were they
developed to their full potential. At the same time, the EU's internal institutional and legal frameworks also changed as a result of different treaties
and enlargements. These internal changes affected EU relations with Latin
America both positively and negatively. On the one hand, the Iberian
membership of the EU affected EU policy positively towards Latin America;
on the other hand, policy towards Central and Eastern European countries
which culminated in the 2004 enlargement negatively affecting EU–Latin
America relations.

This monograph has analysed the reasons behind the EU's strategic
actions towards Mercosur from 1985. The dependent variable has been the
degree of engagement the EU demonstrated in its policy. It has been assessed
in relative terms instead of absolute terms with the analyses of two criteria:
ambition and commitment.

In relation to ambition, the focus has been on what the actor – the EU
– wanted, desired and aspired to do. This book has analysed ambition by
looking at how far the EU tried to shift away from its status quo, examining

EU policy pronouncements and long-term plans in relation to Mercosur. With regard to commitment, the focus is on what the actors promised to do or say – and a review of how much of this was done. It is crucial to reflect how hard the EU tried to achieve its objectives and at what price it did so. The number of meetings and the rank of the actors present at those meetings are a way of assessing this. Another indicator was the funding or aid agreed by the EU for Mercosur.

More specifically, this study has analysed the way that the most important policy-makers from both the Council and the Commission as a whole, and individuals within each institution, have positioned themselves during different stages of the policy-making process. This has brought new insights on two important fronts: first, it has shed light on the different arguments in the existing literature which seek to explain the development of EU foreign policy towards Mercosur; and secondly, the results have been examined in relation to the findings in wider and more general debates on EU foreign policy, particularly in relation to the notion of the EU as a global actor.

To complement this analysis, this book has examined the different arguments in the literature on EU policy towards Mercosur at the different stages in order to examine their real explanatory capacity over time. In doing so, this study contributes to an incomplete debate on the reasons behind EU foreign policy towards Latin America, and Mercosur in particular. These findings are relevant in that they contribute to what is a puzzling debate on EU foreign policy in terms of both theoretical and empirical issues by paying special attention to the important discussion on the EU as a global actor. Such a debate is so crucial that it is mentioned continually in official EU views, such as those expressed above by Miguel Angel Moratinos.

This monograph finds considerable evidence of how the EU has been a responsive actor to Mercosur demands at the different stages of the relations instead of being a strategic actor that has initiated EU–Mercosur relations. This argument also corresponds with the work of Jorg Monar (1997), who suggests that third parties are the actors who have sought to upgrade EU–Mercosur policies. It also shows how the Iberian membership created a crucial juncture in the development of EU relations towards the region. Finally, this analysis also implies that the EU is far from being interested in the region in general and that the development of this policy was only possible due to the influence of both Spain and Portugal and the proactive behaviour of Mercosur. The actions of Spain and Portugal and the EU's reaction to them in relation to Mercosur can be identified as a consequence of the path dependence created with the Iberian membership. This undermines the argument that considers the EU to be a global actor. As Miguel Angel Moratinos claims, the EU has the capacity but not the will to develop relations with certain regions such as Africa which are treated differently from others; whilst the EU has not developed a clear and coherent strategy in relation to Latin America.

The remainder of this chapter is divided into three sections. The first section will summarize the most important findings provided by this study. It will then translate these findings into a broader discussion on EU foreign policy towards Mercosur in the second section. Other explanations for the development of EU–Mercosur relations that can be found in the existing literature will be examined in the third section. The chapter will then be concluded by developing an analysis of the role of the EU as a global actor.

Empirical evidence of EU–Mercosur relations

In order to understand fully the conclusions reached in this monograph, it is important to summarize the findings presented in the previous chapters. This section will begin by discussing the concept of the strategic actor by focusing on the lack of proper EU strategy towards Mercosur. This will then be followed by a discussion of EU internal actors and an examination of which actors have shown the most interest in developing EU strategy towards Mercosur.

Lack of strategy?

This section discusses the issue of the existence of a strategy to some extent. Without claiming that there is a complete lack of an EU strategy, there are flaws in EU behaviour. In fact, the EU's actions can be seen as being at the lowest degree of 'strategic'. Therefore, it could be said that the EU is strategically weak. We will first focus on the actions of the EU and move on to look at the actions of Mercosur. The actions of the latter will be used to undermine the suggestion that the EU has been a strategic actor.

As this monograph pointed out in the first chapter the conceptual contribution is related to the definition by Smith and Xie (2010) of the concept of strategic actor. As was stated in the introduction, for an actor to hold a strategy, he or she should undertake consistently intentional actions. Therefore, following the definitions of Moore (1959), 'design for action', or Drucker (1974) 'purposeful action', and Mintzberg (1987), who relies on the work of the former, a strategy should have *consciously intended* actions.

In general terms the EU strategy towards Mercosur should have a plan, an objective(s), the resources to reach that objective, the capacity to become a 'EU' plan in the sense that it involves all the EU actors. It must also have a strategy that is flexible enough to accommodate changes in the international scene. This monograph has shown that the EU fails to do this. However, this definition does not cover all the aspects of 'strategic' actor. This definition should have a part dedicated to the 'intentionality' behind the strategy. The actor holding a strategy needs to undertake consistently intentional actions. This study has tried to make a conceptual contribution to Smith and Xie's definition of the importance of 'intentionality'.

Mintzberg himself highlights the part of the definition that Smith and Xie do not develop – 'consciously intended'. As he says, it has to be developed consciously and purposely. The significance of the intentionality behind the action is that otherwise, accidental actions would be considered strategies. This would mean that some actors would seem to be what they are not and would be described as strategic players when it was not the case. It is necessary to explain that the development of patterns of behaviour without previous preconceptions should not be considered strategies, which goes against Mintzberg's argument: 'Thus, the definition of strategy as plan and pattern can be quite independent of each other: plans may go unrealized, while patterns may appear without preconceptions. To paraphrase Hume, strategies may result from human actions but not human designs' (Mintzberg 1987: 13).

Moreover, in the opposite case, inaction should not be considered a strategy either. This monograph argues explicitly that, for example, ignoring Mercosur or not giving Mercosur the attention that would be expected from a global actor such as the EU, should not automatically be considered a strategy, the strategy of 'indifference'. If the EU was doing this on purpose it would have reasons to do so, and a plan that explains that indifference is going to show a pattern due to certain reasons. But, for this to be the case, the EU would have to know Mercosur well and have reasons that support this planned indifference. This point will be developed further in the conclusions.

In terms of 'interest', the actor does not need to have interest in the object affected by its strategy, since it could be part of a bigger plan. In other words, the EU could develop a strategy towards Mercosur as part of a global EU strategy and have no interest whatsoever in Mercosur per se. Mercosur could be the method through which to achieve something and not the end in itself. Therefore, 'interest' is not a necessary part of the definition.

In relation to the EU and Mercosur it is clear that for the period covered in this monograph, there was not a strategy. Drawing on the work of Smith and Xie (2010), the analysis offered here has been contextualized within the framework of what it takes for the EU to be a strategic actor. Smith and Xie argued that the EU 'must demonstrate the capacity to extract and mobilise resources from its Member States and other relevant sources, and to do so consistently over a period of time' (Smith and Xie 2010: 5). The findings in this monograph suggest that there is a consistent extraction/selection of resources towards Mercosur especially in relation to the transfer of know-how, which can be seen in the multi-annual strategic papers delivered by the Commission. However, caution is needed in the analysis of the importance of that fact since this monograph has proved how the actual amount of resources is significantly smaller than those provided to other regions, especially for Central and Eastern European countries since 1989. The pyramid of preferences also proves how Mercosur has been continually placed at the bottom of the pyramid. Smith and Xie also contend that the EU 'must show that it is possible to relate these resources to agreed medium and long term objectives, and to act positively in line with those objectives' (Smith and Xie 2010: 5). The four empirical chapters demonstrated that the objectives of the EU were never part of a clear long-term plan and, in fact, these objectives repeatedly changed over time. Chapter 4 showed how the EU had barely started to consider a policy towards Latin America in general, let alone have specific objectives towards the region. In Chapter 5, the discussion of EMIFCA proved just how unclear the EU's objectives towards Mercosur actually were because the Commission suggested three different policy options. In addition to this, Chapter 6 recounted how it was only at the last minute that the EU reached the decision to start negotiations with Mercosur, which suggests the decision was not well planned and strategically organized. Chapter 7 also demonstrated how it was necessary again to have a Spanish presidency and the interest in Latin America to relaunch the negotiations. Even the Venezuela of Chavez encouraged Mercosur to negotiate with the EU despite this new member of Mercosur being unable to participate in the negotiations. Alongside these negotiations with Mercosur, it has been shown that the EU developed a special partnership with one Mercosur country alone – which challenges the notion of the EU having a well-rounded and coherent policy towards Mercosur as a whole.

Smith and Xie also argue that the EU 'must demonstrate that it is capable of generating a strategic narrative that shapes the expectations of both its member States and other EU bodies and also its key international interlocutors' (Smith and Xie 2010: 5). In Chapter 6, it was shown that the EU did not match the expectations and desires of Mercosur. More specifically, it was shown that both parties were unable to reach an agreement. Chapter 7 demonstrated how it is even more difficult to reach agreement this time, considering the international financial crisis, the new EU members and the situation of Argentina, even though the Transatlantic Trade and Investment Partnership negotiations are certainly putting even more pressure on Mercosur. Furthermore, in Chapter 4 it was also demonstrated that the EU failed to match the interests of member states such as Spain and Portugal, who tried to secure a more substantial set of commitments from the EU. In addition to this, it was suggested in Chapter 5 that there was a clear difference in expectations of the Commission and the Council during the setting up of EMIFCA, where it was apparent that there was clear disagreements within the Council. Smith and Xie contend that the EU 'must be able to adapt its aims, its resource allocations and its strategic narrative to changes in the global context and to challenges that emerge from its developing international activities' (Smith and Xie 2010: 5). The fact that the negotiations in the third stage (Chapters 6 and 7) were so linked to the state of affairs in the WTO proves how inflexible the EU was being in its relations with Mercosur. Interestingly, Smith and Xie recognize that the EU has developed strategies and in fact many of these strategies were developed through the Commission. Nevertheless, this does not mean that the Commission can be referred to as a strategic actor.

The EU did not have a design for action nor a purposeful plan of action because, apart from other reasons, it did not know what to do with Mercosur, as is demonstrated in the different stages. In fact, it was Mercosur that was offering the possible upgrades of policy. The EU did not have any sort of consciously intended actions at all, since it did not know the region; it was brand new to this area of external relations until the Iberian membership. The EU did not have a long-term plan.

This monograph denies the consideration of accidental actions as strategies to avoid the characterization of 'strategic actor' being mistakenly attached to a player when it is not appropriate. The EU's actions are closer to accidental than to anything else due to the lack of strategy over time and the fact that the steps taken were promoted by Mercosur. In a way, the 'brain/thinker' of the strategy/plan was not the EU but Mercosur.

When a strategy remains unnoticed even for the player exercising the strategy, it does not mean that there is not a strategy in itself, but that the player is not conscious of the strategy, which is different from an accidental action. In this case, the EU did not have a strategy; it is not that it was not aware of what was going on because only the Commission knew the plan, or just a few EU states were aware of what was going on. Simply put, there was not a strategy. In fact, with the lack of knowledge of the region, it was impossible that there could have been an unconscious strategy. This lack of knowledge is what makes it easy to prove that the EU did not have a strategy of 'indifference'. In order to have had such a strategy, the EU would have had to know what it was ignoring and why, which was not the case. The EU was ignoring Mercosur countries until the Iberian membership, but this was due to ignorance, not as a consequence of a deliberate plan.

Mercosur's initiatives

This book has also established that there is enough evidence to suggest that Mercosur's demands on the EU were a direct cause of the developments in the relations between the two regions. This supports the argument put forward by Jorg Monar (1997), who suggests that third-party groups take the initiative and ask for upgrades in relations and/or policies with the EU. In the case of Mercosur, it was shown in Chapter 5 that this happened from the very first moment that EU–Mercosur relations started to develop. In fact, before Mercosur became a regional group ratified by its member states, there was a meeting between the EU and the South American group. This sequence of events explains the speed at which things occurred. In March 1991 Mercosur signed the Treaty of Asunción which created Mercosur, although ratification of this treaty did not take place until the end of the year. In April 1991 Mercosur countries met with the EU in Brussels as part of the annual meeting with the Rio Group. This gathering was the first formal institutionalized meeting of the Rio Group. Two days after this meeting, Mercosur met with the European Commission in order for the two groups to develop inter-regional relations. As a result of this meeting, the first agreement on the transfer of knowledge was signed on 2 May 1992. At the EU–Rio Group annual meeting that took place at the end of May, the two groups reached an inter-institutional agreement. However, this agreement was not enough for Mercosur, and after these events, the ministers of Mercosur countries asked the Commission to work on possible ways of improving relations. Mercosur had already criticized the EU's agricultural protectionism. During the annual EU–Rio Group meeting in 1993 there were discussions about improving relations. Once again it was Mercosur who asked the EU for an upgrade of relations/policies, and this upgrade was developed the next year following the next EU–Rio Group meeting.

The upgrade that the EU offered and signed in 1995 required unanimous agreement of the member states of the EU in order to start negotiations. Again the pressure applied by Mercosur countries was crucial over the years and especially in the run-up to the first meeting of the heads of states of Latin America and the EU in 1999, as discussed in Chapter 6. The dynamic of third parties demanding commitments from the EU at the start of relations and their upgrading of these commitments was not only characteristic of EU–Mercosur relations. It was demonstrated in Chapters 4, 5, 6 and 7 that this was in fact characteristic of EU–Rio Group relations as well. This set of findings suggests that there was a lack of proactive behaviour by the EU in terms of developing policies towards Mercosur. It also suggests that the EU was more responsive in its approach to external suggestions. This dynamic could be seen as a consequence of the asymmetries in both groups in terms of economic power, with Mercosur countries being in a weaker economic and political position, as well as the difficulty Mercosur faced when trying to gain access to the EU market.

The discussion so far has explained one half of the argument which suggests that it was Mercosur that showed proactive strategic behaviour towards EU–Mercosur relations, whilst the EU displayed a more responsive approach in reacting to Mercosur's demands. However, the reasons have not yet been discussed. The following section will explore these issues in relation to both the support and opposition for a policy towards Mercosur within the EU.

Iberian interest versus EU lack of interest

Once Spain and Portugal joined the EU on 1 January 1986, EU relations with Latin America changed to the point where a 'before and after' line can be drawn. This monograph has presented enough evidence to suggest that the extraordinary interests of Spain and Portugal in their former colonies in Latin America were crucial in the responsive attitude of the EU to Mercosur's demands. Moreover, given the fact that Spain and Portugal are not the most powerful countries within the EU and that many other EU countries have their own special relationships with their former colonies in Africa, the Pacific and Asia, this policy is almost unexpected. In other words, the Iberian support for Mercosur demands and a very persistent Spanish commissioner in charge of relations with this region made the development of a policy possible against the backdrop of the lack of support and interest in the region shown by the majority of EU member states.

Chapter 4 explained the impact of Iberian membership in terms of official declarations by both the EU and Iberian countries at the time of the signature of the Act of Accession in June 1985. However, the impact that Spain and Portugal could have was lower than expected because of the lack of interest in that region and consequently little more than declarations were achieved instead of real commitments. Iberian support did not only occur at the time of the Iberian membership; it has been a clear feature of the Spanish and Portuguese actions in the different EU institutions over the years. Chapters 5 and 6 have shown how Manuel Marin had to fight within the Commission against the French commissioners and the agriculture commissioner during the launch of the 1995 agreement with Mercosur – discussions which were only resolved by an internal voting issue.

In the Council, Spain and Portugal promised support in areas of interest for the other member states in exchange for other members' support on anything related to Latin America (Interview 6). Chapter 5 demonstrated Spanish and Portuguese support for the creation of the 1995 agreement. The continued Spanish and Portuguese calls for supportive action were persistent, especially during the presidencies of Spain and Portugal. It is not a surprise that many of the negotiators on the EU side were Spanish, and this issue helped to smooth the negotiation, according to a negotiator from the Argentinean team.

However, all the support and attention given by Spain and Portugal was not automatically replicated by the other member states and commissioners for different reasons. Firstly, in relative terms there was not a significant trade interest on the EU side towards Latin America. Secondly, there are other former colonies of other member states such as the UK and France that continue to be prioritized over Latin America in the EU because Spain and Portugal are not as powerful as the UK and France (see Chapters 5 and 6). Thirdly, from the moment that Eastern European countries became independent from the former Soviet Union, the EU focused politically and economically on them until most of them became member states in 2004 (see Chapters 4, 5 and 6). During the second attempt to negotiate the agreement (Chapter 7) these Eastern European countries became part of the negotiating team since they are part of the EU and some of them have a special interest in the agricultural sector (e.g. Poland). What was once EU foreign policy is now part of what the EU actually is, and therefore part of what it wants. In relation to the last two points, the discussion of the substance of the agreements in Chapter 4 highlighted the intentions of the EU in relation to different groups of countries. The legal material in agreements with ACP or Eastern European countries, and the absence of it in relation to Mercosur, shows the lack of interest in that group by the majority of EU member states. Moreover, even in the official documents in which Mercosur is mentioned, it is not clear which kind of interest – if there was any interest at all – the EU showed towards Mercosur (see Chapters 5, 6 and 7). Therefore, the EU had a lack of interest towards Mercosur compared with other external relations, but that should not undermine the importance of Mercosur within the EU–Latin America relationship. Mercosur was such a priority within EU relations towards Latin America that to some extent, as explained in Chapter 3, EU policy towards Latin America was synonymous with EU policy towards Mercosur. And, as has been explained in Chapters 5 and 6, the EU had a clear interest towards Mercosur as a region, an interest slightly superior to its interest in Mercosur countries individually. In fact, the EU prioritized agreements with the region over individual agreements.

Finally, as mentioned earlier, the possibility of the EU having a consistent policy of neglect towards Mercosur could be sustained only if the EU knew Mercosur countries and institutions well, and if the EU disliked the region/countries, and had an argument against the country/region. Central to the argument developed in this monograph is the fact that the EU did not care enough about Mercosur since it had a very reactive attitude and Mercosur had to be the proactive player, together with Spain and Portugal. This monograph it is not claiming that the EU did not care at all about Mercosur because in that case there would not have been a policy at all.

What does the evidence tell us about EU policy towards Mercosur?

The study of the degree of EU engagement towards Mercosur has been developed through the whole of this monograph. At the different stages, there have been different outcomes but, as has been shown, the tendency was to increase both ambition and commitment at each stage, which is paradoxical since the path dependence was created in the first stage. It might have been expected that the EU would have great ambition and commitment at that stage which might or might not have continued.

Ambition

At the first stage, the level of ambition was low. There were some moves towards the development of new guidelines; the declaration of the EU and the Iberian countries independently from the Treaty of Accession – as Spain and Portugal wanted – from a legal point of view, showed a low level of ambition as well. In the second stage ambition was medium, due to several pieces of evidence showing growing ambition on the EU side. The guidelines established new goals towards Latin America and the first proper guidelines towards Mercosur showed a positive ambition. Also the agreement on the association agreement was important for the level of ambition. However, the requests from the Latin American side in relation to loans from the EIB, the institutionalization of the Rio Group and the development of agreements between Mercosur and the EU undermined the EU ambition shown at this stage. The lack of legal content of the EU–Mercosur agreements did not help increase the level of ambition either.

At the third stage the ambition was high, from the plans to achieve association agreement, as the establishment of the Joint Committee showed. However, the pressure to upgrade the existing EU–Mercosur relations again came from the Mercosur side, which reduces the level of EU ambition. Moreover, the linking of the EU–Mercosur negotiations to the WTO negotiations was evidence against a high level of ambition as well as the attitude of the new commissioners in charge of the agreement, Lamy and Patten.

Commitment

The meetings with the EU–Rio Group after the San José process are evidence of low but existent commitment at the first stage which should not be confused with none. The level of aid attributed is another example of the level of commitment. At the second stage, the level of commitment is high since these are the most productive years of EU–Mercosur relations. The amount of aid assigned in the guidelines, the upgrading of the investment facilities and the visits of Delors to the region prove that level. But more importantly the signature of two EU–Mercosur agreements in such a short period of time helps the assessment. On the negative side the reorganization of the GSP and the legal emptiness of the EU agreements with Mercosur let down the EU level of commitment.

At the last stage of the policy the assessment of commitment was high. The Joint Committee did not achieve much due to resistance in the EU towards any progress in the development of the association agreement, and the lack of a final agreement in October 2004 evidences a vague EU commitment since the European side was the one linking the EU–Mercosur negotiations with the WTO negotiations. The relaunch of the negotiations also demonstrates a high level of commitment.

Throughout this monograph there has been a discussion of the arguments that are put forward in the existing literature to explain the reasons behind EU policy towards Mercosur. The different arguments are not completely incompatible with each other, but one thing that they do have in common is that they do not explain the reason behind the development of EU attitudes across all stages of policy development. In some cases they do not really explain the policy at any stage. The last part of this section will discuss these different explanations and why they fail at some stage to explain EU policy towards Mercosur. Table 8.1 shows the final outcomes of the six different arguments in the different stages of the policy.

Counterbalancing the US

Within the existing literature there is an argument that focuses on the influence that the US already had in Latin America and how the EU was trying to minimize this influence by developing agreements within the sub-regions of Latin America. Since Mercosur covered a vast segment of Latin America, involving the most developed countries in the region apart from Mexico and Chile, and because it can be dealt with as a region it is not a surprise that the EU wanted to achieve relations with Mercosur. Unfortunately, this argument fails in the first and third stages of policy development. In the first stage (Chapter 4), the EU had anything but a plan towards Latin America and it was at this stage that the EU was elaborating ideas and plans. In the third stage (Chapters 6 and 7), again this argument cannot be accepted because the EU was not willing to compromise on economic issues during the negotiations in order to achieve an agreement with the region. In the second stage (Chapter 5), there was some interest and consideration of the US and the creation of NAFTA as a force to develop relations. However, this point should be considered with caution. Not all of the members of the Commission or the Council were thinking in those terms, and definitely not the 'father' of the agreement, Manuel Marin. There was a semblance of consideration of this situation within the directorate general of trade. Some member states, though, admitted that not only was the EU not competing against the US, but the EU could not compete with the US since it was in a weaker position.

Global aspirations

In the literature, there are also some thoughts about the EU's global aspirations which imply an increase in its involvement in world politics as a whole. As a consequence, the focus of the EU's actions should be an arithmetic progression in EU relations/agreements/partnerships with *all* the regions in the world. This was not the case during the first and third stages. During the first stage, the EU did not yet have any clear policy objectives

Table 8.1 Competing arguments at the different stages

Independent variable	Expectations	Met at first stage?	Met at second stage?	Met at third stage?	Met at fourth stage?
Counterbalancing the US	If the US increases its involvement in LA, the EU should increase its involvement. ↑US = ↑EU in LA	No	Yes	No	No
Global aspirations	If the EU increases its presence in international affairs, the EU's involvement in LA should also increase. ↑EU in the world = ↑EU in LA	No	Yes	No	No
External federator	If LA becomes more integrated, the EU will increase its relations with LA. ↑LA integration = ↑EU in LA	Yes	Yes	No	Yes
Affinity	An increase of shared values between the regions should develop EU policy. ↑LA shared values = ↑EU in LA	No	No	No	No
Interdependence	If trade and investment between the EU and LA increase, EU policy should also increase. ↑LA trade = ↑EU in LA	No	No	No	No
Iberia	If the influence of Spain and Portugal increase within the EU, then the EU's involvement in LA should increase. ↑SP + PT influence = ↑EU in LA	Yes	No	No	No

Notes: LA = Latin America; PT = Portugal; SP = Spain.

towards Latin America as a region or towards individual countries in the region. In fact, EU external relations were not that developed in general. The notion that the EU held global aspirations during the 1980s would certainly be an exaggeration. During the third stage (Chapter 6), the EU proved again not to have much interest in the ratification of EMIFCA, which was done more 'in extremis' as a last-minute decision before a meeting with the heads of state of Latin America. At the time of making an economic commitment to Mercosur, the EU was again not ready to do so and the negotiations stopped in 2004. The pyramid of preference also clearly shows the unequal treatment of regions and countries by the EU, not due to the countries' needs but a result of the EU's interests. The Central and Eastern European countries became the highest priority for EU external relations after 1989, until they became members of the EU in 2004. There was a prioritization of regions due to the economic, security or political interests that the EU might have towards them.

External federator

The argument which suggests the EU's role was that of an external federator can be accepted in the first (Chapter 4) and second stages (Chapter 5) but not in the third stage (Chapters 6 and 7). Alongside the argument of counterbalancing the US, this is the most common argument in the existing literature. It is clear that the EU had allocated resources to Mercosur institutions and other Latin American regional groups in order to promote regional integration. The EU had even created the Centre for Economic and Financial Research to support regional integration in Montevideo, Uruguay. However, in the second stage of the policy, the EU started to offer agreements to both the Mercosur group and individual Mercosur member states. It is somewhat confusing that the EU was trying to promote different policies with different approaches. By 2007, there was no room for misunderstandings because the EU offered a very ambitious partnership to the biggest country of Mercosur. The EU singled out Brazil, prioritizing it over other countries and placing it at the level of other global players such as China, India and Russia – the BRIC countries. Chapter 7 demonstrates that the EU is not completely against the idea of launching individual agreements with Mercosur countries, rejecting the idea of prioritizing regional integration over trade agreements.

Long-standing political and economic cultural ties

The EU and Mercosur shared cultural ties as a result of the Mercosur countries being former colonies of some EU states. These cultural ties include languages (i.e. Spanish and Portuguese) and political systems. In the area of political ties, again the fact that some countries were former colonies also shaped their political organization. Economically, since the mid-1980s, Mercosur countries embraced open trade policies after the failure of import substitution policies. This argument is not very common in the existing literature and it could be that those political, economic and cultural ties have existed since the creation of the EU (and before) but were not appealing enough for the EU in terms of developing relations with Mercosur. Fundamentally, Latin America did not become any sort of priority for the EU until the Iberian membership.

Interdependence

The argument in the current literature relating to interdependence is similar to the previous argument but is focused on the trade tendencies at the international level. This is related to increased global interdependence and how this influenced EU–Mercosur relations. It appears that this argument is not applicable at any of the three stages because trade numbers show how the importance of trade with Mercosur is, in relative terms, of minimal importance to the EU.

Spanish and Portuguese influence in the EU

The Iberian membership of the EU in 1986 seems to have an effect on EU relations with Latin America since there was a distinct 'before' and 'after' phase. A new set of policies were considered towards Latin America and Mercosur which were developed further after 1986. But Spain and Portugal were not amongst the most powerful countries in the EU because they were the new member states and were only just leaving the 'developing country' tag behind them. The further enlargements of the EU in 1995 and then again in 2004 meant that the EU now had twenty-five member states, which diluted the power of Spain and Portugal inside the EU. Therefore, in the last stage of policy development (Chapter 5), it was not possible for these countries to successfully direct significant policy development towards Mercosur. In fact, it was shown in Chapter 4 that the Iberian countries were crucial but not the only force contributing to the development of EMIFCA.

What does this say about EU foreign policy?

This final section of this chapter will bring together the argument made in the previous two sections in order to develop a wider discussion about the nature of EU foreign policy. Two main arguments will be discussed: firstly, institutionalization/Europeanization as a way of explaining the development of EU foreign policy; secondly, the development of the EU as a global actor.

Institutionalization/Europeanization

The crucial importance of the Iberian membership in 1986 for the development of an EU policy towards Mercosur has been discussed in Chapter 3 and in the first section of this chapter. The bottom-up system/procedure can be used to explain to some extent the influence of Spain and Portugal when they became members of the EU, and even before, in terms of developing the EU's interests in Latin America. As a consequence, since 1986 it seems, to a certain extent, that EU relations with Latin America and Mercosur have become increasingly institutionalized. This monograph has proven that the continued efforts of Spanish officials at the national and European level in terms of developing relations with Mercosur were crucial. The bottom-up explanation not only explains relations when the Iberian countries became members of the EU, it also explains Spain's continued desire to influence the EU in its international relations with Latin America.

Following Wong's (2008) work on Europeanization of the five perspectives of national projection – which include the processes of policy projection, policy learning and policy transfer – this monograph explains the Europeanization of Spanish and Portuguese national foreign policies using the uploading model. According to this school of thought, Spain and Portugal would have tried to bring their national foreign policies to the EU supranational level by influencing the Commission and other EU states about this new policy area. However, the bottom-up approach is limited and there was the indifference and opposition of almost all other EU member states to contend with. It could be said that there has been a partial institutionalization/Europeanization of this policy.

This is not the only time that, as soon as they joined the EU, new members tried to bring their own national foreign policies to the supranational level. When the EU was created the EDF was also created in order to deal with the special relationship between EU member states and some of their former colonies such as France's relation with former colonies in Africa. This approach was further developed once the UK, which had its own relationship with former colonies, also became a member of the EU. It cannot be argued that this is why the bottom-up process never completely materialized. It did not help that there was nothing in Latin America and Mercosur that was of particular interest to the EU. There were no economic incentives because these countries were still developing their economies and political systems. Furthermore, there was not any immediate humanitarian incentive because these countries were the wealthiest countries in Latin America, and Latin America was not, for example, as poor as Africa. Neither were there any security incentives because the problems in Latin America were mainly restricted to local issues which did not threaten EU security as international terrorism would do, for example. Therefore, Latin America is very much a remote region and still very much under the influence of the US. This brings us to the question of whether the EU really is a global actor or a partially global actor in international relations.

Is the EU a global actor? Not really

According to Bretherton and Vogler (2006) the EU's global 'actorness' can be explained in terms of presence, opportunity and capability. Each of these different aspects was outlined in the introductory chapter. In relation to these characteristics, if the EU was to be referred to as a global actor then it needed to behave like a global actor in its dealings with third parties seeking to develop relations with the EU. Secondly, the EU had to want to behave like a global actor. And thirdly, the EU needed to have the capability to behave like a global actor. In its dealings with Mercosur, the EU only behaved like a global actor in terms of developing relations. The EU may have looked like a global actor in terms of its relationship with Mercosur, but did not behave as such despite having the opportunity and capability of doing so. In relation to 'presence', it can be said that in relation to Mercosur the EU did manage to create expectations since Mercosur was the one demanding a relationship and the subsequent upgrading of the relationship. Mercosur's demands could easily be due to the EU presence.

It is in relation to opportunity that the EU failed miserably to achieve its role as a global actor. The EU had nothing to lose with Mercosur. It was not a sensitive issue such as relations with Russia or China, the Cold War no longer constrained international relations and Mercosur was very keen on the development of relations. Therefore, there is no justification for the lack of EU efforts towards Mercosur, other than it was not interested. If that was the case, then the EU cannot use the discourse of global actor. If you are a global actor, that includes the whole world – not everything bar almost a whole continent such as Latin America. It is not that the EU does not want to get involved with a country like Cuba, which for obvious reasons is a very complex and sensitive issue that nobody wants to deal with. But to ignore the whole of Latin America is not justifiable for a global actor; it is justifiable for a regional actor, but that is a different debate.

In relation to capability the EU was not constrained but rather showed a lack of capability since its relations with Mercosur were based on cooperation, political dialogue and trade negotiations at the lowest level possible. The EU cannot justify the lack of agreement with a lack of capabilities.

Conclusion

This chapter started with a quotation from the Spanish minister of foreign affairs in which he admitted that the EU could be a global actor, but there was no political motivation for it to do so. It could be argued that the EU could behave as a global actor but chose not to because it did not have the necessary political will.

This monograph has proved that the reasons behind the EU's actions towards Mercosur were, for a certain period of time, different for the main actors, different EU member states and the Commission. This book has examined the various other explanations of EU foreign policy towards Mercosur provided in the existing literature. For the first time, these explanations have been tested across three distinct stages in the policy development process and as a result this study has contributed to the ongoing debate on EU foreign policy in both general terms and in relation to two specific issues: the institutionalization/Europeanization of foreign policies and the EU's behaviour as a global strategic actor. In conclusion, this monograph has argued that the EU was a responsive rather than proactive actor towards Mercosur over the course of the three distinct phases of EU–Mercosur policy development.

References

Adiwasito, E., De Lombaerde, P. and Pietrangeli, G. (2006) 'On the joint assessment of Andean integration in the EU–CAN relations', OBREAL/EULARO Background Paper, April.

Agence Europe (22/3/1991) 'Unequivocal approbation by the EP for the economic and trade agreement of December 1990'.

Agence Europe (23/4/1991) 'EEC–Latin America: first institutionalized ministerial meeting between the EEC and the Rio Group (26 and 27 April in Luxembourg) – how can concrete form be given to the relaunch of relations? – the EIB problem'.

Agence Europe (26/4/1991) 'EEC–Latin America: opening of first institutionalised ministerial conference between the community and the Rio Group – the final document will be adopted on Saturday'.

Agence Europe (5/5/1992) 'Towards reinforcing links between the EC and Mercosul – imminent inter-institutional agreement, examination of possible links on a formal basis. Guimaraes'.

Agence Europe (29/5/1992) 'EC–Latin America: satisfaction for the economic rebirth of South America and intensified cooperation – imminent presentation of projects to be financed by the EIB – broad debate on the "banana" trading regime'.

Agence Europe (30/10/1992) 'EC/Latin America: meeting of senior officials from the commission and from the Rio Group on the subject of trade policy'.

Agence Europe (10/3/1993) 'President Delors begins an official "political" visit to Chile, Argentina and Mexico'.

Agence Europe (20/3/1993) 'EC/Latin America: President Delors' official visit to Chile, Argentina and Mexico gives him the opportunity of confirming the Community's will to strength relations with this continent'.

Agence Europe (25/4/1994) 'EP/external relations: pressure on India and free trade with some Latin American countries?'.

Agence Europe (16/8/1994) 'In a declaration adopted in early August in Buenos Aires, the presidents of the member countries of Mercosur (Argentina, Brazil, Uruguay and Paraguay) welcome the intention affirmed by the European Council in Corfu to intensify relations with Mercosul'.

Agence Europe (12/10/1994) 'Mr Steichen confirms existence of proposal for area of free trade (which would not cover agriculture)'.

Agence Europe (13/10/1994) 'Mr Steichen tells dialogue partners the EU will not sacrifice agriculture, Buenos Aires'.

Agence Europe (19/10/1994) 'The European Commission proposes establishment of a "pioneer agreement" with this emerging economic region'.

Agence Europe (24/10/1994) 'EP/Latin America: Mr Linkhoorh proposes enlarging US/Latin America dialogue (EU?)'.

Agence Europe (9/11/1994) 'Mercosur foreign ministers (Argentina, Brazil, Paraguay and Uruguay) will meet Mr Delors and Mr Marin on 24 November – divergence over agriculture?'.

Agence Europe (7/7/1995) 'Manuel Marin updates on relations between the Union and different countries or groups of countries'.

Agence Europe (14/2/1996) 'The difficulties in defining the offer to make South Africa confirm that ill thought-out promises in matters of free-trade areas place the EU in an embarrassing situation, especially as most of the countries concerned only seek better access to the European market for their agricultural products – global reflection required'.

Agence Europe (17/4/1996) 'Dialogue with the Andean community, setting up of the EU/Mercosur trade instruments'.

Agence Europe (7/5/1996) 'Council shares presidency's concerns for free trade areas'.

Agence Europe (18/6/1996) 'Agricultural organizations on both sides intend cooperating despite differences of approach on trade issues'.

Agence Europe (9/4/1997) 'Draft calendar for negotiation of trade liberalization – delay in ratification in Europe hinders application of a large part of the framework agreement'.

Agence Europe (19/12/1997) 'Mr Marin confirms the EU's "commitment" to develop before the end of the century an association entailing trade liberalization – some member states doubtful about the state of preparedness of Mercosur countries'.

Agence Europe (16/4/1998) 'Sir Leon confirms that a negotiating brief for trade liberalization with Mercosur will be put before the council in June and argues in favour of the "millennium round" in the WTO'.

Agence Europe (14/5/1998) 'Joint trade committees complete trade analysis, marking the first stage towards liberalization – commission should present a mandate for second stage before summer'.

Agence Europe (24/7/1998) 'France affirms that commission proposal on free trade area does not conform to what was agreed and recommends "other ways" of strengthening relations'.

Agence Europe (27/5/1999) 'European Commission submits eight options to council for banana regime to comply with WTO rules'.

Agence Europe (31/5/1999) 'In the end, the General Affairs Council of 31st May did not reach an agreement due to France refusal'.

Agence Europe (1/6/1999) 'Council calls on Cologne Summit to take stance on projects for liberalisation of trade with Mercosur and Chile'.

Agence Europe (10/6/1999) 'Brazilian diplomat says Latin America should make no concessions if EU does not open up its agricultural market'.

Agence Europe (24/6/1999) 'First summit between 48 European and Latin America heads of government to launch phase of political economic cooperation between the two continents – programme and goals'.

Agence Europe (29/6/1999) 'Summit looks to emergence of more a democratic and balanced form of globalisation – closer political, economic, scientific, social and cultural cooperation'.

Agence Europe (15/9/1999) 'Council adopts negotiating briefs'.

Agence Europe (24/2/2000) 'Mercosur ministers insist that upcoming negotiations must cover all sectors, including agriculture'.

Agence Europe (8/6/2000) 'Patten says he has attained his goal of relaunching debate on EU policy towards third countries'.

Agence Europe (20/9/2000) 'Mr Lamy goes to South America while some Mercosur countries complain of lack of interest'.

Agence Europe (8/2/2001) 'Marset Campos and Salafranca reports call for negotiations briefs to be changed to allow future free trade agreements to be concluded before end of new WTO Round'.

Agence Europe (1/3/2001) 'Parliament calls for modification of negotiating brief for free trade agreements presently under negotiation'.

Agence Europe (7/11/2002) '8th negotiating session for free trade agreement to be held from 10–14 November in Brasilia'.

Agence Europe (14/1/2003) 'Pascal Lamy doubts that free trade areas represent the right formula for trade relations with third countries'.

Agence Europe (5/11/2003) 'Pascal Lamy explains why EU wants moment for reflection before re-launching Doha round'.

Agence Europe (27/5/2004) 'Fidel Castro will not attend Guadalajara Summit – Chris Patten and Enrique Iglesias insist on social cohesion and multilateralism'.

Agence Europe (28/5/2004) 'Ministers and the Commission confirm their aim to conclude the free trade negotiations in October – still no Mercosur offer on public procurement'.

Agence Europe (1/6/2004) 'France thinks EU and Mercosur "still far from concluding" a free trade agreement'.

Agence Europe (29/6/2004) 'Commission prudently optimistic about free trade negotiations'.

Agence Europe (10/8/2004) 'EU/Mercosur'.

Agence Europe (28/9/2004) 'Commission is generally disappointed by new offer received Saturday – EU prepares offer for Wednesday'.

Agence Europe (7/5/2008) 'EU/Latin America', *Europe Daily Bulletin*.

Agence Europe (20/5/2008) 'Lima Summit obtains mixed results', *Europe Daily Bulletin*.

Agence Europe (10/12/2009) 'Council wants increased effort to bring about resumption of talks on EU–Mercosur Association Agreement', *Europe Daily Bulletin*.

Agence Europe (5/2/2010) 'Moratinos says summit with Obama is not urgent – debate with MEPs', *Europe Daily Bulletin*.

Agence Europe (22/4/2010) 'Parliament backs conclusion of negotiations with Central America and resumption of discussions with Mercosur', *Europe Daily Bulletin*.

Agence Europe (15/5/2010) 'Seven countries say resumption of Mercosur trade relations is "highly negative signal" for European agriculture', *Europe Daily Bulletin*.

Agence Europe (18/5/2010) 'Dozen ministers criticise resumption of trade talks with Mercosur', *Europe Daily Bulletin*.

Agence Europe (20/5/2010) 'Summit sees readjustment of EU–Latin American relations', *Europe Daily Bulletin*.

Agence Europe (17/7/2010) 'President Lula wants to conclude EU–Mercosur free trade agreement before leaving office in December', *Europe Daily Bulletin*.

Agence Europe (16/9/2010) 'Karel De Gucht hoping for an agreement with Mercosur in 2011', *Europe Daily Bulletin*.

Agence Europe (18/9/2010) 'De Gucht replies to Le Maire on Mercosur', *Europe Daily Bulletin*.

Agence Europe (23/2/2011) 'Ireland, concerned for its agriculture, raises temperature', *Europe Daily Bulletin*.

Aggarwal, V. and Fogarty, E. (2004) *Between regionalism and globalism: interregional trade strategies of the EU*, London: Palgrave Macmillan.

Aggestam, L. (2008) 'Introduction: ethical power Europe?', *International Affairs*, 84:1, pp. 1–11.

Aldecoa Luzarraga, F. (1995) 'EL acuerdo entre la Union Europea y el Mercosur en el marco de la intensificación de relaciones entre Europa y America Latina', *Revista de Instituciones Europeas*, 22:3, pp. 761–792.

Alecu de Flers, N. and Regelsberger, E. (2005) 'The EU and inter-regional cooperation', in Hill, C. and Smith, M. (eds), *International relations and the European Union*, Oxford: Oxford University Press.

Alemany, C. (2004) 'Diplomacia de cumbers y diplomacia ciudadana en la asociacion birregional desde la perspectiva del Mercosur', *Nueva sociedad*, 190, March/April, http://nuso.org/revista/190/relaciones-america-latina-caribe-y-union-europea-ii.

Alvarez, G.O. (1995) 'Los limites de lo transnacional: Brasil y el Mercosur. Una aproximacion antropologica a los procesos de integracion', master's dissertation, University of Brasília.

Anacoreta Correia, J. M. (1996) *Europa America Latina: 20 anos de documentos oficiales (1976–1996)*, Madrid: IRELA.

Arenas, M. (2002) 'Economic relations of the European Union and Mercosur', *Jean Monnet/Robert Schuman Papers*, 1:9, October.

Ayuso, A. (1996) 'La relacion euro-latinoamericana a traves del proceso de integracion regional europea', *Revista CIDOB d'Afers Internacionals*, 32, pp. 147–164.

Baklanoff, E. N. (1985) *Spain's emergence as a middle industrial power*, Washington, DC: America Enterprise Institute (AEI).

Baklanoff, E. N. (1996) 'Spain's economic strategy toward the "nations of its historical community": the "reconquest" of Latin America?', *Journal of Interamerican Studies and World Affairs*, 38:1, spring, pp. 105–127.

Baklanoff, E. (2001) 'Circumventing the embargo: the strategic context of Spain's economic relations with Cuba', in *ASCE, Cuba in Transition*, Volume 11, Bethesda, MD: ASCE.

Bellier, I. (1997) 'The Commission as an actor', in Wallace, H. and Young, A. R. (eds), *Participation and policy-making in the European Union*, Oxford: Oxford University Press.

Birochi, F. (1999) 'The European Union's development policies towards Asian and Latin American countries', *DSA European Development Policy Study Group Discussion Papers*, 11, February, Manchester.

Bizzozero, L. (1995) 'Aproximaciones: nuevas modalidades de cooperación UE-Mercosur' *Desarrollo y Cooperación*, 4, July–August.

Bizzozero, L. (2001) 'El acuerdo marco inter-regional Unión Europea – Mercosur: dificultades y perspectivas de una asociación estratégica', in de Sierra, G. (ed.), *Los rostros del MERCOSUR: el difícil camino de lo comercial a lo societal*, Buenos Aires: CLACSO – ASDI.

Blanco Garriga, T. (1992) 'Brasil y la Comunidad Europea en el marco de las relaciones CE-América Latina', *Revista CIDOB d'Afers Internacionals*, 23–24, pp. 267–290.

Bologna, N. (2003) 'Comparacion entre la Union Europea y el Mercosur desde un enfoque economico institucional', paper presented at the Historia Actual conference.

Botto, M. (2007) 'The role of epistemic communities in the makeability of Mercosur', paper presented at the GARNET Makeability of Regions workshop, Bruges.

Bouzas, R. and Soltz, H. (2001) 'La formació n de instituciones reginoales en el Mercosur', in Chudnovsky, D. and Fanelli, J. M. (eds), *El desafío de integrarse para crecer, balance y perspectivas del Mercosur en su primera década*, Madrid: Siglo XXI.

Bretherton, C. and Vogler, J. (1999) *The European Union as a global actor*, London and New York: Routledge.

Bretherton, C. and Vogler, J. (2006) *The European Union as a global actor*, 2nd edition, London: Routledge.

Bulmer, T. (2000) 'The European Union and Mercosur: prospects for the free trade agreement and implications for the United States', *Journal of Interamerican Studies and World Affairs*, 42:1, spring, pp. i–iv.

Bulmer-Thomas, V. (2001) *Regional integration in Latin America and the Caribbean: the political economy of open regionalism*, London: ILAS.

Caetano, G. et al. (2010) *Las negociaciones entre el Mercosur y la Unión Europea de cara al 2010*, Montevideo: Centro de Formación para la Integración Regional.

Camino Munoz, C. and Nieto Solis, J. A. (1992) 'La década de los noventa: punto de inflexión en las relaciones Comunidad Europea-América Latina?', *Información Comercial Española*, 702, p. 75.

Cason, J. (2000) 'Electoral reform and stability in Uruguay', *Journal of Democracy*, 11:2, pp. 85–98.

Carranza, M. E. (2004) 'Mercosur and the end game of the FTAA negotiations: challenges and prospects after the Argentine crisis', *Third World Quarterly*, 25:2, pp. 319–337.

Cepal (1999) *América Latina en la agenda de transformaciones estructurales de la Unión Europea*, Santiago de Chile: CEPAL.

Chasquetti, D. and Buquet, D. (2004) 'La democracia en Uruguay: una partidocracia de consenso', *Politica*, 42, pp. 221–247.

Chomsky, N. (1992) *Deterring democracy*, London: Vintage.

Christiansen, T. (2001) 'The European Commission: administration in turbulent times', in Richardson, J. (ed.), *European Union power and policy-making*, London: Routledge.

Cienfuegos, M. (2003) 'Implications of European Union enlargement for Euro–Mercosur Relations', in Barbé, E. and Johansson-Nogues, E. (eds) *Beyond enlargement: the new members and new frontiers of the enlarged European Union*, Barcelona: Instituto Universitario de Estudios Europeos.

Cienfuegos, M. (2006) *La asociación estratégica entre la unión europea y el Mercosur, en la encrucijada*, Barcelona: CIDOB.

Cini, M. (1996) *The European Commission: leadership, organisation and culture in the EU administration*, Manchester: Manchester University Press.

Clarin (2/1/2010) 'Con el fantasma de una crisis que no cede, España presidirá la UE'.

Clarin (7/3/2010) 'Es clave aprovechar la presidencia de Espana'.

Clarin (6/5/2010) 'Francia se opone a las negociaciones e el merocsur y la UE'.

Clarin (15/4/2011) 'La UE acuso a Argentina de trabar el comercio'.

Clarin (5/5/2011) 'Otra incierta ronda con la UE por el comercio'.

Clarin (28/6/2010) 'La UE exige a Argentina que "deje de bloquear" importaciones'.

Clarin (5/7/2010) 'Argentina rechazon en la OMC las acusaciones europeas de proteccionismo'.

Clarin (18/10/2011) 'Merkel impulsara un tratado de libre comercio entre el Mercosur y la UE'.

Clarin (13/12/2013) 'Se trabó la negociación entre el Mercosur y la Unión Europea'.

Clarin (4/6/2015) 'Tabaré echa a su embajador en la UE por diferencias con la Argentina'.

Clarin (9/6/2015) 'Uruguay avanza con su plan de acordar con la UE sin el Mercosur'.

Clarin (11/6/2015) 'Brasil: es inminente el acuerdo de libre comercio con Europa'.

Crawley, A. (2000) 'Towards a biregional agenda for the twenty-first century', *Journal of Interamerican Studies and World Affairs*, 42:2, pp. 9–34.

Cuadros Ramos, A., Cantavella Jorda, M., Fernandez Guerrero, J. I. and Suarez Burguet, C. (1999), 'European Union–Mercosur commercial relations: export function modelling', *Informacion Comercial Espanola. Revista de Economia*, 782, November–December.

Dauster, J. (1996) 'União Européia: rumo à associação inter-regional', *Política Externa*, 4:4, pp. 35–48.

De Pablo Valenciano, J. and Carreretero Gomez, A. (1999) 'El proceso de integración regional Europea y su relación con América Latina', *publicaciones electrónicas programa de mejoramiento de la formación en Economía, PROMEC Documentos de Reflexión Académica*.

del Arenal, C. (2009) 'Las relaciones entre la UE y América Latina: ¿abandono del regionalismo y apuesta por una nueva estrategia de carácter bilateralista?', Real Instituto Elcano, Madrid.

Devlin, E., Estevadeordal, A. and Krivonos, E. (2003), 'The trade and cooperation nexus: how does the Mercosur-EU process measure up?', *INTAL Occasional Paper 22*, ITD-STA.

Dinan, D. (1999) *Ever closer union? An introduction to the European Community*, Basingstoke: Palgrave Macmillan.

Doctor, M. (2007) 'Why bother with inter-regionalism? Negotiations for a European Union–Mercosur agreement', *Journal of Common Market Studies*, 45:2, pp. 281–314.

Dromi, R. and Molina del Pozo, C. (1996) *Acuerdo Mercosur-Union Europea*, Buenos Aires: Ediciones Ciudad Argentina.

Duchene, F. (1972) 'Europe's role in world peace', in Mayne, R. (ed.), *Europe tomorrow: sixteen Europeans look ahead*, London: Fontana.

Dunne T. (2008) 'Good citizen Europe', *International Affairs*, 84:1, pp. 33–48.

Duran, R. (2009) 'Notas sobre las peculiaridades del bilateralismo latinoamericano-europeo', in Caetano, G. (ed.), *Las negociaciones entre América Latina y el Caribe con la Unión Europea Posibilidades e incertidumbres en el 2010*, Montevideo: Cefir.

Drucker, P. F. (1974) *Management: tasks, responsibilities, practices*, New York: Harper & Row.

Dykmann, K. (2006) *Perceptions and politics: the foreign relations of the European Union with Latin America*, Frankfurt am Main: Vervuert Verlag.

EC–Mercosur (1993) 'Second meeting of EC–Mercosur Joint Advisory Committee', 12 January.

Edwards, G. and Regelsberger, E. (eds) (1990), *Europe's global links*, New York: St Martin's Press.

EEC (European Economic Community) (1961) 'Cooperation agreement between the EC and Euratom and the governments of the United States of Brazil on the pacific use of atomic energy', 69/95/Euratom, 9 June.

EEC (European Economic Community) (1973a) 'Commercial agreement between the EEC and the Oriental Republic of Uruguay', 6 November.

EEC (European Economic Community) (1973b) 'Commercial agreement between the EEC and the Federal Republic of Brazil', 19 December.

EEC (European Economic Community) (1975) 'Commercial agreement between the EEC and the Federal Republic of Mexico', 23 September.

EEC (European Economic Community) (1980) 'Cooperation agreement between the EEC and the Federal Republic of Brazil', 18 September.

EEC (European Economic Community) (1985) 'Declaration on the intentions relative to the development and the intensification of the relations with Latin American countries', Offical Journal L 302, 15/11/1985 P. 0479, 12 June.

EEC (European Economic Community) (1992a) 'Regulation (EC) 443/92 concerning financial and technical aid and economic co-operation with the developing countries of Latin America and Asia', 25 February.

EEC (European Economic Community) (1992b) 'Regulation (EEC) 319/92 of 3 February 1992 on the implementation for a trial period of the European Communities investment partners financial instrument for countries of Latin America, Asia and the Mediterranean region', 3 February.

EEC (European Economic Community) (1995) 'Relations entre la Communaute Européenne et le Mercosur: le s'organise une audition des pays concernes', press release, CES/95/100, 7 September.

El País (20/2/1985) 'La CEE abre un período de reuniones permanentes para intentar finalizar en marzo la negociación con España'.

El País (27/4/1985) 'España rechaza la propuesta de la CEE sobre los temas pendientes en la negociación'.

El País (1/11/1985) 'Felipe González defiende una negociación política de la deuda externa'.

El País (23/7/1985) 'Los doce firmarán un acuerdo de cooperación con Centroamérica'.

El País (22/11/1985) 'González cree que la entrada de España en la CEE será positiva para América Latina'.

El País (23/11/1985) 'Yáñez cree que la CEE no quiere dar a España protagonismo en Latinoamérica'.

El País (28/12/1985) 'Kohl considera inaceptable entrar en la CEE y salir de la Alianza'.

El País (31/12/1986) 'España inicia la segunda etapa de adaptación a la CE'.

El País (23/6/1987) 'La CE define una estrategia global frente a América Latina'.

El País (7/3/1990) 'España pierde peso en los órganos de poder de la Comisión'.

El País (9/5/1990) 'La Comunidad Europea duplica las ayudas a America Latina y Asia'.

El País (13/10/1990) 'El grupo de río pide a EEUU un trato equitativo'.

El País (17/6/1994) 'Cita de Cartagena'.

El País (20/11/1994) 'Los suramericanos celebran que la 'UE cruce el Atlántico'.

El País (6/4/1995) 'El mercado común UE-Mercosur supera el obstar culo del comercio agrícola'.

El País (16/9/1995) 'Aznar recorre Ultramar'.

El País (27/10/1995) 'La UE coloca las relaciones con America Latina entre sus prioridades'.

El País (9/12/1995) 'El caso latinoamericano'.

El País (16/12/1995) 'Marin prevé una zona de libre comercio entre la UE y Mercosur en el año 2005'.

El País (11/3/1997) 'Chirac busca disputar a EEUU su peso en America Latina'.

El País (9/7/1998) 'La mayoría de la Comisión Europea apoya un nuevo acuerdo de asociación interregional con Mercosur'.

El País (21/7/1998) 'Los ministros de agricultura de la UE quieren saber el impacto que tendra el libre comercio con Mercosur'.

El País (23/7/1998) 'Bruselas aprueba crear una zona de libre cambio con Mercosur y Chile'.

El País (12/5/1999) 'Francia y el Reino Unido frenan las negociaciones de la UE con Mercosur'.

El País (6/6/1999) 'Chirac dinamito la negociación con Mercosur en la cumbre de la UE'.

El País (22/6/1999) 'La Unión Europea vence la resistencia francesa para abrir negociaciones con Mercosur en el 2001'.

El País (29/6/1999) 'La UE, Mercosur y Chile se comprometen a crear sin plazo fijo un área de libre comercio'.

El País (15/7/2000) 'La UE disminuye su ayuda a la cooperación para Latinoamérica'.

El País (17/11/2002) 'La UE refuerza el comercio con America Latina en tres acuerdos'.

El País (9/7/2004) 'Fischler admite ante la COAG que la reforma del azúcar será negativa para España'.

El Pais (25/11/2009) 'España impulsa el pacto comercial de la UE con Mercosur'.

El Pais (18/4/2010) 'UE-Mercosur, novios otra vez'.

El Pais (7/5/2010) 'Francia se opone a desbloquear la negociación con Mercosur'.

El Pais (18/5/2010) 'La UE y Mercosur buscan cerrar un acuerdo de libre comercio este año'.

El Pais (15/7/2010a) 'Lula impulsa las negociaciones entre Mercosur y la UE'.

El Pais (15/7/2010b) 'Solchaga presenta a Mercosur como un proyecto fracasado'.

El Pais (17/7/2010) 'Los socialdemócratas en Brasil apuestan por un tratado con la UE que no dependa de Mercosur'.

El Pais (9/11/2010) 'De la Vega intenta que Argentina tome impulse en Mercosur'.

El Pais (10/12/2010) 'Uruguay ve a Mercosur en su peor momento'.

El Pais (25/2/2014) 'El sector agrario brasileño da un ultimátum a Argentina en acuerdo UE-Mercosur'.

El País (1/8/2014) 'Es más barato que Brasil ayude a Argentina ahora que sufrir después'.

EP (European Parliament) (1969) 'Resolution in relation to the European Community relations with Latin America', 25 November.

EP (European Parliament) (1973) 'Resolution on the coup d'état in Chile', 10 November.

EP (European Parliament) (1976) Support for the creation of institutions that will help the promotion and the information of the possibilities of these countries', EP Resolution 8, March.

EP (European Parliament) (1982) 'Resolution on the conflict between the UK and Argentina for the Falkland/Malvinas Islands', 22 April.

EP (European Parliament) (1983) 'Resolution on the situation in Argentina', 13 October.

EP (European Parliament) (1985) 'Resolution on the project of cooperation agreement between the European Community and Central America', 13 June.

European Commission (1969) 'The EEC's relations with Latin America: Commission memorandum to the Council', Information Memo P-43/69, August.

European Commission (1990) 'Guidelines for cooperation with the developing countries of Latin America and Asia', COM (90) 176.

European Commission (1991a) 'EC–international partners financial facility for countries of Asia, Latin America and the Mediterranean region', COM (90) 575 final, Brussels, 7 March.

European Commission (1991b) Official Journal, 29 April.

European Commission (1994a) 'Communication from the Commission to the Council and the European Parliament: the European Community and Mercosur – an enhanced policy', COM (94) 428, European Commission External Relations Directorate, Latin America Regional Strategy Paper 2002–2006.

European Commission (1994b) 'Commission press release report on the implementation of macro-financial assistance to third countries', press release, IP/94/529, 14 June.

European Commission (1994c) '1796th Council meeting – general affairs – Luxembourg, 31 October 1994, president: Mr. Klaus Kinkel, minister for foreign affairs of the Federal Republic of Germany', press release, Pres/94/219, 31 October.

European Commission (1994d) 'Mercosur foreign ministers visit Commission', press release, IP/94/1091, 24 November.

European Commission (1994e) 'Signature of a solemn Joint Declaration between the Council of the EU and the European Commission on one side and the member states on the other side', press release, Pres/94/281, 22 December.

European Commission (1995a) 'The European Union and Latin America: the present situation and prospects for closer partnership 1996–2000', COM(95) 495 final, communication from the Commission to the Council and the European Parliament.

European Commission (1995b) '1853rd council meeting – general affairs – Luxembourg, 12 June 1995 – president Mr. Herve de Charette, minister for foreign affairs of the French Republic – Mr. Michel Banier, minister with special responsibility for European affairs of the French Republic', press release, 95/174.

European Commission (1995c) '1844th council meeting – general affairs – Luxembourg, 10 April 1995, president: Mr. Alain Juppe, minister for foreign affairs of the French Republic', press release, 95/114.

European Commission (1998a) 'Relations with Latin America', press release, CES/98/12, 23 January.

European Commission (1998b) 'GSP: the Commission proposes a new multi-annual scheme', press release, IP/98/803, 16 September.

European Commission (1999) 'European and Latin America business and governments to focus on Mercosur and WTO trade talks', press release, IP/99/864, 22 November.

European Commission (2001a) 'EU proposes business facilitation initiative with Mercosur and Chile on eve of negotiations', press release, IP/01/326, 7 March.

European Commission (2001b) 'EU trade commissioner Pascal Lamy to visit Brazil to strength EU/Mercosur and WTO trade ties', press release, IP/01/967, 6 July.

European Commission (2002a) 'Pascal Lamy, European commissioner for trade, facing the challenge of globalisation: regional integration or multilateral rules?', press release, SPEECH/02/87, 27 February.

European Commission (2002b) 'EU and Mercosur conclude successful business forum in Madrid', press release, IP/02/726, 16 May.

European Commission (2002c) 'External Relations Directorate Latin America Regional Strategy Paper 2002–2006', European Commission External Relations Directorate General.

European Commission (2004) 'Outcome of Agriculture/Fisheries Council of May 2004' Agriculture press release, MEMO/04/121, 25 May.

European Commission (2010) 'European Commission proposes relaunch of trade negotiations with Mercosur countries', press release, IP/10/496, 4 May.

European Commission (2015) 'Regional indicative programme Mercosur, mid-term review and regional indicative programme for 2011–2013'.

European Communities (1997) 'Treaty establishing the European Community (Amsterdam consolidated version) – Part Six: general and final provisions – Article 300 – Article 228 – EC Treaty (Maastricht consolidated version) – Article 228 – EEC Treaty', Official Journal C 340, 10 November 1997, P. 0298 – Consolidated version, 11997E300.

European Communities (2001) 'Treaty of Nice amending the Treaty on European Union, the treaties establishing the European Communities and certain related acts', Official Journal, 10 March 2001, C 80/1.

European Communities (2002) 'Consolidated versions of the Treaty on European Union and of the Treaty establishing the European Community', Official Journal, C 325/01.

European Council (1992) 'The European Council Lisbon Summit, Lisbon, 26–27 June 1992 (EU European Council), Conclusions of the Presidency' SN 3321/2/92, 26/27 June 1992.

European Council (1994) 'European Council, 9 and 10 December 1994 in Essen: presidency conclusions', press release, Doc 94/4.

European Council (1998) 'European Community investment partners, ECIP, progress reports, 1995, 1996, 1997. Report from the Commission', COM (98) 752 final, 18 December.

EU–Mercosur (1995) 'EU–Mercosur: Interregional Framework on Commercial and Economic Cooperation Initialled', 29 September.

EU–Mercosur (2000a) 'First Biregional Negotiations Committee: conclusions, Buenos Aires', 6–7 April.

EU–Mercosur (2000b) 'Second Biregional Negotiations Committee: conclusions', 13–16 June.

EU–Mercosur (2000c) 'Third Biregional Negotiations Committee: conclusions', Brasilia, 7–10 November.

EU–Mercosur (2001a) 'EU–Mercosur Fourth Biregional Negotiations Committee: conclusions', 19–22 March.

EU–Mercosur (2001b) 'Fifth Biregional Negotiations Committee: conclusions', 2–6 July.

EU–Mercosur (2001c) 'Sixth Biregional Negotiations Committee: conclusions', 29–31 October.

EU–Mercosur (2002a) Seventh Biregional Negotiations Committee: conclusions', 8–11 April.

EU–Mercosur (2002b) EU and Mercosur conclude successful business forum in Madrid', 16 May.

EU–Mercosur (2003a) 'Ninth Biregional Negotiations Committee: conclusions', 17–21 March.

EU–Mercosur (2003b) 'Tenth Biregional Negotiations Committee: conclusions', 23–27 June.

EU–Mercosur (2004a) 'Twelfth Biregional Negotiations Committee: conclusions', 8–12 March.

EU–Mercosur (2004b) 'EU–Mercosur Thirteenth Biregional Negotiations Committee: conclusions', 3–7 May.

EU–Mercosur (2010), 'Summit joint communiqué: Council of the European Union', 9870/10 (Presse 129), 17 May.

EU–Brasil (2015) 'Spain suggests a "pragmatic" option to EU–Mercosur agreement, says Valor Econômico', 27 April.

Evered, R. (1983) 'So what is strategy?', *Long Range Planning International Journal of Strategic Management*, 16:3, pp. 57–72.

Faust, J. (2004) 'The European Union's trade policy towards Mercosur', in Aggarwal, V. and Fogarty, E. (eds), *European Union trade strategies: between globalism and regionalism*, London: Palgrave Macmillan.

Featherstone, K. and Radaelli, C. (2003) *The politics of Europeanization*, Oxford: Oxford University Press.

Flaesch-Mougin, C. (1990) 'Competing frameworks: the dialogue and its legal bases', in Edwards, G. and Regelsberger, E. (eds) *Europe's global links: the European Community and inter-regional cooperation*, London: Pinter.

Freres, C. (2000) 'The European Union as a global "civilian power": development cooperation in EU–Latin American relations', *Journal of Interamerican Studies and World Affairs*, 42:2, pp. 63–85.

Freres, C. and Sanahuja, J. A. (2005) *Final report study on relations between the European Union and Latin America: new strategies and perspectives*, Madrid: Instituto Complutense de Estudios.

Furtado, C. (1976) *Economic Development of Latin America*, Cambridge: Cambridge University Press.

Galinsoga, J. (1995) 'Balance del proceso de San Jose: logros y carencias', paper presented at the conference Perspectivas del proceso de San Jose, San Jose de Costa Rica, 29–31 May.

Gillespie, R., Rodrigo, F. and Story, J. (1995) *Las relaciones exteriores de la Espana democratica*, Madrid: Alianza Editorial.

Giordano, P. (2002) 'The external dimension of the Mercosur: prospects for North–South integration with the European Union', paper for the Royal Institute for International Affairs, Mercosur Study Groups, London, 23 May.

Gomez Saraiva, M. (2004) 'The European Union as an international actor and the Mercosur countries' *EUI Working Papers, RSCAS*, 2004/14.

Gomez Saraiva, M. and Tedesco, L. (2003) 'Argentina y Brasil: políticas exteriores comparadas tras la Guerra Fría', in Palermo, V. (ed.), *Política Brasileña contemporánea: de Collor a Lula en años de transformación*, Buenos Aires: Siglo XXI.

Grabendorff, W. (1987) 'European Community relations with Latin America', *Journal of Interamerican Studies and World Affairs*, 29:4, pp. 69–87.

Griffith, M. (2006) 'Economic partnership agreements', policy briefing, Tearfund.

Groeben, H. von der (1979) *Die Erweiterung der Europaeischen Gemeinschaft durch Beitritt der Laender Griechenland, Spanien und Portugal*, Baden-Baden, Nomos.

Grugel, J. (2004) 'New regionalism and modes of governance: comparing US and the EU strategies in Latin America', *European Journal of International Relations*, 10:4, pp. 603–626.

Hardacre, A. (2009) *The rise and fall of interregionalism in EU external relations*, Dordrecht: Republic of Letters.

Hayes-Renshaw, F. and Wallace, H. (1997) *The Council of Ministers*, New York: St Martin's Press.

Heywood, P. (1995) *The government and politics of Spain*, London: Macmillan.

Hill, C. (1988) 'Research into EPC: tasks for the future', in Pijpers, A., Regelsberger, E. and Wessels, W. (eds), *European political cooperation in the 1980s*, Dordrecht, Martinus Nijhoff.

Hill, C. (1993), 'The capability-expectations gap, or conceptualizing Europe's international role', *Journal of Common Market Studies*, 31, pp. 305–328.

Hill, C. and Smith, M. (2005) *International relations and the European Union*, Oxford: Oxford University Press.

Hilpold, P. (2003) 'Regional integration according to Article XXIV GATT between law and politics', in *Max Planck Yearbook of United National Law*, vol. 7, pp. 219–260.

Holland, M. (2002) *The European Union and the Third World*, Basingstoke: Palgrave.

Holmes, P. (1983) 'Spain and the EEC', in Bell, D. S. (ed.), *Democratic politics in Spain: Spanish politics after Franco*, New York: St Martin's Press.

Hoste, A. (1999) 'The new Latin American policy of the EU', *European Development Policy Study Group Discussion Papers*, 11, University of Bradford, February.

Howorth, J. (2010) 'The EU as a global actor: grand strategy for a global grand bargain?', *Journal of Common Market Studies*, 48:3, pp. 455–474.

Iprofesional.com (20/4/2015) 'Las negociaciones entre la Unión Europea y el Mercosur están en un "callejón sin salida" '.

IRELA (Institute of European–Latin American Relations) (1994) 'La Union Europea y el Mercosur hacia un acuerdo de libre comercio', IRELA online paper.

IRELA (Institute of European–Latin American Relations) (1995) 'El Mercosur y la Comunidad Europea', IRELA online paper.

IRELA (Institute of European–Latin American Relations) (1996) *Europa America Latina: 20 anos de documentos oficiales (1976–1996)* Madrid: IRELA.

IRELA (Institute of European–Latin American Relations) (1999) *Europe's relations with Latin America: towards a biregional agenda for the twenty-first century*, special report, Madrid: IRELA.

Johnston, M. T. (1994) *The European Council*, Oxford: Westview Press.

Kanner, A. (2002) 'European Union–Mercosur relations: the institutionalization of cooperation', *Jean Monner/Robert Schuman Papers*, 1:8, October.

Kennedy, P. (2000) 'Spain', in Manners, I. and Whitman, R. G. (eds), *The foreign policies of European Union member states* (Manchester: Manchester University Press).

Knill, C. (2001) *The Europeanization of national administrations: patterns of institutional change and persistence*, Cambridge: Cambridge University Press.

King, D. S. (1995) *Actively seeking work? The politics of unemployment and welfare*, Oxford: Oxford University Press.

Kinoshita, F. (2001) 'Mercosur y Unión Europea: consideraciones sobre una zona de libre comercio intercontinental', in Pimentel, L. (ed.), *Estudos em homenagem a Werter R. Faria*, Curitiba: Juruá Editoria.

Kirkpatrick, C. et al. (2006) 'Trade between the European Community and Mercosur', report of Working Group on EU–Mercosur Negotiations Trade SLA EU–Mercosur Partners.

Klom, A. (2000) 'Association negotiations between the Mercosur and the European Union: rivalling Western hemisphere integration or supporting Southern Cone integration?', paper presented at the workshop 'Dollars, Democracy and Trade: External Influence on Economic Integration in the Americas', Los Angeles, 18 May.

Kramer, H. (1980) *Konsequenzen der Suderweiterung fur die Stellung der EG im Nord-Sud-Konflikt, (Stiftung Wissenschaft und Politik)*, Ebenhausen.

Kutas, G. (2006) 'Still the agricultural knot', in Valladão, A. and Guerrieri, P. (eds), *EU–Mercosur relations and the WTO Doha Round: common sectorial interests and conflicts*, Paris: Chaire Mercosur de Sciences-Po.

La Nacion (11/5/2015) 'Fuerte división en el Mercosur para negociar con la UE'.

Laporte Galli, D. (1995) La Unión Europea y el Cono Sur emprenden la reconciliación, Barcelona: Fundacio CIDOB.

Maihold, G. (2009) 'La productividad del proceso de Cumbres eurolatinoamericanas. Una evaluación a diez años de Río', in Caetano, G. et al. (eds), *Las negociaciones entre el Mercosur y la Unión Europea de cara al 2010*, Montevideo: Centro de Formación para la Integración Regional.

Manners, I. (2002) 'Normative power Europe: a contradiction in terms', *Journal of Common Market Studies*, 40:2, pp. 235–258.

Manners, I. (2008) 'The normative ethics of the European Union', *International Affairs*, 84:1, pp. 45–60.

Manzetti, L. (1994) 'The political economy of Mercosur', *Journal of Interamerican Studies and World Affairs*, 35:4, pp. 101–141.

Marin, M. (1995) 'La política comercial común y las nuevas zonas emergentes de Asia y América Latina', *Información Comercial Española*, August–September.

Marsh, S. and Mackenstein, H. (2005) *The international relations of the European Union*, London: Pearson.

Martinez Punal, A. (2005) *El sistema institucional del Mercosur: de la intergubermentalidad hacia la supranacionalidad*, Buenos Aires: Torculo.

Maull, H. (2005) 'Europe and the new balance of global order', *International Affairs*, 81:4, pp. 775–799.

Medeiros Ferreira, C. (1993) 'Portugal em transe (1975–1985)', in Mattosso, J. (ed.), *Historia de Portugal VIII*, Lisboa: Ci Circulo de Leitores.

MercoPress (26/1/2013) 'Mercosur/Paraguay controversy reaches EU/CELAC summit in Chile'.

MercoPress (2/3/2013) 'Mujica says Mercosur is a stalled pachyderm and needs trade accords with third parties'.

MercoPress (18/4/2013) 'Democracy in Paraguay is here to stay: Mercosur and Unasur have become irrelevant'.

MercoPress (23/4/2013) 'Brazil conditions Paraguay's return to Mercosur to approval of Venezuela's membership'.

MercoPress (8/5/2013) 'Maduro promises Uruguay permanent supply of oil and full Mercosur commitment'.

MercoPress (14/5/2013) 'Under Brazilian suggestion, Maduro says he is prepared for political dialogue with Capriles'.

MercoPress (20/5/2013) 'Brazil trapped by Argentina and Venezuela economic mismanagements'.

MercoPress (27/5/2013) 'Paraguay demands respect from Mercosur, "if not leave us as we are"'.

MercoPress (16/6/2013) 'Venezuela is not part of Mercosur; it was not ratified by Paraguayan congress'.

MercoPress (30/5/2015) 'Mercosur/EU officials will assess trade talks in Brussels on 11 June'.

MercoPress (12/6/2015) 'Rousseff denies being upset with Argentina over Mercosur and trade policies'.

MercoPress (18/6/2015) 'Mercosur/EU hope "for positive news in third quarter" despite members' domestic problems'.

Mercosur European Union Business Forum (MEBF) (2004) 'Brasilia declaration', Brasilia, October.

Meunier, S. (2000) *Trading voices: the European Union in international commercial negotiations*, Princeton: Princeton University Press.

Meunier, S. and Nicolaidis, K. (2005) 'The European Union as a trade power', in Hill, C. and Smith, M. (eds), *The international relations of the European Union*, Oxford: Oxford University Press.

Mintzberg, H. (1987) 'General strategy concept I: five Ps for strategy', *California Management Review*, 30:1, pp. 11–24.

Monar, J. (1997) 'Political dialogue with third countries and regional political groupings: the fifteen as an attractive interlocutor', in Regelsberger, E., de Schoutheete, P. and Wessels, W. (eds), *Foreign policy of the European Union: from EPC to CFSP and beyond*, London: Lynne Rienner.

Moore, D. G. (1959) 'Managerial strategies', in Warner, W. L. and Martin, N. H. (eds), *Industrial man: businessmen and business organizations*, New York: Harper & Row.

Moratinos, M. A. (2010) 'Europe as a global actor: view from the Spanish presidency', speech by M. A. Moratinos at CEPS, Brussels, 20 January, www.ceps.be/content/europe-global-actor-views-spanish-presidency.

Murilo de Carvalho, J. (1987) *Os bsestializados: o Rio de Janeiro e a República que não foi*, 2nd edition, São Paulo: Companhia das Letras.

Nicholson, F. and East, R. (1987) *From the six to the twelve: the enlargement of the European Communities*, Harlow: Longman.

Nugent, N. (1999) *The government and politics of the European Union*, Durham, NC: Duke University Press

Nugent, N. (2003) *The government and politics of the European Union*, 5th edition, New York: Palgrave Macmillan.

Paemen, H. and Bensch, A. (1995) *From the GATT to the WTO: the European Community in the Uruguay Round*, Leuven: Leuven University Press.

Pena (2009) 'Grietas estructurales en el Mercosur ¿Es posible adaptar algunas de sus reglas de juego a las realidades actuales?', *Newsletter sobre relaciones comerciales internacionales*, November.

Pendle, G. (1963) *A history of Latin America*, Harmondsworth: Penguin Books.

Peters, G. (2001) 'Agenda-setting in the European Union', in Richardson, J. (ed.), *European Union power and policy-making*, London: Routledge.

Peterson, J. and Bomberg, E. (1999) (eds) *Decision-making in the European Union*, London: Palgrave Macmillan.

Petiteville, F. (2004) 'L'Union dans les relations internationales: du soft power à la puissance?', *Questions internationales*, 7, May/June, pp. 63–72.

Piening, C. (1997) *Global Europe the European Union in world affairs*, London: Lynne Rienner.

Pierson, P. (2000) 'Increasing returns, path dependence, and the study of politics', *American Political Science Review*, 94:2, pp 251–267.

Pollack, M. A. (2005) 'Theoretical and comparative insights into EU policy-making', in Wallace, H., Wallace, W. and Pollack, M. (eds), *Policy-making in the European Union*, Oxford: Oxford University Press.

Quille, G. (2004) 'The European security strategy: a framework for EU security interests?', *International Peacekeeping*, 11:3, pp. 422–438.

Ravenhill, J. (2002) 'Back to the nest? Europe's relations with the African, Caribbean and Pacific group of countries', *PEIF Working Papers*, 9.

Regelsberger, E. (1990) 'The dialogue of the EC/twelve with other regional groups: a new European identity in the international system?', in Edwards, G. and Regelsberger, E. (eds), *Europe's global links: the European Community and inter-regional cooperation*, London: Pinter.

Ribeiro Hoffmann, A. (2004) 'The EU foreign policy towards Latin America Southern Cone states', paper presented to the Second Pan-European Conference Standing Group on EU Politics Bologna, 24–26 June.

Robles, A. C. (2008) 'The EU and ASEAN: learning from the failed EU–Mercosur FTA', *ASEAN Economic Bulletin Negotiations*, 25:3, pp. 334–344.

Rodo, J.E. (1922) *Ariel*, trans. with introductory essay by F.J. Stimson, Boston and New YorkL Houghton Mifflin Company/Riverside Press.

Royo, S. (2006) 'The European Union and economic reforms: the case of Spain', *Elcano Newsletter*, 25, 30 May.

Rüland J. (200a) 'The European Union as an inter – and transregional actor: lessons for global governance from Europe's relations with Asia', *National Europe Centre Paper*, 13, presented to the conference 'The European Union in International Affairs', National Europe Centre, Australian National University, 3–4 July.

Rüland J. (2002b) 'Interregionalism in international relations', conference summary, Freiberg, Germany, 31 January and 1 February.

Russau, C. (2005) 'Investment regimes in the EU–MERCOSUR negotiations', paper for the Forschungs- und Dokumentationszentrum Chile-Lateinamerika project 'Free Trade and Industrial Development'.

Sanahuja, J. A. (1999) '25 años de cooperación interparlamentaria entre la Unión Europea y América Latina, 1974–1999', Luxembourg: European Parliament, POLI 107 (ES), March.

Sanahuja, J. A. (2000a) 'Trade, politics, and democratization: the 1997 global agreement between the European Union and Mexico', *Journal of Interamerican Studies and World Affairs*, 42:2, pp. 35–62.

Sanahuja, J. A. (2000b) 'Asimetrías económicas y concertación política en las relaciones Unión Europea-America Latina: un examen de los problemas comercial', *Revista Electrónica de Relaciones Internacionales*, 1, pp. 1–19.

Sanahuja, J. A. (2003) 'De Río a Madrid: posibilidades y límites de las relaciones Unión Europea-América Latina', *Observatori de Política Exterior Europea Working Paper*, 45, Institut Universitari d'Estudis Europeus, Barcelona, April.

Sanahuja, J. A. (2004) 'Un diálogo estructurado y plural. La dimensión institucional de las relaciones Unión Europea-América Latina', *Nueva Sociedad*, 189, pp. 80–96.

Sanchez Bajo, C. (1999) 'The European Union and Mercosur: a case of interregionalism', *Third World Quarterly*, 20:5, pp. 927–941.

Santander S. (2002) 'EU–Mercosur interregionalism: facing up to the South American crisis and the emerging free trade area of the Americas', *European Foreign Affairs Review*, 7, pp. 491–505.

Santander, S. (2003) Las negociaciones UE-Mercosur: un juego con pocas cartas en la mesa?', *Revista de Derecho Internacional y del Mercosur*, 2, pp. 41–51.

Santander S. (2005) 'The European partnership with Mercosur: a relationship based on strategic and neo-liberal principles', *European Integration*, 27:3, pp. 285–306.

Schalk, J., Torenvlied, R., Wessie, J. and Stokman, F. (2007) 'The power of the presidency in EU Council decision-making', *European Union Politics*, 8:2, pp. 229–250.

Sewell, W. H. (1996) 'Three temporalities: toward an eventful sociology', in McDonald, T. J. (ed.), *The historic turn in the human sciences*, Ann Arbor: University of Michigan Press.

Simancas, F. (1999) 'La integración argentino-brasileña y el Mercosur', *Revista Venezolana de Analisis de Coyuntura*, 5:1.

Sjöstedt, G. (1977) *The external role of the European Community*, Farnborough: Saxon House, Swedish Institute of International Affairs.

Skidmore, T. (1967) *Politics in Brazil 1930–1964: an experiment in democracy*, Oxford: Oxford University Press.

Skocpol, T. (1992) *Protecting soldiers and mothers: the political origins of social policy in the United States*, Cambridge, MA: Belknap Press.

Smith H. (1995) *European Union foreign policy and Central America*, London: Macmillan.

Smith, H. (1998) 'Actually existing foreign policy – or not?: the EU in Latin and Central America', in Peterson, J. and Sjursen, H. (eds), *A Common Foreign Policy for Europe?*, London: Routledge.

Smith, K. (2003) *European foreign policy in a changing world*, Cambridge: Polity Press.

Smith, K. E. (2004) *The making of EU foreign policy: the case of Eastern Europe*, Basingstoke: Palgrave Macmillan.

Smith, M. (2001) 'The EU as an international actor', in Richardson, J. (ed.), *European Union power and policy-making*, London: Routledge.

Smith, M. (2006) 'The European Union and international political economy: trade, aid and monetary policy', in Jørgensen, K., Pollack, M. and Rosamon, B. (eds), *Handbook of European Union politics*, London: Sage.

Smith, M. and Xie, X. (2010) 'The EU and China: the logics of "strategic partnership"', paper presented at the ECPR Standing Group on the EU Conference, Porto, Portugal, 24–26 June.

Soderbaum, F. and Van Langenhove, L. (2005) 'Introduction: the EU as a global actor and the role of interregionalism', *Journal of European Integration*, 27:3, pp. 249–262.

Soderbaum, F., Stalgren, P. and Van Langenhove, L. (2005) 'The EU as a global actor and the dynamics of interregionalism: a comparative analysis', *Journal of European Integration*, 27:3, pp. 365–380.

Sondrol, P. (1992) 'The emerging new politics of liberalizing Paraguay: sustained civil-military control without democracy', *Journal of Interamerican Studies and World Affairs*, 34:2, pp. 127–163.

Talberg, J. (2006) *Leadership and negotiation in the European Union*, Cambridge: Cambridge University Press.

Thomson, R. and Hosli, M. (2004) 'Who has power in the EU? The Commission, Council and Parliament in legislative decision-making', *Journal of Common Market Studies*, 44:2, pp. 391–417.

Tonra, B. (2001) *The Europeanization of national foreign policy: Dutch, Danish and Irish foreign policy in the European Union*, Aldershot: Ashgate.

Torrelli, C. (2003) 'Mercosur for sale? The EU's FTAA and the need to oppose it', *Corporate Europe Observatory (CEO) and Transnational Institute (TNI) Info Brief*, REDES, Uruguay, August.

Torrent, R. (1998) *Derecho y práctica de las relaciones económicas exteriores en la Unión Europea*, Barcelona: CEDECS.

Torrent, R. (2005) 'Las relaciones Unión Europea–América Latina en los últimos diez años: el resultado de la inexistencia de una política', OBREAL-EULARO.

Valenzuela, A. (1997) 'Paraguay: the coup that didn't happen', *Journal of Democracy*, 8:1, pp. 43–55.

Vasconcelos, A. (2001) 'European Union and Mercosur', in Telo, M. (ed.) *European Union and new regionalism*, Aldershot: Ashgate.

Wallace, H. (2000) 'The policy process', in Wallace, W. and Wallace, H. (eds), *Policy-making in the European Union*, Oxford: Oxford University Press.

Wallace, H. and Young, A. R. (1997) (eds) *Participation and policy-making in the European Union*, Oxford: Clarendon Press.

Warntjen, A. (2008) 'The Council presidency: power broker or burden? An empirical analysis', *European Union Politics*, 9:3, pp. 316–338.

Waylen, G. (2000) 'Gender and democratic politics: a comparative analysis of consolidation in Argentina and Chile', *Journal of Latin American Studies*, 32, pp. 765–793.

Wessels, W. (1997) 'The growth and differentiation of multi-level networks: a corporatist mega-bureaucracy or an open city?', in Wallace, H. and Young, A. R. (eds), *Participation and policy making in the European Union*, Oxford: Clarendon Press.

Westlake, M. (1995) *The Council of the European Union*, London: Cartermill.

Westlake, M. and Galloway, D. (2004) *The Council of the European Union*, London: John Harper.

Weyland, K. (1993) 'The rise and fall of President Collor and its impact on Brazilian democracy', *Journal of Interamerican Studies and World Affairs*, 35:1, pp. 1–37.

Wiarda, H. (1989) *The transition to democracy in Spain and Portugal*, Washington, DC: AEI.

Wong, R. (2008) 'Foreign policy', in Graziano, P. and Vink, M. (eds), *Europeanization: new research agendas*, New York: Palgrave Macmillan.

Woolcock, S. (2005) 'Trade policy', in Wallace, H., Wallace, W. and Pollack, M. (eds), *Policy-making in the European Union*, Oxford: Oxford University Press.

Young, A. R. (2004) 'The incidental fortress: the single European market and world trade', *Journal of Common Market Studies*, 42:2, pp. 393–414.

Young, A. R. (2010) 'The European policy process in comparative perspective', in Wallace, H., Pollack, M. A. and Young, A. R. (eds), *Policy-making in the European Union*, 6th edition, Oxford: Oxford University Press.

Youngs, R. (2000) 'Spain, Latin America and Europe: the complex interaction of regionalism and cultural identification', *Mediterranean Politics*, 5:2, pp. 107–129.

Index